Kiss Me Deadly

Feminism & Cinema
for the Moment

Kiss Me Deadly

Feminism & Cinema
for the Moment

edited by
Laleen Jayamanne

POWER PUBLICATIONS
SYDNEY

© Power Institute of Fine Arts 1995

Published by
Power Publications
Power Institute of Fine Arts
University of Sydney
NSW 2006
Australia

General Editor
Julian Pefanis

Managing Editor
Elisabeth Schwaiger

Cover Design
Aaron Rogers

Cover image:
Lisa Lyon as femme fatale in Raul Ruiz's *Three Crowns of a Sailor*.

Printed by
Southwood Press

National Library of Australia Cataloguing-in-publication data:
  Kiss me deadly: feminism and cinema for the moment.

  ISBN 0 909952 26 4

  1. Women in motion pictures. 2. Women in popular culture.
  3. Feminism and motion pictures. 4. Women in the motion
  picture industry. I. Jayamanne, Laleen. II. Power
  Institute of Fine Arts

791.43082

Contents

Introduction

Strange Encounters

ROBERT BRESSON: *Bring together things that have as yet never been brought together and did not seem predisposed to be so.*[1]

NICOLAS O'SULLIVAN: *What is cinema?*
RAUL RUIZ: *I tried to answer that, let's say thirty five years ago — and I don't know yet. Not me, not Walter Benjamin, not Langer, not Mitchell, not Bazin.*[2]

The encounter between feminism and cinema over some 25 years, across different continents, has been and continues to be determined by a crystallisation of desires, imaginations and powers of contemporary women. With this sense of a short but intense history it might seem intriguing and puzzling to the reader that this volume characterises this encounter as "momentary." Let me clear any possible misunderstanding across cultures. The idea of the "moment" is not a self-effacing antipodean gesture, suggesting that the force of these essays will fade even as you read them. Nor is it on my part a South Asian conceit on the transitory nature of all endeavour. Rather, it is a way of imaging the conditions that have enabled the work of this volume and a way of thinking of how we apprehend that elusive "object" film, through our viewing, reading and writing practices. I wish to call up both the everyday connotations of the word "moment"[3] as well as two theorisations of it via the image. A moment has no specific tense, no specific duration, only a sense of transience. While "wait a moment" could mean a few seconds, with a hint of caution, the moments of the various paradigms of feminist film theory (sketched below) encapsulate a variety of temporalities. A moment can be instantaneous like Walter Benjamin's idea of "a flash of light"[4] wherein an image constellation can form between the past and the now through the operations of involuntary memory. The happy conjunction of the eye and looking in the German word for moment, "augenblick," is worth mentioning here because of how this suggests the potential intensity of such a temporality, which is very cinematic. It can also be read via Raul Ruiz's theorisation of the "cinematic moment" which he sees as multiple and not determined in any way by apparatus time (i.e., twenty-four frames per second).[5] This elastic notion of the moment, which can sustain a sense of multiple durations, memory, and incommensurable temporalities, a sense of the passing of time and perhaps its concomitant urgency, is important to this work.

The idea for this publication came from a one-day conference called Kiss Me Deadly: Feminism and Cinema Now, held at the University of Sydney in 1991 as part of the Dissonance project, a retrospective on Australian feminism in the arts over the last twenty years. Because from its very inception feminist-influenced film scholarship in Australia has engaged productively with both British and American work, we invited Patricia Mellencamp to give the keynote address as a way of creating a cross-cultural exchange. One of the first things she did after accepting the invitation was to ask to see a selection of Australian films by women and a bibliography of feminist writing on cinema. So there is a nice irony here in the fact that the only essay which engages with Australian work is that by Mellencamp. However, not all of the papers delivered at that event are published here, while others, written subsequently, some of them influenced by the conference, have been included.

Why does a collection of essays on feminism and cinema carry the title of a famous 1950s Hollywood independent film noir by a director who had a reputation for being misogynist? Partly because Robert Aldrich's *Kiss Me Deadly* has been read in contradictory ways from within the problematic of feminist film theory itself.[6] Also because of his great inventiveness and wit in casting a range of "B-girls" in this film, so that the 40s image of the femme fatale is powerfully modified, enriching the lineaments of this generic type who can no longer be seen as the double of the noir man in search of the death drive[7] but as the double of a new social type, "the teenager," while still retaining her characteristic fatality, a truly toxic combination. As well, the phrase "Kiss me deadly" encapsulates perfectly a certain local feeling of ambivalence that has been a part of the feminist project in cinema from at least the mid-80s. For those of us who came to study feminist film theory in the late 70s and early 80s in Sydney, there was, after the initial exhilaration, something like an experience of terror that the very theory that set out to explicate and transform our understanding of "Woman" in cinema was killing a certain experience of cinema. For some of us, cinema was at least as important as feminism, and there seemed to be something wrong in the way the two terms were brought together, like a kiss of death. This title leaves the ambivalence unresolved as a reminder of the dangers that attend a certain kind of blind, non-mimetic[8] epistemophilia, a will to mastery that is best exemplified for me by the rather unappealing figure of the daughter Helen played by Anna Massey in Michael Powell's *Peeping Tom*.

The engagement between feminist film theory and cinema has at times been joyous and at others sad. The joyful encounters have produced actions that have transformed our understanding of cinema, while the sad encounters have decomposed the cinematic body by prioritising theory, leaving a few dull programmatic statements. An encounter which should be an interrelation, even a conflictual, difficult one, has in some unfortunate instances devoured the object. The metaphors of "kiss of death" and "devoured object" may suggest that this volume proposes a naive view of the object's plenitude, a view unaware that in the field opened up by post-structuralist theorising all acts of criticism in some way mark the object with a mutation, a death of sorts. On the contrary, the writers are keenly aware of the function of criticism as a staging of an encounter in which both subject and object mutate. So there is no pre-theoretical nostalgia for the lost object here. Just as there is now, say in philosophy, a desire to bring the body out from the shadow of the mind, to bring practice out from the shadow of theory in all its autonomy and dignity, to try to discover what it can do;[9] there is a desire in this volume to bring film out from the shadow of feminist film theory to discover what it can do for feminism. In legitimating my claim by citing philosophical antecedents, I wish to signal swiftly and unequivocally that this volume does not accept the history of feminist film theory as received wisdom, nor does it simply reject its achievements as being dated. Rather there is a desire to stage encounters between theories and film/s without prioritising theory. This is one common notion that holds the multiplicity of this collection and gives it some coherence, a certain force of necessity for the moment.

I want to give a linear account of the three major shifts of paradigms within feminist film theory in order to contextualise the work in this volume. The first moment was marked by "the images of women" or the "women and film" approach. University courses were formulated on this theme and I remember a stirring Sydney film festival forum on the subject in the late 70s. This moment has its historical importance in creating an awareness of a problem which was until then invisible. Its methodological limitation became evident when all it could do was to look for positive or negative characterisation of women in film. The next period was marked by a major shift in theorising the notion of "woman" as sign, and of cinema as a popular industrial art form. This is the period when psychoanalytic theory became important in theorising the notions of the cinematic apparatus and the viewing subject posited as an effect of a certain deployment of that technology. Claire Johnston, Laura Mulvey and other British "cine-feminists" made pioneering contributions in thus shifting the terms of the debate. This is also the period of "frame-by-frame analysis" of films which became institutionalised via American work. The moment when the psychoanalytic model was hegemonic was marked by certain important internal debates within feminist film theory itself vis-à-vis avant-garde cinema and popular cinema. In this brief sketch of the major shifts in paradigms I can only signal the complexity of the feminist work within this period marked by an intense concern with notions of film as text and textual system, the limitation of which was a certain hermeticism. The need to understand film, a major temporal popular art, as being governed by the vicissitudes of time, created the third paradigmatic moment of feminist film theory. Work on spectatorship within specific periods in specific cultures, especially foregrounding the constellation Cinema-Woman-Modernity, was taken up. Exemplary are the work of Patrice Petro on Weimar melodrama and Miriam Hansen on American silent cinema.[10] Both Petro and Hansen use psychoanalytic concepts but the terms within which they are used have changed. The work in this collection may be situated within this third moment, but the specificity of these essays may rest on an awareness of the disjunct moments of viewing/reading/writing.

This linear account of one exhausted paradigm being abandoned for another within a period of some two decades does pose several problems, one of which was suggested to me in passing by Patricia Mellencamp at the "Kiss Me Deadly" conference. She said that there seemed to be three generations of women scholars speaking there that day. Thinking back on that has some pertinence now because the media have recently highlighted the generational conflicts within Australian and American feminisms. A generational conflict has been reported within American feminism on issues related to sexual harassment especially on campuses. In the case of Australia the conflict was voiced on the occasion of the launch of the updated version of Anne Summers' 1975 bestseller, *Damned Whores and God's Police*,[11] a feminist analysis of Australia's colonial history, which interestingly includes a letter to the next generation, documenting the pioneering work she and other Australian feminists undertook in the 70s.

> The almost 20 years since this book was published ... has also been a time when we have accomplished much in this country—mainly due to the unique partnership between the women's movement and the Government—and has made us the envy of women in many other industrialised countries.[12]

It may be worth taking a cue from Summers' letter alerting the next generation to the need for making strange alliances (like the one between feminists and the state) and sustaining public memory. This Australian notion of strange alliance may just be the durable form of the strange encounters from which I take my title. In this conflictual context the question of how the generational knowledge of feminist film theory is to be transmitted becomes an interesting one. Of course there can be no question of handing down intact the previous generations' hard work as received wisdom to the next, nor can the exhausted paradigms be entirely forgotten. I am, however, often tempted to do the latter and when I did so once, a student told me that however boring it might be to say it, sometimes it is necessary to say that X image is "negative," is unacceptable, and then move on.[13] Do we then allegorically emblematise certain methods in order to show how time has ruined them?

Toni Ross' reading of Nicolas Roeg's *Bad Timing; A Sensual Obsession*, as an allegory of a "riven authorship" indicates how timing is crucial to the act of theorising and criticism. In all probability, such a reading as hers could not have been done when the film was first released in the early 80s because, as she points out, there was a timely coincidence between cine-feminism's work with the psychoanalytic trope of the gendered gaze, the feminine and the logic of the cinematic apparatus, on the one hand, and the work of this film, on the other. It had an immediacy then which would have made it resistant to an allegorical reading. Now, however, the film on each viewing seems dated, ruined, compelling Ross to simultaneously engage with the ensuing effects of this temporal declivity, while retaining the memory of its original impact, refusing to quite forget those heady times. In so doing, her mode of writing is itself attuned to the temporality of allegory as a perpetual flux. Ross reanimates *Bad Timing* by specifying its conflicting aesthetic allegiances, one of which is to Romantic theories of art and authorship. In doing this she is able to show how the sign "woman" functions in different aesthetic regimes, such as Neo-Classicism, Romanticism and Modernism; more specifically, how Woman operates within the figuration of Roeg's authorship as allegorised by *Bad Timing*.[14] The historical work on aesthetics she draws from points to largely untapped areas of research that can be as productive for film theory as they have been for literary theory. The way she analyses how the sign "woman" can figure in a sublime encounter between the sexes also points to an area of possible future work.

Needeya Islam's paper on Kathryn Bigelow and the action films works within the tradition created by Claire Johnston and its insistence upon the importance of a feminist engagement with the reworking of popular film genres.[15] Johnston's work on Dorothy Arzner and Nelly Kaplan established the gains to be made by engaging with the richness of a coded, instantly recognisable set of scenarios, gestures, and images. Islam shows how Bigelow insinuates herself into genre and works within it in a manner which does not offer a safe place from which to receive it. Whereas, say, with Robert Altman's critique of Hollywood in *The Player* one knows exactly where one stands, then as Islam argues, in Bigelow's work "the viewer is rarely instructed as to whether or not to take an ironic stance, although this is a tone which is notably apparent in a general sense." The "uncomfortable viewing" which this entails also obliges the critic to be implicated in such difficulty. She formulates this difficulty as the enabling condition of the film. What this suggests to me, as reader, is that criticism cannot, when encountering such an object, function according to a sensory-motor logic. Just as in *Blue Steel*, Megan Turner, the cop played by Jamie Lee Curtis, cannot assume the role of cop with one hundred percent sensory-motor efficiency, the critic too has to disengage her habitual sensory-motor action[16] schooled via previous genre films and theoretical discourses on how to read them. She has to invent a set of rules or practices suggested by the films themselves.

Islam's argument suggests an irresistible scenario which can be stated thus: between the gun and its being fired (which is its proper sensory-motor link), the female hero's body and the critic's body insert themselves in a manner that makes trigger-happy behaviour problematic. A scenario emerges from the necessary hesitation between a sensation and a possible action. In such a moment there is a necessity to stretch or halt, as in a pause, the link between the "image of woman with a gun" and what can be done with it or said about it. This moment of hesitation would be a way of letting thought arise when confronted by an image invested with the senses. An image invested with the senses before action takes hold of it is, according to Gilles Deleuze, one of the preconditions for the emergence of the time image.[17] Islam's piece offers a way of thinking criticism as something other than sensory-motor. This I propose as another common notion that unifies this heterogeneous collection. Indeed this volume as a whole offers a possibility of this kind within the history of feminist film theory. The female hero, author, critic, transforms what it is possible to do, show and say with (action) cinema by stretching a little, or halting, or displacing, the habitual (i.e., sensory-motor) retinal and critical moves.

Michelle Langford's "Film Figures: Rainer Werner Fassbinder's *The Marriage of Maria Braun* and Alexander Kluge's *The Female Patriot*," critiques two familiar readings of these films and offers alternatives which have methodological implications for film analysis. Langford deftly uses Kluge's own theories as tools with which to negotiate his film. Kluge's film theory has been very finely explicated by Stuart Liebman and others,[18] but it is less common to find readings of his work that are able to enact in their very movement the fragility and fleeting process of thinking with images essential to the economy of Kluge's cinema. Langford suggests that the viewer has to learn how to enter the gaseous image-world of Kluge's montage sequences by taking a cue from his allegorical figures. Learning here is not sensory-motor (automatic), but more like how children play on scrap heaps, putting together stuff in as yet uncoded configurations. Walter Benjamin calls this childlike capacity "ontogenetic mimesis," to distinguish it from "phylogenetic mimesis."[19] Theodor Adorno's pupil Kluge offers us a rare contemporary example of how the mimetic faculty may be reschooled-retooled via cinema (its last refuge?).[20] Langford's delicate quirky passage through *The Female Patriot* is attuned to a reading in flux. In reading *The Marriage of Maria Braun* via Deleuze's concept of deep-focus as a recollection image as well as via a notion of the undoing of melodrama as cliche, Langford is able to take the concept of the deep-focus shot into other dimensions, including sound. In pursuing the imbrication of genre and this particular filmic technique she is able to show how this film can create historical memory without simply representing the past.

Lesley Stern's essay "Meditation on Violence" brings together two apparently dissimilar films, Martin Scorsese's *Raging Bull* and Michael Powell's *The Red Shoes*, as though there could be a neat fit between boxing gloves and ballet shoes. "Fit" is not the right word for what Stern does in bringing these two films together. She cuts one film with the other, she cuts into them, makes them bleed into each other through a sustained descriptive force. The writer's obsessive descriptive drive which mimics the cinematic and thematic obsessions of the two films may be read via Gilles Deleuze's reading of the time image as description. Here description does not give the original object in its plenitude, instead it repeatedly returns to the object, erasing and redrawing its countenance. As someone said, the colour red looks different according to whether it is next to black or white; similarly after Stern's operations of "irrational cuts" between the two films, neither will be the same again. She bleeds one film into the other and in so doing offers insights into the moments of seepage between the possessed body of the performer and the everyday body, across gender lines. This apprehending of one film by the other I take to be a mimetic process by which she draws a series of correspondences between the two.[21] Psychoanalysis offers useful knowledges here but works in a performative relationship to the films and not as meta-commentary on them.

Jodi Brooks' "Between Contemplation and Distraction: Cinema, Obsession and Involuntary Memory" explores contemporary modes of cinematic fascination. Brooks draws on Miriam Hansen's work[22] on the cinematic and redraws the lineaments of cinematic spectatorship as an amorous encounter.[23] Brooks opens up a temporal moment in Hansen's exegesis so as to be able to delineate the shape of cinematic fascination. She does this via a cluster of Benjaminian concepts, "aura," "correspondence," "involuntary memory," "distraction-contemplation" which she then reconstellates by bringing them to bear on Benjamin's notion of "collecting." Collecting, according to Brooks, is the process by which the contemporary viewer of videos, films, television, converts images into wish images via an erotics of encounter. What is delicious in Brooks' argument is her mode of writing, the way she apprehends auratic European experiences in the vernacular, so that the famous Proustian madeleine becomes a "soggy pastry," and the high bourgeois activity of collecting rare things becomes thinkable in terms of a way of charging, i.e. "renewing," the banal contemporary gaseous image-world with the intensity of experience as duration.

Melissa McMahon's " 'Fourth Person Singular': Becoming Ordinary and the Void in the Critical Body Filmic" shares with Jodi

Brooks' essay a certain facility for casually and yet pointedly redrawing the contours of mythical European scenarios so that they become accessible to contemporary manoeuvres. In this regard McMahon's redramatisation of the mythical founding moment of the modern city and the function there of the phantasmatic figure of Zobeïdes is exemplary in its hilarity and theoretical astuteness. What she is concerned with is the possibility of viewing, reading, writing practices in relation to cinema that do not subordinate a body to a transcendent concept and by extension she addresses the wider question of how to think the cinematic body itself without subordinating it to theoretical categories. She is interested in a form of thinking which is not a "philosophy of capture." To this end she draws from Gilles Deleuze and Félix Guattari's work a way of thinking about the cinematic body and bodies as operating in movement and time.

Here I wish to make a distinction between McMahon's use of Deleuzian concepts in relation to certain films and Steven Shaviro's in his book *The Cinematic Body*.[24] While both Shaviro's and McMahon's choice of films are personal and idiosyncratic, both refer to the work of Robert Bresson and Shaviro deals with him in some detail. Despite Shaviro's admirable critique of the reification of concepts in film theory (especially psychoanalytic ones), in his introductory chapter and his offer of an alternative to theory fetishism, that is exactly what happens in his own analysis of films. The work of directors such as George Romero, Jerry Lewis, David Cronenberg, Robert Bresson, Andy Warhol and Rainer Werner Fassbinder, are all analysed via concepts derived from Deleuze and Guattari's work (though significantly not from Deleuze's two books on cinema). But finally every single chapter of the book concludes with a sentence that is more or less a variation of the following from the introduction: "Film should be neither exalted as a medium of collective fantasy nor condemned as a mechanism of ideological mystification. It should rather be praised as a technology for intensifying and renewing experiences of passivity and abjection."[25] The imperative in this final sentence in repeated as a summary of a range of films. Here is the concluding sentence of the chapter on Bresson: "Bresson grasps the flesh with such directness and such intensity that he necessarily presents a vision in which grace is indistinguishable from suffering and abjection."[26] The valorisation of passivity, abjection and surrender to the image as an escape from mastery leads Shaviro to a simple reversal where all films re-enact his favourite scenario, of masochistic, abject surrender.

For McMahon, more attuned to the temporality of the image, what fascinates is not what confirms a privileged affect but that which in the image makes her unsure of what to say, what to do, what she calls "the undecidable space of the body and its involvements." Here the critic seems to be aware that she does not yet know what a body can do and makes that temporal moment the enabling condition of her subsequent reading. So she bears witness to this in Mouchette's suicide, when she describes the Bressonian economy thus:

> Gestures accumulate and contradict each other without cancelling each other out. They are evocative while maintaining their status as fragments, as parts of a texture, without coalescing into moral messages or unambiguous determinations of motive or psychology, even in the event of Mouchette's suicide which, like the murder in Jeanne Dielman, so closely approximates a banal gesture. Its restraint is shocking, but it leaves us with nothing to say.

Whereas Shaviro always already knows what to say in the end, his "Deleuzian" reading is sensory-motor, habitual, automatic.[27] McMahon's mode of reading is akin to the way a perception is said to take hold of us or of a filmic body, so that it does not get transformed into an action immediately.[28] So through an act of memory or imagination or both she reads across the cuts, between the out-of-frame tumescent male organ of the truck driver and his monologue in Akerman's *Je tu il elle*, and thereby produces an amazing description of the hand-job sequence as an eroticisation of the sentence, the speech act. This kind of reading is not an application of Deleuzian concepts, it is more like taking a cue from Deleuze so as to begin a critical time-movement of her own.

Patricia Mellencamp's paper, "Five Ages of Film Feminism," is marked by at least three kinds of gestures. First, there is the desire to read her own personal and intellectual history in relation to the history of feminist theorising of cinema. In doing this she activates a feminist gesture, fluently articulating the conditions that make fluency in life difficult for intellectual women. Also, in mapping the five stages of film feminism as she sees it, she performs the very difficult gesture of criticising a canonical feminist film, Yvonne Rainer's *Privilege*.[29] In Australia such a critical gesture has always been difficult but thought to be necessary. The other gesture is the one by which Mellencamp connects the work of the Australian Aboriginal film-maker Tracey Moffatt and that of the African-American film-maker Julie Dash in terms of their interest in filmically articulating the experience of cross-cultural violence, exchange and the creation of memory via film.

My own piece on the work of Raul Ruiz explores two canonical figures of feminist film theory, the femme fatale and the maternal, but constructed here as allegory. I use Benjamin's theory of allegory in relation to Ruiz' filmic allegory to examine how late twentieth century allegory works in two particular sequences of *Three Crowns of a Sailor*. A concern of this piece is to describe the operations of allegorical figuration and to note with surprise how in pursuing the femme fatale[30] I stumbled on the marvellous secret that she nestled between two avatars of the maternal. The piece is also haunted by the question of why Deleuze does not in his books on cinema even mention the name of the Chilean/French filmmaker Raul Ruiz whose contributions to a cinema of the time-image was so available to him. Allegorical embodiment offers feminist film practice and criticism a rich array of possibilities away from problems of the iconicity of the image.

There is in fact something like a methodological imperative in these essays to make the relationship between theoretical ideas and the experience of cinema a productively difficult one. All of the essays are predicated on a fascination with the cinematic and are governed by a desire to sustain that fascination in the very act of writing. Whether successful or not, this writing aims to maintain a certain kind of mimetic relationship with the object of analysis.[31] This aspect distinguishes it from most American writing in the field of feminist film theory.

This is an idiosyncratic collection dealing with the cinema of such directors as Chantal Akerman, Kathryn Bigelow, Robert Bresson, Jane Campion, Julie Dash, Alexander Kluge, Tracey Moffatt, Michael Powell, Yvonne Rainer, Nicolas Roeg, Raul Ruiz, and Martin Scorsese, among others. And it is by chance, certainly not design, that five out of the eight essays work with concepts derived from Deleuze's books on cinema. Two of the essays work with Benjamin's concepts of allegory and the image and memory. The theories of two of the most philosophically attuned film-makers, Alexander Kluge and Raul Ruiz, are used as tools with which to apprehend their images. The two essays that are outside this nexus may also be aligned with them insofar as they are concerned with cinematic memory to some degree. Concerns of time and memory have been brought to the fore by Deleuze's work on the cinema and much of the work in this volume is preoccupied by them. Why then do I insist that this volume is eclectic and heterogeneous rather than "Deleuzian?" Because of the logic of the strange encounter of concepts and films which do not simply apply Deleuze but use his concepts (among others) to make something happen. The encounters between films and theories staged here are not unified by any programmatic intention, some are in fact (in their choice of films and methodologies) foreign to the semi-official canons of feminist film theory. I have, however, used some Deleuzian concepts in reading these essays, and if my reading (rather than the essays themselves) has a programmatic ring, then it is one that has to be invented each time one stages an encounter between a film and a concept. I think this volume offers useful guidelines, but no guarantees, on how to negotiate this moment, for that is a matter of invention.

It is hoped that the analytically rigorous, historically alert, intuitive and imaginative filmic-textual, theoretical elaborations of these essays will be taken up and re-constellated by others wishing to stage strange encounters of a third kind.

This project has been supported by the Mari Kuttna Bequest and grants from The University of Sydney and the Australian Film Commission. But a text such as this is also always the result of collaboration, goodwill and time freely given. Particular thanks are due to: Julian Pefanis, Elisabeth Schwaiger and Rod Ritchie at Power Publications; to Lisa Trahair and Colin Hood for their careful reading of the text; and to Meaghan Morris for her advice and unstinting support.

1　Robert Bresson, *Notes on Cinematography*, trans. Jonathan Griffin (New York: Urizen Books, 1977), 22.

2　Paul Garcia, David Bolliger, Nicholas O'Sullivan, "Cinema, Prosthetics, and a Short History of Latin America: Raul Ruiz Interview" (22 February, 1993, Sydney, unpublished).

3　My thanks to Chris Caines and Toni Ross for their observations.

4　Walter Benjamin, "Thesis on the Philosophy of History," *Illuminations*, ed. Hannah Arendt, trans. Harry Zohn (Glasgow: Fontana Collins, 1977), 257. See Michael Taussig, *Mimesis and Alterity, A Particular History Of The Senses* (New York/London: Routledge, 1993), 39–40, and 71, for a reading of this idea and also note 49 of my essay in this collection for further discussion.

5　Garcia et al.,"Cinema Prosthetics". See note 45 of my essay in this collection for a brief account of Ruiz's ideas on cinematic temporality derived from this interview.

6　Carol Flinn, "Sound Woman and the Bomb: Dismembering the 'Great Whatsit' in *Kiss Me Deadly*," *Wide Angle*, vol. 8, no. 4 (1986), 115–157. Kaja Silverman, *The Acoustic Mirror, The Female Voice in Psychoanalysis and Cinema* (Bloomington and Indianapolis: Indiana University Press, 1988), 65–66. Laleen Jayamanne, "They are becoming us or they are becoming other: they are at a dangerous point," *Dissonance; Feminism and the Arts 1970–90*, ed. Catriona Moore (Sydney: Allen and Unwin 1994), 184–190.

7　This is Slavoj Zizek's argument about the femme fatale in " 'The Thing

That Thinks': The Kantian Background of the Noir Subject," *Shades of Noir*, ed. Joan Copjec (London, New York: Verso, 1993), 199–226.

8   Mimesis is used here via Taussig, as a form of sensuous knowing. See Taussig, *Mimesis and Alterity*, 20–23. In this respect Helen's blind mother, played by Maxine Audley, may be regarded as one who apprehends cinema sensuously, i.e. mimetically.

9   Michael Hardt, *Gilles Deleuze; An Apprenticeship in Philosophy* (Minneapolis, London: University of Minnesota Press, 1993), 107.

10   Patrice Petro, *Joyless Streets, Women and Melodramatic Representation in Weimar Germany* (New Jersey: Princeton Universitiy Press, 1989). Miriam Hansen, *Babel and Babylon, Spectatorship in American Silent Film* (Cambridge: Harvard University Press, 1991). An Australian text that doesn't quite fit into this schema is *"Don't Shoot Darling!": Women's Independent Filmmaking in Australia*, eds. Annette Blonski, Barbara Creed, Freda Freiberg (Victoria: Greenhouse Publications, 1987).

11   Anne Summers, *Damned Whores and God's Police*, rev. ed. (Ringwood, Victoria: Penguin, 1994).

12   Anne Summers, *The Sydney Morning Herald*, 25 January 1994, 2. Subsequent to the launch of her book there were a series of articles and letters in the Sydney press which opened up a debate on the problems of the generational knowledge and achievements of Australian feminism.

13   My thanks to Cassandra Robertson for her timely comment.

14   Ross has also addressed the theme of authorship and allegory in the photocopy portraits of the Australian artist Jane Richens, in "Portrait of the artist as photocopier; Jane Richens," *Continuum*, Special Issue on Electronic Arts in Australia, vol. 8 no. 1 (1994), 339–345.

15   See Meaghan Morris' reading of Claire Johnston's work as constituting an activist ethic and creating public memory, in "Too soon, too late: reading Claire Johnston, 1970–81," in Moore, *Dissonance*.

16   I wish to thank Thomas Engesser for his notion of "sensory-motor *criticism*" which he derives from Gilles Deleuze's description of the action image as being governed by a sensory-motor logic. In Deleuze, the sensory-motor schema offers an explanation of how action is organised in genre cinema in terms of responses to certain stimuli. According to this schema, perceptions and actions are always adequate to each other. See *Cinema 1: Movement Image* (Minneapolis: University of Minnesota Press, 1986) especially 205–215. For the moment, I think Engesser's notion of sensory-motor criticism offers a useful cautionary, "Hey! wait a minute."

17   See Gilles Deleuze, *Cinema 2: The Time-Image* (Minneapolis: University of Minnesota Press, 1989), 4. In the context of showing how the time image emerges in Italian Neo-Realist cinema Deleuze makes the following observation, "So the situation is not extended directly into action: it is no longer sensory-motor, as in realism, but primarily optical and of sound, invested by the senses, before action takes shape in it, and uses or confronts its elements." The implication here is that these new situations cannot be encountered via habitual responses and that some other mode of appre-

hension has to be developed. The agent of sensory-motor action is therefore replaced by the seer in Neo-Realist cinema. In this regard Deleuze writes of the importance of the child in Neo-Realist cinema who is characterised by a certain motor incapacity but sensory maturity. Deleuze, *Cinema 2*, 1–8.

18 *October*, no. 46 (1988), Special issue on the cinema and theory of Alexander Kluge, ed. Stuart Liebman.

19 Walter Benjamin, "On the Mimetic Faculty," *Reflections: Essays, Aphorisms, Autobiographical Writings*, ed. Peter Demetz, trans. Edmund Jephcott (New York: Schoken Books, 1978), 333.

20 Theodor Adorno says, "Art is a refuge for mimetic behaviour," in *Aesthetic Theory*, trans. C. Lenhardt (London and Boston: Routledge and Kegan Paul 1984), 79.

21 For a similar "descriptive" mimetic writing see the following articles by Lesley Stern, "The Oblivious Transfer: Analysing *Blue Velvet*," *Camera Obscura*, no. 30 (1994), 77–91; "When the Unexplained Happens: On Tracey Moffatt," *Photofile*, no. 40 (1993), 36–38; "*Opening Night*: The Acting-out of Gena Rowlands," a paper presented at the Fin de Siècle Feminisms Conference; "Gender, Art and Theory at the End of the Century," 18 September 1994, University of New South Wales, Sydney.

22 Miriam Hansen, "Benjamin, Cinema and Experience: 'The Blue Flower in the Land of Technology,' " *New German Critique*, no. 40 (Winter 1987), 179–224.

23 See Jodi Brooks' work on cinematic fascination as it operates in a diversity of filmic practices. "Consumed by Cinematic Monstrosity," *Art & Text*, no. 34 (1989), 79–94 and "Fascination and the Grotesque: *What Ever Happened to Baby Jane?*" *Continuum*, Special issue: *Film: Matters of Style*, ed. Adrian Martin, vol. 5 no. 2 (1992), 225–234.

24 Steven Shaviro, *The Cinematic Body*, (Minneapolis and London: University of Minnesota Press), 1993.

25 Ibid., 65.

26 Ibid., 252.

27 Deleuze, *Cinema 2*, pp 1, 2, 5. See Deleuze's re-reading of Bazin's reading of a famous sequence from De Sica's *Umberto D*.

28 Deleuze, *Cinema 1*, 215.

29 See "Discussing *Privilege*: An Interview with Yvonne Rainer," by Gabrielle Finnane in *Continuum*, vol. 5 no. 2 (1992), for a very detailed discussion of the performative strategies of the film.

30 Ruiz and Lisa Lyon have certainly reworked this great European archetype so that she cannot be recouped by psychoanalysis as Zizek does in the article cited above without revealing the reductive nature of that enterprise.

31 I am here indebted to Susan Buck-Morss' exegesis of Adorno's conception of mimesis as exact fantasy. *The Origin of Negative Dialectics; Theodor W. Adorno, Walter Benjamin, and the Frankfurt Institute* (Sussex: Harvester Press, 1977), see the section, "Exact Fantasy: Mimetic Transformation," 85–88.

Five Ages
of Film Feminism

Patricia Mellencamp

"What are we like, my generation of 1941?—romantic,
idealistic, fiercely partisan about politics and equality
of the sexes, determined to change our world."
Dorothy Hewett, *Wild Card*[1]

"It's hard to be politically conscious and upwardly mobile
at the same time ... To think there was a time when
we actually thought we were going to change the system."
Jane Wagner/Lily Tomlin (1983)
The Search for Signs of Intelligent Life in the Universe[2]

In her brilliantly funny script, Jane Wagner writes a history of the U.S.
women's movement through the diary of Lyn, a character created by
Lily Tomlin. In an euphoric 1970 entry, Lyn recalls "The 'Women's

Strike for Equality' March ... Betty Friedan says: 'We, today ... have learned the *power* of sisterhood!' And we did! ... It was worth risking our lives ... We're going to form a consciousness-raising group just like thousands of women all over the country are doing."[3]

Lyn's last scene, fourteen years later (1984), is a garage sale. Lyn is an unemployed, middle-aged, single mother, with a history of marriage, childbirth, divorce; she has experienced activism, meditation, and entrepreneurship. To her doctor's diagnosis of pre*mens*trual syndrome, Lyn replies that she and her mother are both getting divorced, "I'm raising twin boys. I have a lot of job pressure—I've got to find one ... my husband is involved with a ... woman ... who's quite a bit younger than I am ... And you think it's my *period* and *not* my life?"[4]

Our thoughts and friendships make up women's history—a series of everydays become big events over time. For Wagner, girl talk, personal experience, and popular culture are legit grounds for theoretical speculation. This is a women's epistemology, a logic, which unravels language and contradiction. Along with Wagner's and Tomlin's wit, Monique Wittig's materialism,[5] her call to move away from sexual difference, to "destroy the categories of sex in politics and philosophy," and the economics and factual irascibility of Virginia Woolf's *Three Guineas*, a piercing argument akin to Wittig, inspired these remarks.[6]

Not surprisingly, these powerful thinkers are similar. They acutely realise the hold of words and "logics" on our thoughts and hence on our daily lives. All three writers (simultaneously artists and critics) recast language, including personal pronouns. This is not deconstruction, that back-door, additive pleasure which always finds more. This is demolition, a frontal attack on everyday thoughts, on politics and economics, which is reductive. For women, there is usually less than meets the eye. Wagner, Wittig, and Woolf reveal that the purloined letter of women's inequality is in plain view. All we have to do is see it once. And then remember it—turning it into history. Writing can be the *practice* of liberation. But first we have to change the way we think.

The politics of Meaghan Morris, Laleen Jayamanne, and Tracey

Moffatt—as they tackle neo-colonialism or "multiculturalism"—take
me into the 1990s. My thoughts travel from youth to age, from anger
to compassion, from sexuality and desire to history and knowledge,
from sex to money, from difference to sameness, and from the U.S. to
Australia—where I read and admire the adventurous life, and the
courage to live it, of Dorothy Hewett. "Lucky Country" indeed! The
five ages of feminism can be taken historically, personally, and
descriptively. To be sure, this journey is idiosyncratic, particular.[7]

Taking the High Road

So there I was in 1974 (precisely like Lyn in Wagner's play), just after
the Civil Rights movement and the Vietnam War protest, in the midst
of the women's movement and sexual liberation, getting divorced,
raising two children as a "single parent," creating a film program,
organising conferences, and then ... discovering Lacan's subject divided in language ... through, of all places, film feminists! *This* is comedy!
The split subject of Lacan might have been news to men, but to working mothers? In retrospect, the elegant patina of theory made women,
and talking about women, legit, big-time academe. The irony of
women turning to men for answers *and* for legitimation is not new (or
over)—although it is a bit of a cringe. We still second class our experience and thought. What ensued was predictable: films by radical filmmaking mothers starring their children and titled "The Mirror Phase,"
after Lacan. No wonder women's history repeats every twenty or
thirty years.

The Scylla and Charybdis of semiotics and linguistics, cinema's *la
grande syntagmatique*, were not royal roads paved with golden nuggets
of knowledge about women, but rather arduous detours, tests of stamina and mettle akin to being trapped between a rock and a hard
place. Plucky feminists explored male subjectivity, male desire embedded in obscure words. Only the stalwart and sturdy, like Kaja

Silverman and Teresa de Lauretis, survived the prickly thorns of semiotics' terms. For many, terminology was terminal, leading nowhere. I can still recall the cranial exhaustion after reading essays on inner speech and suture in *Screen*. The new language of theory was a mixed blessing: theory (Barthes, Foucault, Deleuze) broke open academia along with the text, letting women into the debates; and theory took us as objects, even as absence (Lacan). Go figure.

I noticed, however, that many of the emperors were at least semi-naked. While looking outside, at great male systems for answers, I eventually saw that even the frog prince of theory, film theory, had a brazen history of ignoring women—unless they were femme fatales or pin-ups. Bazin spoke of pin-ups, perhaps imitating Kracauer and his analysis of female chorus lines and techniques of capitalism. Even Eisenstein, the theorist of my dreams, ignored women, including the fabulous and feisty female hero of *The Old and the New*. Barthes and Foucault followed suit, but showed me the path through the forest.

Gradually, like Dorothy, home from the exoticism of Oz or the wilds of the Prague School, and with Foucault's guidance, I realised that the answers were right in front of my eyes, in women's everyday lives—I just couldn't see them because they were covered-up by Art and Theory or framed as contradictions, a logic which I had learned as a girl in the 1950s. "Gradually" is a bit of an understatement—this took me almost twelve years to notice. Staring at grand theories of vision, I didn't see what was right in front of my eyes, the nose on my face gambit: women's personal experience, the drudgeries, delights, and dramas of our everyday life, our history of thought and action which we pass on to our daughters, to our sons, to our students.

Focusing on women's everyday lives, including the domestic regime, is not a trivial pursuit, as scholars like Paul Bove suggest.[8] Social problems like drug addiction and "health care" first appear on the women's pages as "women's issues." The Vietnam War was initially a "woman's issue" in the U.S. before it became men's news. After men take over our "issues," they become front page events. Women have "issues," replicated in the current self-help therapy lingo, which they talk about; men have events and take action; women's domain is the private and personal; men's terrain is the public and political.

This distinction between events and issues is complicated by Morris, writing on Claire Johnston. The key terms are experience, activism, history. "Whatever their differences, most feminisms have been marked (at least in their creative political phase) by an experimental approach to the present, a desire to shape the future, and an enterprising attitude to representing the past."[9] For the intrepid Morris, feminism is a struggle "to name a different temporality ... to bring about change and to contest what constitutes change."[10] What Morris calls feminism's skeptical and constructive attributes has made "feminism untimely" for many social historians. She concludes that Johnston's thought was eventful, "a temporal art with social implications; she was an activist, in the sense that she made things happen."[11] Feminists act, they *make* history; historians react, they *record* history. Unlike Johnston (and Woolf), we must live to tell about it.

Many women, even Johnston, thought that psychoanalysis or other theories of male subjectivity would provide the answers for women. They were dead wrong. Or, in *Thriller*[12] and so many Hollywood films including *Vertigo*, they were just plain dead.

A 1950s Parable

In *Vertigo*, the inscrutable Kim Novak as Madeleine/Judy lures us and the story on a false trail—into the mysterious secret of female sexuality and identity. First the film goes to the art museum for clues and then to art historians and the bookstore for answers. Jimmy Stewart/Scotty Ferguson tracks the victim of his desire to an art museum. Kim/Madeleine poses, presumably unaware of surveillance, transfixed by a painting of a woman. A dramatic series of point of view shots of Scotty looking and interpreting is a false trail. Madeleine is the lure who possesses knowledge, not Scotty.

However, this is known only in retrospect. For now, we are led to believe that the secret, which is both cause and effect, question and answer, is sex, that the woman's sexual identity, her story, lies in the painting and perhaps psychoanalysis. So, off to a bookstore and a scholar for answers: the painted woman is Carlotta Valdez, an enigma of Spanish eroticism, Madeleine's heritage, a figure who is both mysterious and mentioned only in passing.

What is critical is that women's history and identity, and maybe scholarly answers, mean absolutely nothing to the story. The trick is to make us believe women are significant while the only thing that matters is obsessive male desire. This is the con artist's shell game, or the magician's sleight of hand. In fact, Madeleine is not who she appears to be—something we learn late in the film. She can only be a masquerade, can only be what he wants her to be. Madeleine exists because of men. By herself, as herself, she doesn't matter. Along the way, a wife is murdered; even at the inquisition, nobody cares. Male obsession drives the film; female sexuality is only a screen, neither cause nor effect.

From the early 1970s through the 1990s, from Mulvey to Modleski, feminist film critics have been brilliantly investigating female subjectivity in Hitchcock films.[13] Feminist film theory begins with Judy/Madeleine, luminous and revolutionary work but still a blind alley, perhaps a dead end.

When she was very young, Hewett wrote, "Sexuality has taken the place of intellect. I resent his power over me but can't keep away ... While I share his obsession, these experiences hardly rate a mention in my diary. It is still full of unconsummated romance."[14]

(St)Ages One and Two: Intellectual Feminism and Irascible Feminism continued *Vertigo's* quest for glamour girls via the secret of sex, looking in the same few pages of the *Standard Edition*, Lacan's mirror, Hitchcock films, and other 1940s film genres.[15] Historically, this inscription of female subjectivity, particularly in the debates over

female spectatorship, was an astonishing and radical move. Nowhere in the history of film theory are women mentioned as subjects—extraordinary given the power and presence of female stars and women in the audience. Like the consumer courted by capitalism, *she* is absolutely *essential* and rarely mentioned. Thus, to add female subjectivity to the agenda, along with noticing the absence of women from so many texts, were great and brilliant moves.

What now appears so apparent to any undergraduate in the 1990s had, in 1975, been overlooked for eighty-five years. In "The Purloined Letter," the "principle of concealment," to paraphrase Poe, is "the excessively obvious"—which escapes observation. The "intellect ... passes unnoticed considerations too obtrusive, too self-evident." Sometimes the most "sagacious expedient" is "not concealing something."[16]

However, as productive as the feminist focus on sexual difference has been, it has continued, unabated, as sexuality and pleasure, for almost twenty years, with diminishing returns on a great investment. In spite of countless dead ends and warnings, "whatever you do, don't go into the forest," we spoke about sex constantly while maintaining it as the secret, the key to identity.

We didn't heed the good wolf, the Virginia Woolf, who forcibly talked money, work and knowledge in *Three Guineas* (1938) rather than sex and power, and urged us to "shut the bright eyes that reign influence, or let those eyes look elsewhere." Nor did we heed the grand wizard Foucault who saw through repression as the invisible cloak of sex —the emperor Freud wearing no clothes.[17] Rather than sex being repressed, as Freud died arguing, we were obsessed by it, speaking about it constantly. Deleuze and Guattari saw a white man's face superimposed over theory, and, like the little boy and the emperor, railed against what they perceived to be Freud's singular answer of Oedipus and castration for virtually everything.[18] Most feminists in the U.S. still ignore their trenchant critique of Freud.

For women, female sexuality is not an enigma, or a mystery.

Authority and the money economy are, along with power which, in
capitalism, is granted through money. Sex is only a mystery to children and, it would appear, to men. But like the purloined letter (and
the inequities of the money economy), there to be seen, we ignored
ourselves (and power/money), off chasing fantasy women via models
of male desire and subjectivity. In Poe's tale of a letter which passes
among men in an attempt to blackmail a woman, the contents of the
letter, which are never revealed, don't matter to the reader. By never
questioning the contents, we presumed the Queen's guilt—a tactic of
blaming the victim, like rape, which in fact becomes Lacan's metaphor
when analysing this tale. We imagined that we were all form, the eternal riddle of the sphinx, signifiers of glamorous mystery, a masquerade
or mask, that the thoughts and emotions and actions of our daily lives
didn't matter. Personal experience, our logic, was banished from the
kingdom of theory. (Never say "I.")

So was history, for a time, and economics. We watched hard working actresses on the screen while declaring women's absence as subjects. Why didn't we analyse, for example, Barbara Stanwyck's contract negotiations, her "conditions of production"? She was an independent agent, apparently choosing projects when it was
uncommon.[19] Why didn't we read *Mildred Pierce* in terms of the
money rather than (or in addition to) the sexual economy? Mildred's
greatest talent, along with being a devoted mother, was, after all, her
amazing ability to make money, to support herself and her daughters,
something the whining men around her fail to do. However, sexuality
was, in the late 1970s, given the urgency of radical politics, the surrealists' road to liberation. We failed to see that the endlessness of
Lacanian desire is similar to Freudian obsession—which is about fear
and anxiety, not libido, not freedom. Significantly, money is at the
base of obsession.

What is true of *Vertigo* and the MacGuffin of female sexuality might
be true of feminist film theory—ensnared in the form of secrecy—
speaking of hysteria and pleasure, primarily visual, circling obsession

and anxiety, mainly aural. We learned little about the Queen of Poe's tale, maintaining her as a mysterious, guilty enigma. Seeing ourselves as the seen rather than the seer, as the object rather than the subject, might not have been as empowering as it initially appeared to be.

We forgot that when the Queen grew older, she would be discarded, replaced by a younger dream girl, or relegated to the place of old crone of the fairy tale. Fantasy women are thin, smooth, young, and in most U.S. states, still Anglo (in Hawaii, she is Asian). Aging women and, until recently in the U.S., women of colour, need not apply.[20]

This aging riddle must be weary of being unknowable, of being seductive, of being guilty. What an anguish never to speak one's mind. What a drag to embody desire all the time—as Juan Davila impersonating Kim Novak in Jayamanne's *A Song of Ceylon* must know. But what a source of profit for the lingerie, cosmetic, fashion, and weight-loss industries. Why have we spent so much time on this old story? Is this what we wanted to be? Is this how we fancied ourselves? Are feminists in denial when it comes to romance? Feminist film theory has heavily invested in the sexual economy at the expense of the money economy, a divestiture which sold off history. Precisely as women gained political force, sex took on the contours of an obsession.

Paradoxically, intellectual feminism, so reliant on psychoanalysis, has paid scant heed to Freud's work on obsession, about which he wrote more than on any other topic, devoting fourteen major papers to it. His first was in 1894; his most famous in 1909, "Notes Upon a Case of Obsessional Neurosis" (the Rat Man [a.k.a. Dr. Ernst Lanzer]), in which rats are equated with money, then children; *Beyond the Pleasure Principle* and "The 'Uncanny.' " in 1919; and in 1926, the substantial and, for women, important revision, *Inhibitions, Symptoms, Anxiety*. For Freud, "Obsessional neurosis is unquestionably the most interesting and repaying subject of analytic research."[21]

One explanation for the oversight of this work is the emphasis of feminist film theory on vision more than sound or thought; Freud linked hysteria to *visual memory* while obsession is tied to *thoughts*, to words. *Studies in Hysteria* states that whereas memories of hysterical patients usually return in pictorial form, the memories of obsessionals return as thoughts.[22] By *Totem and Taboo* (1913), hysteria is a "gesture language" and obsession a "thought-language" with hysteria "similar to the picture-language of dreams,"[23] hence a logical basis for a film theory predicated on vision (equated with knowledge: "to see" as "to understand.")

The differences between logics of hysteria and obsessional neurosis are instructive. Hysteria satisfies opposing impulses simultaneously, and obsession satisfies opposing impulses through sequential acts. As Freud argues in Rat Man, in "hysteria two birds are killed with one stone. In contrast, a contiguity marks the diphasic obsession, acts where a first activity is undone by a second."[24] At the base of hysteria is conflict; at the base of obsessions are what Freud called reproaches (guilt, shame, hypochondria)—which have a lot to do with women. Both are the result of holding opposing or contradictory thoughts. Both logics apply in different measures to films, constructing different thought processes, different subjectivities.[25]

As Henry Jaglom's infuriating and fascinating film *Eating* suggests, food has replaced sex as women's obsession. The obsession is exacerbated, perhaps triggered, by the delusions of romance—that men, beauty, and possessions make women's lives meaningful. In *Eating*, self-help meets upper class anthropology; over-eaters anonymous goes Hollywood. An arty surveillance camera is wielded by a male witness in the treacherous wilds of a Beverly Hills home filled with fairy tale princesses of all ages, years later, like a Grimm sorority reunion. Women at a birthday party are almost an alien species of obsessional neurotics. Only one bingeing twenty year old and a seventy-five year old mother (Candice Bergen's real mother) eat any of the six cakes. Here, all the women are full of blame, self-pity, self-hatred. Women are only their vacant bodies, bingeing, aging, dieting. In spite of their apparent beauty, and variety, they are ensnared in common self-loathing.

Obsession—so central for an analysis of *Vertigo* and so operant in contemporary U.S. culture—shifts from desire to anxiety, from the unconscious to the conscious, moving away from Oedipus and castration and toward loss and the female subject. This is a model of anxiety rather than pleasure, an economics of money more than libido, and a logic of contradiction that, for me, captures women's experience within commercial culture. This is the epistemology we need to break through, this is what keeps us captive to desires, others and our own.

However, romance or envy are sometimes the repressed of feminist film criticism; both share mechanisms with obsession. The story of romance—a genre that serves male desire and fantasy—and the tactic of envy which divides women against each other and consequently against our selves, so permeate popular culture that extricating oneself is not easy. Like obsession, romance is not an innocent pastime—it teaches us to relentlessly define ourselves by outside standards, our central measure of self, being desirable for someone else. Like obsession, it takes up more and more time, to the exclusion of other concerns.

For Ann Barr Snitow, romance novels produce a "pathological experience of sex difference"—Wittig's analysis with a twist: women are subjects; men are objects, mysterious, unknowable.[26] The heroine waits for the hero's next move, occupying her time with tourism and consumerism, wondering what to wear, and existing in a constant state "of potential sexuality." She has only one thing on her mind— *him.* "Pleasure for women is men." However, this is not pleasure but anxiety. Romance verges on obsession: "the pleasure lies in the ... waiting, anticipation, anxiety." The heroine waits, fears, and speculates, in a fever of "anti-erotic anxiety."

Women's great adventure is romance, "the one they are socially sanctioned to seek," and to which they constantly "return in imagination." The transcendent moment, as TV soaps so well know, is "the first phase of love." "Unlike work, which leads to development, advancement, romance depends on passivity, on not knowing ... Once the heroine knows, the story is over. Nothing interesting remains."

The premises of heterosexual romance are, for Helen Taylor, not unlike lesbian romance novels—"they *feed* certain regressive elements in the female experience."[27] She argues that there is a feminist reworking of "romance novels," and "a growing market for new lesbian romances." Women now desire women. For Barr and Taylor, romance speaks to women's fantasies, desires, and longings. I see most romance differently—as inscribing (male or female) desire/sex at the core of women's lives. Herein is the kinship of romance with intellectual feminism.

The trouble with men's dream girls—the flip side of self-loathing—is that, like Madeleine, they are so boring, so caught up in obsessions which are not even their own. Yet, dream girls can become interesting and intelligent women, living by their wits and their bodies—which are aesthetic and erotic pleasures, not problems or masquerades. There is more to the mystery of women's lives than sex.

In *(St)Age Two:* Irascible Feminism, words become weapons. Women have discovered their "lack" or absence and are furious. If words could kill, the academic death toll would be high. These whip-cracking women also go to Hitchcock and other male experts for answers which are used against them—with superb wit and arch anger. However, it is still a man's world. The fascination is male subjectivity which feminism can dominate and then replace. Little changes except that women, not men, run things. Woolf advocated radical change—women should enter the professions to change institutions, altering, not replicating, power structures and values.

We thought this is what we were doing as we complained about generic men or skewered famous men. But by blaming men, we assumed victimhood; we gave power away. We learned little about the Queen of Poe's tale, nothing about Madeleine/Judy, and next to nothing about ourselves. The problem with anger is that it tries to regain old ground rather than staking out new territory and making new claims. Rage is thus tautological, producing more of the same, which might explain the *déjà vu* of much current scholarship. (As one of Jane Wagner's characters says, "I've lost the same ten pounds so many times, my cellulite is experiencing *déjà vu*.") Stages One and Two remain within the terms of the theories they critique—an uneasy consonance. This was my stance in "Sexual Economics" and in "Oedipus and the Robot in *Metropolis*," the nagging victim manoeuvre, a stance of negativity, of self-pity.

As Dorothy Hewett writes of her activism in the Australian communist party, "I was already well on the way to becoming that most dangerous and humourless of creatures, a martyr to a cause. I actually wanted to suffer in the cause of the working class. But I couldn't help lingering in front of shop windows, lusting after the latest fashions."[28]

I am no longer interested in dream girls, in theories of sexual desire, or in secrets. Warhol was right; with enough repetition, sex becomes boring. I am interested in women's knowledge and in the money, along with the sexual, economy—why we have more knowledge and less authority (and money). I suspect we have been led astray—down a garden path of theory.

(St)Ages Three and Four shift the point of view to women—to the Queen, to Madeleine. This shift is marked for me by Sally Potter's *Thriller*, a 1979 film which (1) interrogates the romance of classical texts, along with envy between women, and (2) inscribes history and women's points of view, including women of colour.

I wonder how Judy felt—only a few seconds are from her point of view, in fact, one look in the mirror and a flashback, and then all we know is that she knows that Scotty knows. For Judy, like Thelma and Louise, men are fatal. However, Thelma and Louise *choose* death—an heroic rather than sacrificial, inadvertent death like Judy's. And Judy was alone, without female allies. Potter is right on in *Thriller* when Mimi of *La Boheme* wonders why she died, why she and Musetta didn't get together. Mimi concludes that her death was murder. It served male desire to be "the hero."

What if the nun who appears in the tower during the death scene in *Vertigo* was a feminist detective and had saved Judy at the end? Or, like *Sunset Boulevard*, we told the tale from the dead Judy's point of view, splattered over the mission's floor. This would be a dissection of male obsession comparable to Gloria Swanson's obsession with youth. What Norma Desmond really wanted was to work, acting in films, her profession. While the balding Cecil B. DeMille, looking 70, is at the studio, working, playing himself, Norma Desmond, not looking a day over 40, is encased in her mansion, too old to be an actress. Talk about double standards. What about Midge, surrounded by the sexy lingerie she is designing, who is barely noticed in *Vertigo*? Imagine Midge and Judy joining a therapy group on codependency and sexual obsession and becoming friends. After all, who needs this crazed looking, aging guy with all these problems?

(*St*)*Age Three:* Experimental Feminism, multiplies differences—homo-, trans-,bi-, from hetero-sexual; African-, Hispanic-, Asian-, Native American from Anglo-American. Film audiences replicate the on-screen declarative prefixes. However oppositional, the sexual body is the focus. Teresa de Lauretis, for example, argues a theory of lesbian fantasy modelled on Sheila McLaughin's film, *She Must Be Seeing Things*, and Laplanche and Pontalis's model of psychoanalysis. De Lauretis also draws on Wittig's notion of the lesbian body as "not a woman" because "what makes a woman is a specific social relation to a man, a relation ... called servitude ... economic obligation."[29]

In certain ways, these arguments retain the oppositional edge (and many of the premises) of early feminist film theory. In 1974, when all this began, the concept of sexual difference embodied a radical politics, similar to the social differences between what Woolf calls in 1938 the sons and daughters of educated men. As oversights were pointed out throughout the 1980s, cultural and racial differences multiplied. Eventually and subtly, sexual split off from difference, becoming "sexuality" which multiplied into bisexuality, transsexuality, lesbian, gay sexuality and then divided, hetero- versus homo-. However, Wittig aside, the body, whether metaphorical or not, is still the focus, and sexual discourse the source of intellectual pleasure. This can be oppositional politics. But even resistant sexuality can work to conceal discrepant economics. (Fashion speeded things up by turning race, multiculturalism, and queer theory into trends, marketing ploys, best selling books, and TV talk show topics.) Because the political stakes and personal risk were high, prefixes verged on identity. One specificity waged intellectual struggle with another. Commonality was gained for each, a good thing, and common purpose was lost for all.

To my 1986 assertion and belief that "differences are productive," I would add, "up to a point." Unless differences are driven by a common goal, they separate us. Commonalities unite us, creating unity in diversity (and in adversity).

Privilege

Yvonne Rainer's *Privilege*, a crossover film of noble intent, is on the cusp of this stage, and this quandary.[30] It addresses race, touches on lesbianism, and is about aging. However, it is a film of positions rather than experiences—a paradox in that so many women talk. Amidst all the information, it fails to listen and it speaks for others. It can't hear because its mind is on something else—men as the central story of women's lives. Caught up in the tenets of heterosexual romance, *Privilege* enacts what it attempts to critique.

Jenny is the middle-aged protagonist, discussing menopause and aging with over sixteen women, conversations interrupted by her memory (a 25 year old secret of a rape told in flashback) and intercut footage of educational medical films. Computer text, along with voice-over, adds information on aging to the collage. Women's daily lives provide the setting—a docu-drama of staged conversation. The flashback adds elements of psycho-drama. The film feels like a treatise *and* self-help therapy—*Eating* goes to Soho.

The central problem is the central character—Jenny (Alice Spivak), the film's star who has no last name unlike Yvonne Washington (Novella Nelson), Rainer's African-American alter-ego. While *Privilege* is about aging (its biology and its gendered inequities), it dramatises women's immaturity: Jenny's desire to be desired is fatally uninteresting. At heart, Jenny is still a girl, wondering where youth and Daddy went and what to do without it and him. She feels empty, the romantic heroine thirty years later.

A life spent in pursuit of *him* would indeed be a life wasted, a life to regret. But Jenny is not that far along. Amidst fashionable political issues, *Privilege* tells the same old story—without men, women are nothing. Race and aging become subordinate to the film's real concern. The *big* question is: "So what do I do now that the men have stopped looking at me. I'm like a fish thrown back into the sea, longing to be hooked. I still want them to look, proud of being looked at. It's a chronic disease that you never get over."

Jenny doesn't lament once or twice about her new, imagined undesirability. "Must a woman's feelings about herself depend on a man's assessment of her body?" (By now, she is driving me nuts! *Where have you been?*) Jenny sounds like a recovering intellectual feminist, in denial all these years about how much the male gaze and desire *personally* mattered while *intellectually* attacking it. Jenny: "My biggest shock in reaching middle age was realising that men's desire for me was the linchpin of my identity." What makes Jenny pathetic is defining herself in relation to men and her body rather than her mind or accomplishments.

What is really at stake in *Privilege* is the loss (rather than the gain) of male heterosexual desire—the passing of that determination in our lives. Yet Rainer takes this blessing as a problem. Why do we continue to limit ourselves to our bodies, real or metaphorical? Are sex and male desire all that matter?

Age (49) is menopause, hot flushes, hysterectomies. Biological determinism prevails in spite of the economic and social arguments.

Fear of aging drives the film in spite of its upbeat denials: "When you're young, they whistle at you; when you're middle-aged, they treat you like a bunch of symptoms; and when you're old, they ignore you." Heterosexual desire, determined by men (which, for me, is the key, not simply heterosexual desire per se), propels the women's anxiety. The double standard, linked to biology (sex, race, and age) rather than social contradiction, drives the film's logic.

African and Hispanic American women come to the rescue of the aging, white heterosexual (who could be on her middle-aged way to homo-). Like sex, race is an enigma and a solution. Digna, the Latino woman, is in the unconscious (or the back seat of the car), waiting to rescue Jenny from her heterosexual history. Class is romanticised. "Whiteness" appears as natural, it is what Michele Wallace criticises as "an unmarked term." For Wallace, the film is "depressing in its inability to take seriously the subjectivities of women of colour."[31] Yvonne Washington, Rainer's super-ego, rarely speaks. The African-American woman is silenced *while* represented—making the silence even louder. (In contrast, Digna talks so fast, in translation, that her words run together.)

In an interview, Rainer candidly conceded this point: "In Australia … there was a woman in the audience, who was Aboriginal I think. She was critical that all the material about race was mostly rhetorical or literary, and all the documentary interviews were about menopause."[32]

Wallace calls this a "structural problem." I think it is an inability to *hear* women. Wallace notes, "The positions from which women of colour speak … are qualitatively different from and inferior to positions from which white women, white men, and men of colour speak."[33] This is also the problem with difference; it operates through hierarchy which we internalise, against our best efforts. There is no "equality in difference." As Wittig suggests, "Women should do without the privilege of being different."[34]

What is also troubling is the linkage of men of colour with the rape

of white women—which Hazel Carby has argued, via the 1890s jour-
nalism of Ida B. Wells on lynching, historically served white men. The
victim of the flashback rape is a (white) lesbian, but the story and trau-
ma of the rape belong to Jenny, the witness. Wallace points out that
"the historical rape of the black woman—which literally founded the
African American race" is ignored.

As Wallace writes, "Rainer establishes a hierarchical continuum
along which the individual's potential capacity for privilege and vic-
timisation is carefully calibrated. According to this view, white men
can't be victims any more than a Latino woman of colour can have
privilege."

Privilege is determined by sex and male desire. For Jenny, who used
to be "advantaged sexually," now, "having passed the frontier of
attractiveness to men, she is now on the *other side* of privilege." (Jenny
comes up with this just after her scene in bed with Robert, the
Assistant DA. While her memory is young, her body is middle-aged.) If
privilege is granted to women by men, then privilege is servitude by
another name. And these are not the negative privileges of history —
class and race, but of sex and desire; not the privileges of work—education and profession, but of sex and attractiveness.

For me, under the influence of Morris, the economics and politics
of privilege circle around money and power. When women age, they
move to the margins of power; when men age, they become CEOs,
Presidents, making big decisions and big bucks. Money and property
could assuage many side-effects of menopause and many inequities of
race.

I suspect that the contradictions of daily life are more difficult to
notice than those of art and theory. Here the secrets are not glamorous. Few of us see our lives as heroic. Yet "we were the ones who
gave birth, who had blood on our hands ... We were the ones who held
things together. We were the ones who, if the cupboard was bare,
faced the open mouths of our children ... We knew the story of daily
life, the price of bread, the story of a bargain." Through great lines like

these, *For Love or Money*, the Australian documentary, revises history, of which Woolf was deeply suspicious. Like *Three Guineas*, the film collects evidence, statistics which paint a different picture of the world, one which includes Aboriginal women. The film charts the repeated struggle for equal pay. It is about daily, heroic life—work and money and why we have less.

Fairy tales also depend on the everyday and on the present which becomes magical, incalculable, a bit irrational. They start from the familiar, with a beginning and an end in the familiar. I have always preferred the small pleasures to the big ones. For me, the familiar is delightful—books in bed at night and coffee in the morning. In fairy tales, the familiar and the unfamiliar collide. The everyday becomes a world of wonder and surprise rather than the repetition and boredom often ascribed to women's daily lives.

Fairy tales also have a critical flaw—happily ever after. It is that happily ever after, the satiation granted by the passage into men's arms, that is questioned by *Thelma and Louise*. To her great surprise, Rapunzel was not taken to a palace and a life of luxury as "kingdom" would imply. Instead, she was dumped in the suburbs and named Thelma. Rather than huge and airy white spaces, her house is cramped, brown, and impossible to keep clean. Instead of the prince and servants catering to her every pleasure, she waits on the gold-chained, beer drinking salesman, appeasing his every nasty, petty, violent whim, only doing what he wants, and, according to him, doing nothing well. How did this happen? She used to have a mind, and a body, and a *life* of her own, didn't she? She can't remember. Happily ever after, after all, has turned out to be a nightmare of entrapment and anxiety.

Thank God the sorceress, Louise, now working as a waitress at a diner and driving a convertible, was her close friend. Louise's life hadn't been perfect, either—including a rape in Texas about which she wouldn't speak, and an OK but unspeakably boring guy, an Elvis wannabe who can barely speak. Within the first five minutes of the film, Thelma and Louise leave for a weekend at a cottage. Little did they know that lecherous wolves, and their own confused desire, would dog their every move, luring them off the track, with the ultimate trap laid in the film's end. Little did they expect that the film would be a media event—of pro and con, feminist or not—and that "thelmad and louised" would become a phrase for violent action.

Thelma and Louise

The film's first shot is of the road, in the West. Neither "the road" nor "the West," locations of adventure, have been spaces for women's movement. In both genres, women were static. In the Western, they were confined to the schoolroom, the saloon, or the ranch kitchen (although this is changing). Rather than taking to the open road as male authors did, women remained behind, waiting; or they were way stations along the way. Thelma and Louise are on the road, in the West. The car is a place of talk, of friendship which leads to insights. This Thunderbird convertible becomes an icon of freedom. The men remain behind, waiting.

The black and white photo of the opening image turns to colour, the camera pans up, the image darkens. Is this the road to nowhere or the road to freedom? Are they running away or moving forward? Or both? The film runs along two tracks. There is the linear narrative, the outer journey or chase, accompanied by dramatic camerawork and directed by Ridley Scott, and an inner journey into feminist self-awareness revealed by behaviour, gesture, appearance and talk and written by Callie Khouri.[35] What the men back home imagine (like many in the audience) is different from what is happening to Thelma and Louise. They are coming together more than running away, facing reality rather than escaping it, becoming self-reliant and heroic rather than helpless and scared, being courageous not violent. This interior journey more than the narrative destination is what matters. This doubled, simultaneous "action" explains the polarity in responses generated by the film.

The film's move from dependence on men to independent women is marked by numerous stylistic touches. As Thelma and Louise change, everything around them changes, even the density of the air (and possibly the film stock). *Thelma and Louise* proceeds from clutter and confinement to open space, from noise and city trucks to silence and the desert, from high-necked blouses and skirts to open necks and jeans, from coiffed to loose hair, from stasis to movement, from indecision to decisiveness. They look and act completely different at the end.

The film mirrors their internal state, it reflects their thoughts. The deafening sounds of the trucks' horns after the rape-killing are blaring, frightening—like their confused minds. They pass through hard-edged, loud, transient spaces—motels, gas stations, truck stops. The rock and country songs on the track play out their lives, their moods. Gradually, the film becomes quieter, as do Thelma and Louise, until it reaches the solitude and soft focus of the end.

Thelma and Louise traverse a dangerous gamut of sexism. Men have been separating women for years—a scenario replayed through Daryl, then Harlan, and J.D. They are all *bad* choices for Thelma, which she, like so many women, continues to make. Believing they cannot make it without men no matter how pathetic, women give their lives away, often without knowing how it happened. Here, however, each encounter with men is a lesson which threatens their very survival. As "the law" and men lose their control over women, men up the ante and the technology. Parallel editing of the escalating and cowardly actions of the police and Daryl (holding the men in confined spaces) shows us what particularly Thelma is escaping.

In the beginning, these women measured their lives and defined themselves by men's desire which was claustrophobic. Their first shots are in the kitchen —Thelma in her brown suburban home and Louise in the crowded diner, calling Thelma. At the country rock bar, Thelma flirts with Harlan, drinks too much Wild Turkey, and goes outside with him, without Louise. Male desire turns violent. Louise rescues Thelma, by holding a gun to Harlan's head. Louise doesn't shoot Harlan after the attempted rape. She kills him after he says "suck my cock," after she has turned and begun to walk away. Harlan was not cowed or remorseful. He tried to get the last word, as will the obnoxious trucker. Words are taken seriously in this film.

Thelma repeats her destructive behaviour, looking for meaning and pleasure in men, by picking up the drifter/petty criminal, J.D. Again, men come between women. While Thelma is telling Louise about her first orgasm, J.D. steals Louise's money—which they needed for Mexico. Romance and sex, which can be self-destructive, have serious consequences for women. (Instead of focusing on men and sex/romance, they should have kept their eyes on the money and themselves.) At the same time, sex is liberating. The women's roles shift; Thelma begins to initiate action and make decisions. She learns from experience.

The soundtrack is dense, with effects and music. The words are few and illuminating, intelligent. Through words, their lives come into clarity. "All he wants me to do is hang around the house." "I can't go back. Something has crossed over." Thelma begins to take responsibility for her actions: "We couldn't go to the police ... no one would have believed us. I'm not sorry ... I'm having some fun ... I'm just sorry you did it and not me."

The critical choice is on the soundtrack. "Do I want to come out alive. I don't know." Women's desire for freedom, for independence, can turn them into heroes. Louise: "We've got to decide if we want to come out dead or alive." "I feel awake ... wide awake." During the miraculous escape under the bridge, "Whatever happens, I'm glad I came with you." The key scene is the surreal night of anguish in the desert, which foreshadows the end, daybreak, their turning point. These poetic scenes of decision wherein characters wrestle with their own conscience usually belong to men. "It happened to you, in Texas, you were raped." After this respite, the peace before the end, the car glides silently through space. They have entered historical time. There is no one in the universe but them, moving through darkness and history.

As I suggested, women have not moved through this open, Western space very often in films. They wore heavy skirts and petticoats and sat in the wagon or made flapjacks in the kitchen. The film's aerial shots are not like John Ford's Monument Valley, conquering the land, triumphant over space. Thelma and Louise almost become part of the land, neither conquered nor conquering. The huge scale of the landscape is intercut with intimate, personal shots. The editing begins to dissolve close-ups of them into each other. "You're a good friend." "You, too, the best." "This is the first chance you've had to express yourself." The parallel tracks of the film merge into one.

Grand Canyon looms before them. The Thunderbird is cut off by helicopters and a small army of police. Women's choice is between a rock and a hard place. Or perhaps it is between freedom and confinement. Louise: "I'm not giving up." Thelma: "Let's not get caught ... Let's keep on going." These are key words. Death allows them to "keep on going." Life would have meant confinement in prison or marriage. Louise: "You sure?" In a series of extreme close-ups, they are smiling, without fear, looking at each other, laughing. They hold hands and kiss, the polaroid they took at the beginning flies away, the car is held in a freeze frame over the canyon. In the end, Thelma and Louise defy gravity, gaining mastery of themselves, becoming triumphant over death. The ending is courageous, profound, sublime.[36]

Thelma and Louise take their authority from death, as Potter does in *Thriller*. According to Walter Benjamin:

> It is characteristic that not only a [wo]man's knowledge or wisdom, but above all [her] real life—and this is the stuff that stories are made of—first assumes transmissible form at the moment of [her] death ... Death is the sanction of everything that the storyteller can tell. [S]He has borrowed [her] authority from death.[37]

The film's relation to history, to women's past, is comparable to Morris' analysis of Claire Johnston: "She saw the past as a 'dynamic' vital to any struggle, but ... this dynamic must have nothing to do with lost heritage, and everything to do with creating effective ways of action in the present."[38] For *Thelma and Louise*, the rape initiates their journey, it pushes them forward. They become fearless. For *Privilege*, the flashback rape is a primal scene, holding Jenny back, making her timid. For Johnston and Thelma and Louise, "memory was a practice ... of becoming."

Angel at My Table

In an interview in the *Village Voice* for the opening of *Angel At My Table*, the New York film release of the TV series, Jane Campion ("startlingly frank for a public figure") said she had searched for "a grammar of the brain that had to do with story."[39] I like this phrase, a "grammar of the brain," an epistemophilia. Of the author, Janet Frame, Campion said that the "mythologies of our lives ... begin with childhood images." For Frame, these images are related to fairy tales which also have a dark to nightmarish side. For years, Frame was institutionalised for schizophrenia, receiving hundreds of shock treatments, only to learn that she had been misdiagnosed. In Frame's work, the princesses and sorceresses are all locked up in institutions— another version of Rapunzel.

Her novels (made available in the U.S. after the film's release) are about the difficulty of language, of speaking. For example, in *Scented Gardens for the Blind*, Erlene Glace is either unable or unwilling to speak. Her mother, Vera, presumably writes about her mute daughter: "a living fable, with no spinning wheel to prick her finger upon, dropping blood to the snow, no underground stream where at midnight the old soldier will ferry her to the palace for dancing." Vera Glace is "one of the many sorceresses in Frame's work," sorceresses who can

shift the point of view, and come back from the dead. The fact that
Vera "has been a mental patient, childless, unable to speak, for the last
30 years," emerges only at the end. Like Campion, Frame is not "afraid
of loose ends," of ambivalence or ambiguity.[40] Contradictions remain
amidst multiple narratives.

Angel at My Table is the story of Janet Frame's life. The television
series was made by women—produced by Bridgit Ikin, edited by
Veronika Haussler, written by Laura Jones, directed by Jane
Campion—and stars the point of view of women. It was released in the
U.S. as a single film divided into three sections, replicating its televi-
sion origins—a coproduction with The Australian Broadcasting
Commission, Channel Four, and Television New Zealand.

Part I, "The Is-Land," "This is the story of my childhood" is, like
the rest of the tale and Campion's style, told in snatches, in glimpses
which include death: of Frame's twin, who died in 1924, of shots of
the "loonies," of extreme close-ups of a child's eyes, of chewing gum in
school and being punished, of sleeping four abed in a New Zealand
farm home, of Janet outside, watching. The everyday, particularly the
New Zealand landscape, is magical, menacing, strange and familiar.
The rural family contains daily tragedies as abrupt, unexpected, and
normal as life itself. School is the regime of disciplinary, discomforting
space. While the production is big, with a huge cast in many locales,
the drama is intensely subjective, intimate.

Freda Freiberg perfectly describes Campion's style—"images
which disquiet if not jar. Through bizarre or even grotesque framing,
jolting cuts, and a *mise-en-scène* which often verges on the surreal, her
films invest everyday, domestic, and trivial scenes and situations with
an edge of menace."[41] The "edge of menace" is a wonderful phrase.
Kate Sands describes the films' narrative obsessionality—quoting
Freiberg—bizarre, surreal, with an atmosphere of menace, often
linked with sexual obsession and sexual perversity—to say nothing of
sexual abuse.[42]

The "terrible and telling significance of minor detail"[43] is, for me, the key. However, I do not agree that the details are minor (unless this is minor in the Deleuzian sense, as was Kafka). Rather they are embedded in a complex style—there but not battering us over the head, like an exquisite, hand-tailored, designer suit rather than a flashy one off the rack. High style is always in the details.

> When I begin to read I people the world of the
> farm with characters from ... Grimm's *Fairy
> Tales*... . I both love and fear them.[44]

Walter Benjamin said that "The first true storyteller is, and will continue to be, the teller of fairy tales."[45] When I was a little girl, my grandmother read "The Twelve Dancing Princesses" to me every night. For her sake, I would try with all my might to pick another tale, but I always chose this story, of the princesses who danced every night on the opposite shore, their whereabouts unbeknownst to the King, their father. It was far and away my favourite. I was delighted when Janet read this story, a metaphor for the film, to her sisters in bed. While our histories are different, and we come from distant parts of the world, Frame and I loved the same story about clever princesses who had adventures and stuck together until they were separated by the prince, with his cloak of invisibility.

A bit later in the film, Janet stages the story with her sisters in the woods at night. It is dark and scary, they wear costumes, the owls hoot. Janet notices her older sister's growing breasts, sees her smoking, and then watches her having sex in the woods. Death, not a prince, intervenes. After a family outing, including the four bathing beauties posing for a photograph, Myrtle drowns at the baths. Janet had been studying her, imitating her, then she was gone.

Although I was a very social being who loved parties and had hundreds of dates, I recognised myself in Janet—particularly her love of books which she holds, caresses. I also recognised my shy son in Janet. She is the outsider, watching, isolated. At school, the popular girls are together, she is off to the side, awkwardly aware of her body. Being in public spaces is painful. At home at night is violence, the war, death. Her shyness and discomfort are misdiagnosed as mental illness. She writes, reads, and then leaves for college.

In Part II, "An Angel at My Table," Janet has books but no life with people. She withdraws, even from her sisters, until she is alone, fearful. During an observation of her teaching, she panics and is speechless—formerly my fear. Finally, she is hospitalised in the psych ward, diagnosed as a schizophrenic. Massive electro-therapy is a violent assault on her body—a body which has not been glamourised, which is not the sexual body of film theory. A voice-over tells us that in eight years she had two hundred shocks. Then, the magical event, she wins a prize for her book *The Lagoon*—her lobotomy is cancelled and she moves into a cottage to write—her salvation. Yet, she is still watching, not living, life. She believes that she needs experience so leaves for adventure and Part Three.

"The Envoy from Mirror City" begins with a memory—of the four sisters at the sea, singing "To France." Janet travels to London, to Spain and tries to be part of an intellectual group. She has sex with Bernard—who is from Ohio. After she returns to London, despair, and a miscarriage, she discovers that she never had schizophrenia in the first place. Nothing was wrong with her. Academia, psychoanalysis, and finally romance and sex failed Janet, all seeing her as a problem which needed a cure.

After her father dies, she begins to write again. Defining herself as "well," Janet takes responsibility for her life. She discovers that meaning comes from within. We make our lives what they are. Janet returns home, to the spectacular New Zealand countryside. She sees the swimsuit photograph of the four sisters, the dancing princesses united, does the twist, and begins her own life, liberated at last. For in the end, this is the only struggle and goal. *Angel At My Table* is a happily ever after fairy tale—of heroic survival and freedom which has nothing to do with a prince or someone else's desire. No longer awkward, Janet is quite beautiful. This transformation has not been through the prince's eyes, an external standard, but through Janet's mind. This exceptional story is also the story of our daily lives.

Benjamin tells us that storytellers speak of the "circumstances" they have directly learned or they "simply pass it off as their own experience."[46] Like my friend, Morris and her tall tales, story is elided with personal experience, or what in Australia is an anecdote. This emphasis on *mutual* experience creates a reciprocity between speaker/listener, a companionship and familiarity central to Benjamin. The story comes "from oral tradition" and shared experiences—the stuff of which Moffatt, Dash, and Campion films are made. The experience can be the storyteller's or "reported by others. And [she] in turn makes it the experience of those who are listening to [her] tale." Thus, the listener has a stake in hearing and in remembering the story, which exists in "the realm of living speech," of shared "companionship."[47] This living speech, forged in mutual experience, is intriguing for feminism—a hearing as much as a seeing, a history as much as a fiction.

Benjamin's distinction between the novel and the story suggests Deleuze and Guattari's distinction between major and minor literatures. Morris details this in relation to Johnston, but it could also work for what Morris calls experimental feminism: "living and writing, art and life, are opposed only from the point of view of a major literature."[48] For Benjamin, "the novelist has isolated himself" from the realm of shared experience.[49] As Morris points out, the minor is not "marginal"; "it is what a minority constructs *in a major language*," "a model of action from a colonised position *within* a given society,"[50] like Hollywood, feminism, and *Thelma and Louise*; like Frame, Campion, Moffatt, and Dash. Minor films are a mode of becoming with no opposition between art and life. (For Bakhtin, carnival crosses "the self-conscious borderline between art and life, making little formal distinction ... between author and co-creating reader."[51])

In every case the storyteller ... has counsel for [her] readers. But if today 'having counsel' is beginning to have an old-fashioned ring, this is because the communicability of experience is decreasing ... after all, counsel is less an answer to a question than a proposal concerning the continuation of a story which is just unfolding."[52] Rather than being over, as postfeminists declare, I see women's stories, feminists' stories, as unfolding and continuing.

(St)Age Four: Empirical Feminism. The first question to be asked of history, and narrative, is what is missing. Women per se are not always missing—but what they think and do are. Not women's bodies, but women's knowledge and work need reclamation. In many ways, the dominant model of feminist film theory is wrong. Women have been watching, from the sidelines, for years. They often possess the gaze but not the economic means. They see and know, but it doesn't matter; they have no authority.

Empirical feminism unravels, consciously, the historical *experience* of economic, social contradictions, including those of race—in which appearance is not a clue to buried or biological secrets and concealed meanings but rather a question—there to be seen. Sex is not an answer, and perhaps not even a question. Rather than consonance with men's theory, there is a disquieting dissonance with history.

When the intonation, the enunciation shifts into women's minds and into our history (which includes our experience)—an epistemophilia, a desire to know as well as a scopophilia, the desire to see—we cease thinking like victims and become empowered, no matter what happens. As Collette Lafonte asks in *Thriller*, "Would I have wanted to be the hero?" That is the question for women. *For Love or Money* answers: "We find heroes only in monuments in public parks but I think the real heroes are us." This has been a big step for feminist film theory, one which recapitulates early feminist activism—from 1890 through the 1920s, in the 1940s, and again in the 1960s, the twenty year, cyclic rediscovery that women have minds of their own and can take action. As Jayamanne notes, we must prevent "the erasure of memory and of our capacity to remember."[53]

The empirical avant-garde destabilises history through the experimental, granting women the authority of the experiential (which includes knowledge and memory). The self—of the maker, of the audience, and of ancestors—is invoked in a spirit of cultural continuity rather than rupture. The focus is on *becoming*, on *relations*, on what happens *between* experience and thought, between "sensations and ideas," between sound and image, between cultures, between women. This is not a logic of "either/or" but a logic of "and," of connections, of actions. Becomings, according to Deleuze, are "actions which can only be contained in a life and expressed in a style."[54]

In *The Audition*, a short film by Anna Campion, the mother and daughter beautifully live out the dramas of art and everyday life. Taking a ride in a car is a poignant, tense, and lovely scene which perfectly captures the not so gentle struggle between mother and daughter. The aging mother, portrayed in close-up, rehearsing for a scene in her daughter's film (*Angel at My Table*) petulantly plays childish games which her gorgeous daughter (Jane, the director) generously hears, tenderly accepting her mother. This is an important move against the divisiveness of envy, or the demand that our mothers be perfect, who we want them to be instead of who they are.

The camera is not a curious bystander, an ethnographer of "others," but rather a knowing observer and a loving participant who walks about the house, cherishing the details and conflicts of daily life in the editing. This is not a romantic view of mother and daughter—but a loving tug of war for control, for independence, for freedom. The roles have shifted, been complicated, with age. The daughter, the film director, is the adult—she has made the passage into wisdom and acceptance.

The struggle between mother and daughter is painful, complicated by race and age in the extraordinary *Night Cries: A Rural Tragedy*. The

images of the old, dying, withered, unseeing white mother and the
voluptuous, middle-aged Aboriginal daughter, trapped by history,
their own and their nation's, in a dry, orange, saturated desert *mise-
en-scène*, enduring pain and facing death, are intercut with scenes of
childhood memory on the beach, when they were both young. The
affect that is high pathos comes from a collision—the personal crashes
into the historical. As Adrian Martin has noted, echoing Eisenstein,
"form can move content through a whole series of complex attitudes
and contradictory positions,"[55] not the least of which is the struggle
between mother and daughter, in tandem with the tragedies of colonial history.

Martin has described a tradition of Australian independent film
which also reminds me of Eisenstein who was fascinated by all forms
of popular culture. For Martin, the energy lies in its "impulse to incor-
porate—in however dislocated or perverse a way—vivid fragments of
the cultural environment—TV, music, cinema." Unlike "deconstruction," this tradition is "less overt critique and more emotional."[56] It is
very aware of cultural contexts and meanings.

Both Tracey Moffatt and Laleen Jayamanne have been deeply
influenced by the history of cinema, including Hollywood movies.
Moffatt: "I learned to make films by watching them. A childhood spent
glued to the television, then a diet of very commercial cinema through
to avant-garde films."[57] She watched 1960s Disney films, tied to personal memory, for example, *Mary Poppins*, which had

> very high production qualities, quite artificial and cartoon like.
> I remember *Mary Poppins* (because Daphne, my real Mother
> took us out to see it). There were the B-grade Hollywood bibli-
> cal epics—Anglo Saxon actors wearing lots of eyeliner and
> darkish pancake makeup to look 'Middle Eastern.' The sets
> were minimal and lighting hard, very stagy. I'd stare at these
> images for hours. I don't know why I liked them.[58]

These images are reflected in the *mise-en-scène* of *Night Cries*.

For Jayamanne, the highly stylised, excessive melodramas of Sri-Lankan cinema—completely amazing films which make Sirk look like Zola—have been influential, along with performance art. At the same time, as Moffatt says, "Whatever sort of film it is, whatever it's about, it's showbiz."[59] The specific movies their work recalls, *Vertigo* for Jayamanne, and *Jedda* for Moffatt, are 1950s technicolor features—rather than 1940s Hollywood for the first generation film feminists. Both *Jedda* and *Vertigo* portray male desire as an obsession which is deadly for women. These films are completely revised—to focus on women and history rather than male subjectivity and sex.

These women have no illusions about lost grandeur or the good old days. Jayamanne has no patience with nostalgic theories of pristine, colonial others, no sentimentality about lost origins. She tells a story about returning to her parents' grave in a Sri Lankan fishing village. Although they were middle-class and therefore had a gravestone, it had vanished. No matter, she had a photograph of herself standing beside the grave marker. "I have the photograph, not the real place." Her place of origin, Sri Lanka, is a place of memory tied to "images and sounds" instead of a real place. "I do not see this as impoverishing ... I am neither marginalised nor in a state of deprivation ... I straddle two traditions with a degree of comfort and a tolerable degree of discomfort. I like it."[60] There is nothing ambivalent here. Bivalent, multiple knowledges are more accurate than current theories of difference as lack or ambivalence.

Moffatt is equally matter-of-fact. "My people grew up on an Aboriginal mission outside of Brisbane ... I was fostered out to a white family along with my brother and two sisters ... . It wasn't against my mother's will."[61] "My work may feature brown faces but it could be anybody's story." Moffatt wants to be taken as an artist, not an Aboriginal artist. "Yes I am Aboriginal, but I have the right to be *avant-garde* like any white artist."[62]

Jayamanne's and Moffatt's films return to the compelling, colonial moment, cast as scenes of childhood memory. The past, a question of memory *and* history (which is intimate and emotive), haunts the present of their films like a primal scene. Having said this, I am not thinking of Freud but of something he (and many postmodern women) could never understand—the mutual struggle of women for independence, of mothers and daughters to love *and* to let go, to be together and separate. This lifelong journey, away from and with the mother, is taken into history, resulting in what Eisenstein would call a qualitative leap understood as a transition from quantity to quality. A transition marked by an emotional quality.[63]

Eisenstein, read through Deleuze and feminism, reverberates in this work. And this is logical. His is a theory of affect, of emotional intensities, a theory permeated by *inter*national cultures. Colonial subjectivity is hybrid—like separate hieroglyphs fusing into ideograms.[64] This emotional fusion is what Deleuze and Guattari call the one in the many, or what Eisenstein calls "unity in diversity."[65]

Rehearsing

Rehearsing, a simple Super 8mm film on video, begins with photographs and film stills (for Jayamanne, poses of ecstasy), recombined with critical texts, stylised performance, and music, then recycled in photo-essays and moving pictures. *Rehearsing* refers back to *A Song of Ceylon* and anticipates a feature film in the dreaming stage. The setting is the sparse kitchen of a Sydney flat, a space rendered through details in close-ups. Two men and a woman are sifting through photographs, talking about a story—a film and a life. Jayamanne's voice over declares her presence, sets the scene, and gives direction. She tells a story about a photograph. It is a melodrama. The godfather who threw himself at the train, his body flung in pieces along the railway tracks, is the young boy in the photo, the brother of the young girl, Laleen's grandmother. "This is the man you will talk about who killed himself." Of the story she says, "it's all possible because of the child," the child being her mother as a baby.

History is private and political. The men discuss Sri Lankan racial politics, colonial disputes. Tamil is the indigenous name of people in Southern India and northern Sri Lanka; Sinhalese is the majority language and dominant culture of Sri Lanka. The history between the two continues to be bloody. The men briefly rehearse an awkward scene of confrontation—which has sexual and violent dimensions. Jayamanne is in charge—until the photographs take over, although the camera keeps passing quickly over them as if it isn't ready to stop and look, not wanting to be nostalgic, sentimental.

The still photograph, glimpsed early on, which becomes the focus of the last section, is of Jayamanne's grandmother, who died in childbirth, on her death bed, surrounded by her family. The infant is her mother. We see other photographs of Davila, the famous Chilean painter/performer, an exile living in Sydney, who impersonated Kim Novak in *A Song of Ceylon*. This handsome, sweet-looking gay man paints huge, shocking works about terrorism, death, mutilation, and ecstasy. Davila—a displaced artist and Jayamanne's alter-ego—is the main performer. Jayamanne describes this piece as "a combat of sorts between two men and eight photographs or a rite of passage dramatising homoeroticism's debt to the maternal conceived not simply as the dead mother but also as virtual space."[66]

The film moves from glance to story, from opera to Louis Armstrong singing "Summertime," from preparation to rehearsal—a film not yet performed, not yet made. The last words on the soundtrack are "Your daddy's rich and your mamma's good looking. One of these mornings, you're gonna rise up singing, you'll spread your wings," which is the future, what the feature film will represent for Jayamanne.

John Berger's valuable distinction between private and public photography suggests something of the simple richness of this film. The private preserves context and continuity unlike the public photograph which is "torn from context," a "dead object" lending "itself to any arbitrary use."[67] For Berger, like Andre Bazin, photographs are relics, traces of what happened. To become part of the past, part of making history, they "require a living context." This memory "would encompass an image of the past, however tragic ... within its own continuity."[68]

Photography then becomes "the prophecy of a human memory yet to be socially and politically achieved."[69] The hint of the story to come "replaces the photograph in time—not its own original time for that is impossible—but in narrative time. Narrated time becomes historic time" which respects memory.[70] The film begins from something remembered—as Freud says, "every affect is only a reminiscence of an event"—and then begins to construct what Berger calls "a radial system" around the photograph in "terms which are simultaneously personal, political, economic, dramatic, everyday, and historic."[71]

> Jayamanne calls the photo a "maternal tableau" which has been generative for me. I have used it since 1979, first in an obsessively biographical mode ... but I've moved out of that and am able to fictionalize it. Juan found the image fascinating because of the virtual space, that empty space running from the dead woman's face. The baby is my ma—her mother died at 18 in childbirth. During *Rehearsing*, I saw the young boy for the first time. I saw him only through the Super 8mm camera. When I am stuck, that image seems to help me to move on. So it's not a primal scene in the Freudian sense. I dream of using it in a 35mm film in Sri Lanka. Photos or magical appearances that come to life to complicate the plot is standard stuff of our family melodramas.[72]

Jayamanne's larger project is to render visible cultures undergoing transformations. Her metaphor is "the body under duress," like Ceylon, "the body neither here nor there," a body which, for her, "did not exist before the technology of cinema."[73] Her film bodies are renderings of classic postures and gestures of Western cinema, in spaces haunted by the history of vanishing cultures.

Jayamanne's theoretical comments also describe Moffatt's work—the tactic of "post-colonial hybridization," despite what she calls the "efforts of chauvinistic forms of nationalisms to erase such heterogeneity and regress into some mythical ideal of pure identity, whether of nation or gender. We have seen the bloody aspect of this in the history of Sri Lanka in the last decade."[74] Jayamanne and Moffatt "use the messy inheritance that is exacerbated by the introduction of electronic media into postcolonial societies."[75] With cinema, one cannot work with the "pristinely national" any longer.

Moffatt's films are a politics and an aesthetics of assimilation—"matter of method and also of survival ... Survival not in a cultural ghetto but in the market as well as in the domains of cultural visibility and legitimacy."[76] Hybridisation/assimilation is history which is neither pristinely indigenous nor completely other.

Although much history is not recorded in print or film, particularly in indigenous cultures, it cannot be erased. For Moffatt, history comes back to haunt us. Like age, we carry our history, our forebears, on our face, their spirits indelibly imprinted in our memory. History can be reincarnated, recollected, its spirit given new life as living memory. This is history of recognition. This is the history told by *Night Cries: a Rural Tragedy* (and *Daughters of the Dust*). This history of presence is inhabited by the filmmakers; their lives are spiritually connected to their forebears—as if they know them, and love them. This is also what Eisenstein would call ecstatic history, a history of pathos. It might resemble Walter Benjamin's Messianic time, or Deleuze's "virtual" time.

Space is not empty but full of meanings—particularly the black space of the frame in *Night Cries*. Like Aboriginal landmarks we cannot see, space is filled with history, haunted by sound, it is the space out of which forgotten figures can emerge, and recede back into.

Moffatt, like Julie Dash, sees history as an empty canvas, full of forgotten actants, a cast waiting to be remembered, recollected.

Form and story are equivalent in value—including the collision between sound and image, the formal work on the minimalist sound track. Moffatt: "It's not enough to just be black and a film-maker and right on, you have to be responsible for exploring film form at the same time."[77] Like Jayamanne's critique of anthropology, Moffatt reacts against ethnography, the realist tradition of representing Black Australia. "It's black, we can't experiment with form ... it was always a gritty, realist approach representing black lives."[78] "I don't believe in talking down to Aboriginal people."[79] As Moffatt says "I am not concerned with verisimilitude." "I am not concerned with capturing reality, I'm concerned with creating it myself."[80]

For women of colour, the history of representation is being made. By inscribing what has always been there but missing in representation, by a shift in enunciation, telling the tale from the point of view of women, history changes. This is Moffatt's tactic in her short film, the acclaimed *Night Cries: A Rural Tragedy.*

Night Cries refers to Australia's historical policies toward Aborigines by remaking *Jedda* (1955), a big technicolor, cinemascope film directed by Charles Chauvel. *Jedda* begins briefly, in the ranch home of a cattle station, an Australian homestead. Jedda is the adopted Aboriginal daughter, living with her mother, father, and Joe, the ranch-hand, "half-caste." Like Jedda, he has been "civilised." Outside the "civilised" culture of the ranch are untamed Aborigines—the space of the unknown, desire, danger, and death and Marbuk, the lead character played by Robert Tudawali, an Aboriginal actor. As Marcia Langton, the star of *Night Cries* notes, he is the "primitive," "condemned to death by his own tribe" (not by the white coloniser) which is the "inversion of the truth."[81] Marbuk performs rituals and seduces Jedda. The rest of the film is a chase scene through the desert landscape—the attempted rescue of Jedda by her father and Joe (or conversely, the pursuit of the Aboriginal by white men) until Jedda dies—

dragged over a cliff by Marbuk.

For Langton, an Aboriginal activist and political leader who plays the Aboriginal daughter of *Night Cries*, *Jedda* expresses "all those ambiguous emotions, fears and false theories which revolve in Western thought around the spectre of the 'primitive' as if none of the brutality, murder and land clearances occurred."[82]

Night Cries, however, is concerned only with *Jedda's* prologue, with its portrayal of the brief relationship between Jedda, the Aboriginal daughter, and her white foster mother. For Chauvel, this scene, set within the ranch house, women's space, is only a prologue, prelude to the capture, chase, and death of Jedda. For Chauvel, Jedda's relationship with men determines her life, her identity. For Moffatt, on the other hand, the mother is the central figure in women's history: "I took two of the film's characters, Jedda, the black woman, and her white mother, and aged them as if thirty years had passed. In the original film, Jedda is thrown off a cliff and killed. I wanted to resurrect her."[83] The actress playing Jedda remarkably resembles Moffatt: "As I developed the script, the film became less about them and more about me and my white foster mother. I was raised by an older white woman and the script became quite a personal story. The little girl who appears in some of the flashback sequences looks a lot like me. That was quite intentional."[84]

An aged white woman is facing death in a landscape that is almost deserted. Her middle-aged Aboriginal daughter (Marcia Langton) cares for her—wheeling her to the outhouse, feeding her, tenderly then aggressively. Her resentment for her entrapment is palpable. The flashbacks of the little girl on the beach who can't see her mother are terrifying. The beautiful child, with seaweed wrapped around her neck, panics; her sobbing captures all the pain and fear of childhood —of death, of separation. This is a terror that can paralyse us, can haunt us, no matter how our bodies mature and age. This terror comes from the fear of leaving and the horror of staying, of being trapped in one's life and in history. When the mother dies, the daughter re-enacts the pain of this incalculable loss, in a scene which remembers birth.

The painted studio landscape of *Night Cries* is filled with memory—including childhood remembrances of Hollywood movies. As Australian film critic Ingrid Periz explains, space is "inhabited by memory—of a once great cattle station fallen victim to a changing agricultural economy, of foregone hope, of resentment and familial obligation"; Moffatt's inscription of memory is very economical—"a brief shot of old photographs, an abandoned railway platform, echoes of a ghost train, and flashbacks to childhood ... Memory constricts this space, a space of recollection."[85] The film opens with a quote from Rosalind Russell, who stars in *Picnic*, a film which suggests a stifling scenario of entrapment, of failed expectation, of waiting. Periz concludes, "Dreaming of escape, they wait for whatever life will deliver them." "*Night Cries* shows what happens after *Picnic*."[86]

For Langton, *Night Cries* "can be read as an autobiographical exploration of Moffatt's relationship with her own foster mother. The film asks questions about the role of 'mother' in adoptive mother/daughter relationships."[87] But Langton's interprets this relationship differently from white interviewers and critics. Langton possesses the cultural knowledge of experience, and I will quote her at length. Langton:

> Moffatt's inversion of colonial history is to play out the worst fantasies of those who took Aboriginal children from their natural parents to assimilate and 'civilise' them. Perhaps the worst nightmare of the adoptive parents is to end life with the black adoptive child as the only family, the only one who cares.[88]

As I said earlier, this domestic scenario portrays national politics. Langton argues that "Moffatt's construction of that nightmare is subversive because the style and materiality of the homestead set is so reminiscent of Aboriginal poverty." She continues: "Chauvel's once privileged homestead now resembles the inside of a humpy ..." The White ranch/homestead ("extracted from the slave labour of the Aboriginal men and women on the Australian pastoral station") now turns to "Aboriginal poverty ... all the excesses of the historical/economic moment of the Australian cattle station are collapsed."[89]

"What Moffatt was trying to *correct* in the text of *Jedda* is the Western fascination with the 'primitive.' Moffatt's inversion forces the audience to look not at the desire of Chauvel's *Jedda* but at death, and at the consequences of Western imagination of the 'primitive.' "[90] Langton inscribes subject positions based on cultural difference.

Moffatt's style is suggested by the horror of the whipping scene which is then followed by the softness of the daughter washing the mother's feet. Eisenstein has never been more applicable: for the sound, it is "not strictly fitting to say: 'I hear.' Nor for the visual overtone: 'I see.' For both, a new uniform formula must enter our vocabulary: 'I feel.'" This is the "Filmic Fourth Dimension."[91] Moffatt's films have found what Eisenstein calls "an inner synchronization between the tangible picture and the differently perceived sounds."[92]

The film's use of close-ups evokes Eisenstein's essay "Dickens, Griffith, and the Film Today." This 1944 essay—which includes an analysis of the differences between the close-ups of D.W. Griffith and Eisenstein—is a key text of Deleuze's *Cinema 1*(and becomes, I think, the basis for Deleuze and Guattari's notion of faciality in *A Thousand Plateaus*, a concept which links face, race, and cinema. There is a close affinity between the notion of faciality and photography).

For Deleuze, cinema is thought. "The great directors of the cinema may be compared ... with thinkers." ("Preface to the French Edition.")[93] For Eisenstein, "Montage thinking is inseparable from the general content of thinking as a whole."[94] Moffatt *thinks* through montage. Her films and her series of photographs embody what Eisenstein calls "an inner unity," not the "outer unity of story."[95] This explains *how* Moffatt signifies historical scope and why her work elicits such strong response. We don't just witness history, we *experience* history *as* memory. This is the "secret of the *structure of emotional speech*"[96]—*affective logic*, "inner speech,"[97] "sensual thinking."[98] In this film without speech, without dialogue, Moffatt works on a deeply emotive level akin to the affective logic of inner speech.

Eisenstein's distinction between "contemplative dissection" and "emotional fusion"[99] helps me to understand how Moffatt's work differs from the usually male romantic avant-garde. "Contemplative dissection" concerns contrasts, juxtapositions, before and now—what Eisenstein calls *"un-crossed parallelisms."* "They are united neither by a unity of composition nor by the chief element, emotion."[100] "Emotional fusion" involves "some *new quality.*"[101] This "qualitative leap" is enabled by feminism and, perhaps, Deleuze.

Although distinguishing historically between cinema of movement and, later, cinema of time, Deleuze's way of thinking about cinema is *cinema*tographic, not psychoanalytic, it focuses on topography more than narrative. Regarding Deleuze's first observation, movement is not limited to the cause-effect logic of narrative, or to figures "moving" through space, or to cameras dollying, tracking. Action is only one kind of movement; the others are perception and affection. Deleuze took the phrase "self-moving thought" from Henri Bergson, what Deleuze calls "one of the most difficult and finest bits of Bergson's thought ... I don't think it's ever been quite absorbed."[102] Deleuze points out that these thoughts came to Bergson when cinema was "taking shape;" they coincide with, rather than reflect upon, cinema, specifically a cinema of narration. Later, particularly post World War II, came "time images," which "have nothing to do with before and after, with succession. Succession was there from the start as the law of narration. Time images are not things happening in time, but new forms of coexistence, ordering, transformation."[103]

For many Australian women, feminist theory, in lockstep with academia, has soured to formulaic careerism, what Jayamanne calls "a rhetoric of validation," "the same set of propositions recycled with

snazzy marketable titles ... bereft of all energy ... not to mention political effectiveness."[104] As Lesley Stern has said, "There's a kind of generic predictability about the enterprise that has to do with academic disciplines," a "restrictive repertoire" to which she has developed "an
abhorrence." [105]

Certain works break this "restrictive repertoire." By making history, women are enabling theory to move on. I prefer "unity and diversity" to theories of difference and ambivalence. Through "emotional
fusion," the "montage removes ... contradictions by abolishing ... par-
allelism in the realms of sound and sight."[106] Form—which is intensity, energy—infuses history with the complexity and clarity of experience. In the collision and fusion between sound and image, a visual
and acoustic space is revealed out of which historical figures, virtual
figures, can emerge and can be heard.

BeDevil

BeDevil, "A Trilogy of Designer Spook," is Moffatt's 1993 feature
length film. It has little to do with linear narration and succession.
Rather, the three tales are "time images." Past and present, youth and
age, Aboriginal and White Australia, the personal and the national
"coexist," one transforming the other: time periods are superimposed
on each other; place is haunted by time. Beneath white commercial
culture and real estate are the ghosts of an older, displaced culture.
Beneath cinema is another image, another story. Beneath the postmodern *surface* is a face, an older, darker face which haunts (and is
haunted by) Australia's colonial history which exists in the present.
As Moffatt says, "the ghosts are real."

BeDevil begins with the post World War II expansion of commercial culture—the white postmodern world of suburbs and popular culture—movies and particularly television. "The [three] stories are contemporary accounts of events which appear to be from the early

1950s, the early 1960s, and the 1970s, respectively" told in flash-
backs.[107] In fact the film goes into the 1990s consumer culture of
roller blading and designer logos. "*BeDevil* comments on 1950s' consumerism, property development and cultural appropriation, but over-
whelmingly it concerns articulation of place."[108] From the indigenous
point of view, postmodernism might be the accelerating spread of
white culture on Aboriginal (and Native American) land, eradicating
one history by another, all the while looking away from what has happened. Looking away from exploitation is denial, disavowal, which
prevents action. The film resonates with the current Aboriginal land
rights debates and legislation in Australia.

But from another point of view, White Australia, this island continent is an inter-racial nation, a hybrid culture. English colonists came
first, then the U.S. military during World War II, Eastern European
immigrants, and finally, Asians. As Moffatt says, "I have Chinese characters, Italian, Greek, and so on... very multi-cultural."[109] While the
white characters are *very* white, the characters are predominantly
Aboriginal. Who is haunting whom depends on point of view and
knowledge. For Penny Webb, Moffatt's concerns are "the black history
of white Australia, the magic of cinema, and an evident love for strong
women."[110] Her style is "magic realism that includes the unsaid and
the unseen." (Although she is a great interview subject, Moffatt leaves
many things unsaid, including the depth of her activist politics. She is
a savvy artist, talking art, fashion, and entertainment, with an eye on
her career.)

In this film, the "unsaid and unseen" can be *experienced*, felt.
Aboriginal characters don't simply see or look as much as they *witness*
or *evade*. They don't speak as much as they *testify* or *parody*. Blacks
have depth and possess knowledge, which is not visible to everyone.
The audience either gets it or doesn't. What we get depends on cultural knowledge. Aborigines are petty thieves, aging women, drunken
relatives; they are human. Whites are caricatured, limited, but subtly
so. Like postmodernism, they are surface, without depth or insight.

But in interviews and in person, Moffatt refuses to polarise or politicise. "The stories are inspired by family ghost stories I heard as a child, stories which come from both sides of my background."[111] These childhood ghost stories can also be taken as allegories of "nation." The studio style vaguely resembles an earlier allegorical program, Rod Serling's TV series, *The Twilight Zone*. But Moffatt's imitations of TV styles reveal television's formal artifice which has become so conventionalised to be foolishly taken as "everyday."

BeDevil's stunning *mise-en-scène* of place is filtered through movies as well as television, painting and memory. Moffatt returned to Brisbane to "remember" the feel of the tropical North.[112] One inspiration was *Kwaidan*, the 1964 Japanese film by Masaki Kobayashi, a film with an "abstract soundtrack" and painterly studio sets.[113] (Countless film directors have done this, from Fritz Lang to Alfred Hitchcock, to Francis Coppola in *One From the Heart* and *Dracula*.) Another was Nicolas Roeg's *Walkabout*.

> I saw *Walkabout* [1971] when I was thirteen and the visuals have always stuck with me ... I think I am the only Aborigine in Australia that will admit to loving this film ... because of its open texture ... its play with time ... the kids are in a desert one minute and walking through a forest the next.[114]

For Moffatt, films should be experimental and popular at the same time, which is what Roeg's works accomplish. "The key word is unpredictability—never let the audience know what is coming next."[115]

"The first story is on an island. The characters are in a mangrovey, swampy, mosquito-infested island in Queensland."[116] "The new swamp set looks fab, what a thrill to work in it tomorrow. A forest of thin tea tree trunks against a pukey green [Linda Blair] painted sky, beautiful, ugly, you can almost hear the mosquitoes whine." "The second story is in a desert with location stuff ... The third story [is a] decaying dockland area." All three are set in Queensland, where Moffatt grew up.[117] "The film gets funnier as it progresses. The first story is quite hard, the second rather funny, but the third is actually comedy with slapstick."

The trilogy begins with an eerie tracking shot from the edge of the water, through tall grasses, to a murky, misty swamp where three Aboriginal children are playing. The film, like this opening shot, is an archaeology, peeling away layers of time. *BeDevil* is "about the mystical Australian landscape of my imagination ... childhood memories."[118] In *Mr. Chuck*, "[a] mad American GI during WW II accidentally drove his army duck ashore and into a swamp. He sank without a trace. It was said his ghost haunted the swamp."[119] Later a film theatre will be built over the swamp by a cross-section of Australian mates and their supervisor, a blonde, very white man with two very white, very clean children. (At one point, the White Father's face turns into a lizard.) The Aboriginal children watch the clean, perfect White family from the sidelines. Aborigines are on the outskirts of town, outside commerce.

This story is told in direct address by two characters in the present: Shelly, a local white woman in her seventies who lives in a suburban housing development; and Rick, "once handsome, now a jailbird with lots of attitude," in his "late thirties."[120] The contrast between the white skin and black skin of the tellers is intense, as is the contrast in *mise-en-scène*. White is clearly marked *as* white. Shelly was kind to Chuck as a child, but she ignored the beatings he was receiving. "We all knew ... we could have helped." Aborigines watched and understood. White colonists saw and knew but did nothing. Rick says: "I hated that place, that island." Shelly says, "I loved the island ... full of American soldiers." Swooping aerial shots of the island suburbs, beachfront real estate filled with cars, ranch-style homes, and waterways resemble commercial travelogues—garish bright colours, cheery music. The tone of these shots are in contrast to Rick's story.

Moffatt stars in the second ghost story, *Choo Choo Choo*, as Ruby

Morphet, "twenty five, Aboriginal, beautiful, tough." "Documentary characters recount the tale of the ghost train and girl who haunt a local railway siding. We meet older Ruby [in her mid fifties] and her rowdy gang of women friends as they return to the old siding for a picnic of designer bush food." The style is like TV, "Cooking with Wine." Maudie, "a very bossy chef, speaks only Aboriginal language." "These Aboriginal women confound any notion of the stereotypical TV subject. We see Ruby in flashback living with her young family at the siding."[121]

The tale opens with women friends riding in a truck in the country, and joyously singing. We are in the truck, riding along with the women. Then the point of view is disembodied. A tracking shot down city streets resembles the point of view of a civic parade. All the participants are white folks. Like the island aerial shots, this footage is sunny, bright, cheerful, without a located point of view, like the "neutrality" of TV and history. A cheerful Asian man beckons to the camera and invites us into his shop. "Want to hear a spooky story?" He tells us about the strange gesture all the townsfolk were making for the tracking camera. It is about the haunted train: "Choo, choo, they hear them but they can't see them."

In contrast to the location footage, the studio set is ominous, of darker, muted hues. The set of the railway siding is hot, tense, with strange shapes, weirdly beautiful rocks. "I play my mother who actually lived out west in a ramshackle house like the one in the film. My family were gangers on the railway and at night they would hear this ghost train coming up the track, but never see it."[122] A blind girl had been killed on the tracks. At the end, Ruby sees the Aboriginal ghost of the blind girl, walking. "This figure, the ghost of a white girl, personifies the culture/race distinction" that is central to "place."[123] Like the two children in the opening sequence, this is the white/black hyperreal imaginary of childhood, the mystery from the Aboriginal's point of view.

The third story is "Loving the Spin I'm In," about a commercial warehouse where young lovers of mixed race tragically lived, loved,

danced, and died—a story right out of *West Side Story*. They haunt the
warehouse where an Aboriginal family still lives. The owner is trying
to sell the real estate to Japanese businessmen, and moves out the
Aboriginal family, leaving the ghost dancers behind. But the Asian
businessmen run away, frightened silly by the ghosts. The roller-blad-
ing boys skate around a shiny spinning automobile shot by an over-
head camera, a high-tech TV commercial for Japanese cars.

The ghost stories are about national economics, a critique of
progress as another layer of archaeology. From the U.S. soldier in the
1950s to Asian business in the present, Aboriginal culture has been
displaced and endured, dispossessed and relocated. The colours of the
colonisers change but the spirit of the past remains, haunted or haunting. It all depends on point of view and cultural knowledge, experience.[124]

(St)Age Five: Economical Feminism:

Daughter, sister, lover, wife, mother, grandmother ... I will be
suborned into all of these roles ... but I have my vocation. It is
outside sex, and yet my sex is part of it.[125]

The old crone of the tale is a savvy sorceress with some money and
time to herself. If asked, she will caution princesses about depending
on the prince or another princess to make her happy. She urges
women to say what they want and need, rather than to leave this up
to the guesswork of others or history. She is the only critic who knew
that Thelma and Louise were dead the minute they lost the money,
that sex was the wrong choice. Fortunately, she is on the other shore
of desire—whether hetero or homo—knowing some history and able
to learn from experience. She has recovered from romance and shed
the constraints of femininity. Liberation, like wisdom, also comes with
time.

Woolf wrote *Three Guineas* when she was older and wiser. She
wants equality in everything, including money and property. Woolf's

1938 argument anticipates Monique Wittig; both thinkers interlock the money economy and the sexual economy. Woolf's appeal is to "facts" and experience rather than "dangerous theories of psychologists or biologists."[126]

Wittig's key point is that "the doctrine of the difference between the sexes" produced by heterosexuality justifies women's "oppression."[127] For Wittig, "woman" and "man" are economic and political categories. "For what makes a woman is a specific social relation to a man, a relation ... which implies ... economic obligations." Woolf's model figure was Antigone. Her problem was not sexuality, it was that "she had neither capital nor force behind her."[128]

Early on, Woolf tackles the economic divide of public/private. Men's work in the public sphere was paid, and counted. Women's work in private was not paid, thus didn't matter. Later on, she writes that the "public and the private worlds are inseparably connected," the "tyrannies and servilities of one mirror the other."[129] Woolf advocates the formation of an Outsider's Society, where the daughters of educated men can be "working in their own class" for "liberty, equality and peace."[130]

Daughters of the Dust

I concluded my talk at the *Dissonance* film conference in Sydney, September 1991, with these exact words:

> If our journey were not into the arms of men, the singular happy ending, then the separation from mother would be another story, a feature film rather than a prologue—one of subjectivity, of identity, of adulthood rather than perennial childhood, a mature and life-granting scenario which would embrace *and* separate from the mother. Perhaps then the image of the self in old age would no longer be haunted or

made inadequate by the memory of the little girl—who doesn't have the knowledge that comes with age. We would then live in the present and not forget the past. For women, this would be collective, loving autonomy. We could grow up and be women with brains rather than dream girls with bodies. Otherwise, we will be just aging bimbos, bimbsters all. And we must not waste time. When it comes to women, and history, memory is short.

Six months after I returned home, I saw Julie Dash's *Daughters of the Dust* with my brilliant twenty-three year old daughter, Dae, in a theatre in the Village in New York. The event marked a personal turning point in our lives. *Daughters* realises "collective, loving autonomy" and sold out every show. It was still playing, eight months later. The movie theatre was filled with beautiful women of colour who all understood the historical importance of the moment, of this exceptional film.

Daughters of the Dust is history—a successful feature film directed by an African-American woman, Julie Dash, and a commercial film which doesn't sacrifice form (including duration), doesn't compromise on style, and adheres to personal values whether fashionable or not. It is experimental, experiential, and empirical—a triple threat like Dash who wrote, produced, and directed the film—which took time to find a distributor. Unlike the films by African-American men, this is a tale told from the multiple points of view of women of all ages, including the spirits of the unborn—modern women, present-day women. *Daughters* is about love and respect rather than fear and hatred, about the spiritual world within the material world.

The setting is historical: the Sea Island Gullahs off the coast of South Carolina at the turn of the century. Due to its isolation, Africans maintained a distinct culture which is recreated—recollected. A voice over, of Nana Peazant, the old woman, the powerful head of the family-clan, speaking through the ages, says: "I am the first and last, I am the whore and the holy one ... many are my daughters. I am the silence you cannot understand. I am the utterances of my name." After invoking the ancestors, the spirits of the unborn, we go to Ibo Landing, the Sea Islands of the South, in 1902.

The landscape is paradise, a splendid tranquillity composed of pastels, the pale blue sky, the golden beach, the azure ocean, sounds of water. Mary, the prodigal daughter, is arriving, returning home from the mainland. Her family—gloriously dressed in pure white—awaits her on the beach. Some revile her—as a prostitute; most accept and love her. Mary accepts them all, and her life. Hers is the tolerance of experience. This is a celebration not of her homecoming but of the extended family's departure from this island for the mainland. Coming and going, their paths cross. A young photographer has come to record the auspicious event; this is modern history, abetted by photography not memory, by images not spirits.

A young girl's voice sets up the drama in voice-over: "My story begins before I was born. My great-great grandmother ... saw her family coming apart." Thus, the tale is of the past, of history. It is an ending and also a beginning—like life itself. Things end, only to begin anew. Like their ancestors from Africa, this family is beginning a journey to a new land. The girl continues as the storyteller: "The old souls guided me into the new world," as the camera pans the house.

Nana Peazant is the historian, the guardian of legend and the spirits. History comes from oral tradition, from experience. This is remembered history which lives through stories and through spirits. History is spiritualist, perhaps materialist. For Nana, age is wisdom, age is strength, age is to be respected: "We carry these memories inside us. We don't know where our recollections came from." But there is a tragic reason for recollection: "They didn't keep good records of slavery ... We had to hold records in our head. The old souls could recollect birth, death, sale. Those 18th century Africans, they watch us, they keep us, those four generations of Africans. When they landed, they saw things we cannot see." This is the history of survival, not defeat.

The women span several generations—they wear white; Nana wears dark blue as did her ancestors, slaves who worked planting the cotton, dyeing the cloth, staining their fingers dark navy. That past of slavery haunts the present, in scenes of dark blue intercut into the pastel tranquillity of the family celebration. As Nana teaches, our power doesn't end "with the dead." "Respect your ancestors, call on your ancestors, let them guide you." Nana believes in the spirit more than the body. To her grandson's anger about his wife's rape, the parentage of the unborn child not being his, Nana replies, "Ya can't get back what you never owned."

Nana's attempt to fortify the family for their journey, to give them their heritage, is also the film's gift to the audience and to African-American history. This is an empowering film. "I'm trying to learn ya how to touch your own spirit ... to give you something to take north with ya ... Call on those old Africans. Let the old souls come into your heart ... let them feed you with wisdom." Nana calls upon the spirits. We glimpse the young girl, as yet unborn, running. Then we see this spirit enter her mother's body. The spirits are carried by the wind, their presence can be felt, experienced.

An aesthetics of history is inscribed on bodies which dance, stroll, gesture, talk, and listen—a choreography of grace filled movement, poetic voices and words, one group leading to another, then shifting the players. The film is lush with groups shots and closeups of beautiful African-American women, talking, listening, laughing. "I saw Africa in her face," says Nana. The film caresses these faces of many ages, taking time to let us see them, to cherish their presence and experience what they might be thinking. They are so different yet connected, "unity in diversity."

The film asks that we listen, carefully—there is much to hear on the soundtrack. The film respects its oral traditions, it talks poetically, it speaks historically. bell hooks writes that "talking back" meant "speaking as an equal."

[In] the home ... it was black women who preached. There, black women spoke in a language so rich, so poetic, that it felt to me like being shut off from life ... if one was not allowed to participate. It was in that world of woman talk ... that was born in me the craving to speak, to have a voice ... belonging to me ... It was in this world of woman speech ... that I made speech my birthright ... a privilege I would not be denied. It was in that world and because of it that I came to dream of writing, to write. Writing was a way to capture speech.[131]

History is in the conversations which tell the story of our lives. Mary talks about the rape of "coloured woman," there as common as fish in the sea. The voice-over spirit says she needed to convince her father "I was his child." The men recall the slave ships. Mary tells the story about her baby, born dead, so she nursed another baby. Nana—shown in close detail, often apart from the group, old, wiry, tough, a survivor—cannot understand how the family can leave.

The family is divided, momentarily, historically, over spirituality versus Christianity. Nana's daughter-in-law says "I am educated. I'm tired of those old stories ... they pray to the sun, the moon, they ain't got no religion. I don't want my daughter to hear about that stuff." The voice of the spirit girl: "We were the children of those who chose to survive." Shots of clothes drying are intercut. "I was travelling on a spiritual mission, but sometimes I would be distracted ... I remember the call from my great, great grandmother. I remember and I recall. I remember my journey home."

For many viewers, the film feels like "a journey home." The film comes to understand that "we are part of each other ... we are all good women. We are the Daughters of the Dust." Although the family separates, four generations of women remain together. Yellow Mary became active in anti-lynching. The spirit's voice-over concludes this extraordinary film: "My mommy and daddy stayed behind, with Yellow Mary. We remain behind, growing older, wiser, stronger."[132]

1   Dorothy Hewett, *Wild Card: An Autobiography, 1923–1958* (Victoria: McPhee Gribble/Penguin Books, 1990), 84.

2   Jane Wagner, *The Search for Signs of Intelligent Life in the Universe* (New York: Harper and Row, 1986), 193.

3   Ibid., 138.

4   Ibid., 191.

5   Monique Wittig, "The Mark of Gender," *The Straight Mind and Other Essays* (Boston: Beacon, 1992), 76–89. "Mark" refers to the "conventions and rules" of language that "were never formally enunciated." This is not just textual deconstruction, however. "But language does not allow itself to be worked upon, without parallel work in philosophy and politics, as well as in economics."(82) In her succinct style, many of her arguments are in the short essay, "One Is Not Born A Woman," in *Feminist Issues*, Winter 1981.

6   Virginia Woolf, *Three Guineas* (New York & London: Harcourt Brace Jovanovich, 1938).

7   I initially presented this schema at the Australian conference, "Dissonance," in September 1991. I am grateful to Laleen Jayamanne for her invitation and her hospitality. She squired me around Sydney in her car with careening good cheer. The Power Institute of the University of Sydney was gracious and stimulating. I enjoyed the good company of Virginia Spate, the Director. I am indebted to Meaghan Morris, forever, for her intellectual acumen, of course, but especially for her friendship, hospitality and great shopping taste and stamina.

    The five ages have been elaborated in my book forthcoming in Fall 1995, Temple University Press, *A Fine Romance ... Five Ages of Film Feminism (What Cinderella, Snow White et al. Forgot to Tell Thelma and Louise)*.

8   At a symposium on Film History at the Hawaii International Film Festival, Paul Bove argued that the big political questions must be addressed before we can address women's daily life.

9   Meaghan Morris, "'Too soon too late': Reading Claire Johnston 1970–1981," in *Dissonance, Feminism and the Arts 1970–90*, ed. Catriona Moore (Sydney: Allen & Unwin & Artspace, 1994), 127.

10 Ibid.

11 Ibid., 133.

12 This is a 45 minute independent film, written, edited, and directed by the British filmmaker, Sally Potter, in 1979. In 1992, *Orlando*, her feature film, was released.

13 Neither critic would, I think, agree with my analysis. Modleski, in fact, makes a strong case for the centrality of the female spectator in *Vertigo* in *The Women Who Knew Too Much*. And Mulvey would assert Madeleine's passivity, her lack. I take a third tack. In a fairly recent essay, Deborah Linderman has used Freud's essay on the "uncanny" to analyse the film. However, this is just one of Freud's essays on obsession. Equally, Modleski mentions "Mourning and Melancholia," which also has strains of Freud's thought on obsession. Yet, neither critic appears to realise the centrality of

obsession and anxiety to even their own arguments, and how very different this model can be from what has come to be known as "feminist film theory." Robin Wood's latest analysis of the film does mention that the film is caught within the delusions of romance. Thus, I would partially agree with Wood.

Freud's *Delusion and Dream* provides another, but obvious, means of analysis for this film. However, the cure Freud recommends is a "real" woman rather than chasing imaginary dream girls. Freud even suggests that unless men wake up to the real, they will be seriously disturbed. The case mentions fetishism, almost in passing, going on to the more serious implications of worshipping figments of male desire. Strange that feminist film theory has also overlooked this text, perhaps it is too easy a read.

14 Hewett, *Wild Card*, 74.

15 I would estimate that out of the thousands of pages Freud wrote, perhaps only two hundred, *at most*, figure in most feminist film criticism. What most critics call Freudian psychoanalysis comes from film critics' models, not from Freud or even Lacan. It astonishes me how many younger film scholars have never read Freud while imagining they know Freudian theory.

16 This story was central to Lacan, who analysed its schema of vision, of circulation. However, what fascinated Lacan was not its overt logic, which is what fascinated the detective, Dupin. Rather, Lacan looked beneath the surface, at the sexual drama of the letter, not at what was there, but at what was not there. Lacan, in effect, one-upped the master detective, Dupin. Just a reminder: the schema of vision is seeing (and not seeing); interpreting (and misinterpreting); knowing (and not knowing). Thus, the linkage between sight and knowledge is, from the beginning, central. Vision and thought are both determinant.

17 Foucault argues this clearly in the opening of *The History of Sexuality*, Volume I (London: Allen Lane, 1979).

18 *A Thousand Plateaus* includes their more recent analyses of psychoanalysis.

19 I remember hearing Mary Beth Haralovich give a talk about Stanwyck. I believe it was in Glasgow, at the *Screen* conference, in 1991 or 1992.

20 Remarkably few feminist film critics even mention age as an issue, let alone write about age.

21 Patrick Mahony, *Freud and the Rat Man* (New Haven, Connecticut: Yale University Press, 1986), 20.

22 Breuer and Freud, 1955, 280.

23 Mahony, *Freud and the Rat Man*, 169–170.

24 Ibid., 57.

25 For a lengthy explication of obsession, see Patricia Mellencamp, *High Anxiety: Catastrophe, Scandal, Age, and Comedy* (Bloomington, Indiana: Indiana University Press, 1992).

26 Ann Barr Snitow, "Mass Market Romance: Pornography for Women is Different," *Powers of Desire: The Politics of Sexuality*, ed. Ann Snitow et al. (New York: Monthly Review Press, 1983), 247–260.

27 Helen Taylor, "Romantic Readers," *From My Guy to Sci-Fi*, ed. Helen Carr

(London: Pandora, 1989), 58–73.

28 Hewett, *Wild Card*, 94.

29 Monique Wittig, "One is Not Born a Woman," 53. Teresa de Lauretis, *The Practice of Love* (Bloomington, Indiana: 1994).

30 I have debated whether to write about this film which addresses so many important topics and was made by an artist I admire. But I have reservations about *Privilege*.

31 Michele Wallace, "Multiculturalism and Oppositionality," *Afterimage* (October, 1991), 6–8.

32 Lynne Tillman, "A Woman Called Yvonne," *Village Voice*, January 15, 1992, 56. The racial politics of the U.S. and Australia are inverted—with Australia's being one of assimilation and the U.S. being predicated on miscegenation, to say nothing of slavery. Thus, the interpretation of the U.S. in relation to race doesn't apply to other cultures.

33 Wallace, "Multiculturalism and Oppositionality," 8.

34 Wittig, "One is Not Born a Woman," 55.

35 This is the split between the what Barthes has called the "hermeneutic" and "proairetic" codes. He rather disdains the latter, preferring the former.

36 Since I wrote this, Sharon Willis has published an essay on this film, "Hardware and Hardbodies, What Do Women Want?: A Reading of *Thelma and Louise*," *Film Theory Goes to the Movies*, ed. Jim Collins, et al. (New York & London: Routledge, 1993), 120–128. Cathy Griggers also has an essay on this film in the same volume: "*Thelma and Louise* and the Cultural Generation of the New Butch-Femme," 129–141.

37 Walter Benjamin, "The Storyteller: Reflections on the Works of Nikolai Leskov," *Illuminations* (New York: Schocken Books, 1969), 94.

38 Morris, " 'TOO SOON TOO LATE',' " 133.

39 Amy Taubin, "Notes on Campion," *The Village Voice*, May 28, 1991, 62.

40 This is from a review of Frame in *The Village Voice*.

41 Freda Freiberg, "The Bizarre in the Banal: Notes on the Films of Jane Campion," *Don't Shoot Darling: Women's Independent Filmmaking in Australia*, ed. Annette Blonski, et al. (Richmond, Australia: Greenhouse Publications, 1987), 328–333.

42 Kate Sands, "Women of the Wave," *Back of Beyond: Discovering Australian Film and Television* (Sydney: Australian Film Commission, 1988), 11.

43 Ibid., 11.

44 Hewett, *Wild Card*, 16.

45 Benjamin, "The Storyteller," 102.

46 Ibid., 87.

47 Ibid., 100.

48 Morris, " 'TOO SOON TOO LATE',' " (129) quoting Gilles Deleuze and Felix Guattari, *Kafka: Toward a Minor Literature* (Minneapolis: Minnesota University Press, 1986).

49 Benjamin, "The Storyteller," 87.

50 Morris, " 'TOO SOON TOO LATE',' " 130.

51 Linda Hutcheon, *A Theory of Parody* (New York: Methuen, 1985), 72.

52 Benjamin, "The Storyteller," 86.
53 Laleen Jayamanne, "Love Me Tender, Love Me True, Never Let Me Go: A Sri Lankan reading of Tracey Moffatt's *Night Cries: A Rural Tragedy*," *Feminism and the Politics of Difference*, eds. Sneja Gunew & Anna Yeatman (Sydney: Allen & Unwin, 1993).
54 Gilles Deleuze and Claire Parnet, *Dialogues*, trans. Hugh Tomlinson and Barbara Hammerjam (New York: Columbia University Press, 1987), 3.
55 Adrian Martin, "Nurturing the Next Wave," *Back of Beyond: Discovering Australian Film and Television*, 90–105.
56 Martin, "Nurturing the Next Wave," 98.
57 Correspondence with Moffatt, December 8, 1991 and March 21, 1992.
58 Ibid.
59 Shane McNeil, "Relativity, Roeg, and Radical Forms: An Interview with Tracey Moffatt, *Lip Sync*, (Aug./Sep. 1991), 1–3, 14.
60 Laleen Jayamanne, "Image in the Heart," *Framework*, no. 36 (1989), 31–41.
61 Ann Rutherford, "Changing Images: An Interview with Tracey Moffatt," *Aboriginal Culture Today* (Dangaroo Press, 1988), 152.
62 Scott Murray, "Tracey Moffatt," *Cinema Papers*, no. 79 (1990), 19–22.
63 These concepts are found in the following essays by Sergei Eisenstein: "The Cinematographic Principle and the Ideogram," 32, "The Structure of the Film," in *Film Form: Essays in Film Theory*, ed. and trans. Jay Leyda (San Diego, New York, London: Harvest/Harcourt Brace Jovanovich, 1977).
64 Ibid., 30.
65 Eisenstein, "Dickens, Griffith, and the Film Today," ibid., 251. For an elaboration of this theoretical frame, see my "Haunted History: Tracey Moffatt and Julie Dash," *Discourse*, vol. 16 no. 2 (Winter 1993–94), 127–163; and "An Empirical Avant-Garde: Laleen Jayamanne and Tracey Moffatt," in *The Fugitive Image*, ed. Patrice Petro (Bloomington, Indiana: University of Indiana Press, 1995).
66 Laleen Jayamanne, "Passive Competence," *Screen*, vol. 28 no. 4 (Autumn 1987), 107–120.
67 John Berger, "Uses of Photography," *On Looking* (New York: Pantheon, 1980), 56.
68 Ibid., 56–63.
69 Ibid., 57.
70 Ibid., 61–62.
71 Ibid., 63.
72 From correspondence with Jayamanne, December 18, 1991.
73 Laleen Jayamanne, "Do You Think I am a Woman, Ha! Do You?", *Discourse*, vol. 11, no. 2 (1989), 49–64.
74 Ibid., 55.
75 Ibid., 57.
76 Jayamanne, "Love Me Tender, Love Me True, Never Let Me Go," 73–84.
77 Correspondence with Moffatt.
78 McNeil, "Relativity, Roeg and Relative Forms," 2.

79 Rutherford, "Changing Images," 153.

80 Ibid., 155.

81 Marcia Langton, *"Well, I Heard It on the Radio and I Saw It on the Television
    ..."* (Sydney: Australian Film Commission, 1993.) Langton also refers to an
    earlier essay by Ann Kaplan, "Aborigines, Film and Moffatt's *Night Cries—
    A Rural Tragedy*: An Outsider's Perspective," *The Olive Pink Society Bulletin*
    vol. 2 no. 1 (1990), 13–17.

82 Langton, "Well, I Heard It on the Radio...," 45–46.

83 Quoted in Murray, "Tracey Moffatt," 22.

84 Ibid.

85 Ingrid Periz, *"Night Cries*: Cries from the Heart," *Filmnews* (August 1990), 6.

86 Ibid.

87 Langton, "Well, I Heard It on the Radio...," 46.

88 Ibid., 47.

89 Ibid.

90 Ibid.

91 Eisenstein, *Film Form*, 71.

92 Sergei Eisenstein, "Synchronization of Senses," *Film Sense*, 81.

93 Gilles Deleuze, *Cinema 1: The Movement-Image* (Minneapolis: University of
    Minnesota Press, 1986), "Preface to the French Edition."

94 Eisenstein, *Film Form*, 234.

95 Ibid., 235.

96 Ibid., 249.

97 Ibid., 250.

98 Ibid., 251.

99 Ibid.

100 Ibid., 252.

101 Ibid., 251.

102 Gilles Deleuze, "Mediators," *Incorporations, Zone* 6, ed. Jonathan Crary and
    Sanford Kwinter (New York: Urzone, 1992), 280–294.

103 Ibid., 283.

104 Jayamanne, "Image in the Heart," 33.

105 Lesley Stern, *Camera Obscura*, No20/21 (1989), 295.

106 Eisenstein, *Film Form*, 254.

107 Penny Webb, "Tracey Moffatt's *BeDevil*: A Film Inscription of Three Ghost
    Stories," *Agenda*, no. 34 (1993/94), 32–35, 32.

108 Ibid., 32.

109 John Conomos and Raffaele Caputa, *"BeDevil," Cinema Papers*, no. 93
    (May 1993), 26–32, 29.

110 Webb, "Tracey Moffatt's *BeDevil*," 33.

111 Conomos and Caputo, *"BeDevil*," 29.

112 Ibid.

113 Moffatt, fifth draft of the script.

114 Conomos and Caputo, *"BeDevil*," 31.

115 Ibid.

116 Ibid.

117 Ibid., 29.
118 Ibid.
119 Moffatt, Script.
120 Ibid.
121 Webb, "Tracy Moffatt's *BeDevil*," 34.
122 Conomos and Caputo, "*BeDevil*," 29.
123 Webb, "Tracy Moffatt's *BeDevil*," 33.
124 I have said nothing about the soundtrack, particularly the music and
     effects, which are quite dominant. At first the music seemed overdone, too
     much, and not subtle enough. On second thought, the music operates, I
     suspect, on the level of parody (with many cultural references) and critique
     of movie music, contemporary music, and the relationship between sound
     and image. I am not a music scholar. Also, I do not have a videotape and
     thus could not listen carefully. Perhaps the music threads the three stories
     together, as do the common ties of depth/surface/coverup; the subtle quali-
     ties of racism/multiculturalism; and the invention on address/point of
     view, TV/film.
125 Hewett, *Wild Card*, 11.
126 Woolf, *Three Guineas*, 17.
127 Wittig, "One is Not Born a Woman," 20.
128 Woolf, *Three Guineas*, 141.
129 Ibid., 142.
130 Ibid., 125.
131 bell hooks, "Talking Back," *Discourse* 8 (Fall-Winter 86–87), 124.
132 I have elaborated this initial discussion of the film by including the terrific
     essays on this film by Black critics. My initial reading remains the same,
     albeit more informed now. I concluded my essay in *Discourse* with more
     comments by Marcia Langton, plus these words:
          Manthia Diawara emphasises what he calls *Daughters of the Dust*'s
     "religious system," which he states is African, leading to "a Black structure
     of feeling." He links this to Cornel West's recent call for a politics of conver-
     sion, of feeling, which Dash's system of "ancestor worship" resembles.
     (18/19) Let me digress briefly to West who passionately claims that "black
     existential angst derives from the lived experience of ontological wounds
     and emotional scars." (43) Black Americans face a "nihilistic threat"
     whose symptoms include a "sense of worthlessness and self-loathing," a
     "kind of collective clinical depression," "an eclipse of hope." (43) For West,
     recovery from nihilism is analogous to recovery from addiction; all are
     "diseases of the soul." (43).
          For West, "Any disease of the soul must be conquered by a turning of
     one's soul. This turning is done by one's own affirmation of one's worth, an
     affirmation fueled by the concern of others. This is why a love ethic must
     be at the center of a politics of conversion." (43) For West, this "love ethic
     [which is 'universal'] has nothing to do with sentimental feelings or tribal
     connections." Rather, it is generating a "sense of agency," (43) to which I
     would add self-worth and self-love. Against the premises of corporate

enterprise and romance, universal spiritual practices, all predicated on love, illustrate that strength, happiness, and high purpose come only from within, from the heart. Rather than lacking (the premise of desire), or in need of (the premise of obsession), spirituality teaches that we are greater and more self sufficient than we have imagined.

bell hooks speaks of the film's "truth of spirit," the "spirit of unity" (DBh 48). However, she finds this spiritual truth in Native American and Black traditions, what she sees as the "historical overlap between ideas about nature, divinity, and spirit in those two cultures" (DBh 49). Like hooks, I prefer "spirituality" to religion. Spirituality surpasses the exclusions, intolerance, and differences of religious institutions—squabbles represented in *Daughters of the Dust*. And I suggest that the film's spiritual qualities have great affinity with Hindu, Buddhist, and Muslim practices (and Kashmir Shavism, my personal practice of Siddha Yoga), as well as with traditions of Christianity. Spirituality invokes the divinity, the greatness and beauty, within everyone. Through diversity and individualism, spirituality invokes unity and community. For me the spiritual basis of the film, eliciting what Eisenstein would first call *pathos* and later *ecstasy*, is unifying and inspiring—providing another way to think and feel and change history, or create history. Spirituality—in the character of the unborn child, on the soundtrack (in the wind and the music), in the values of love and compassion, in the formal structure—enables an identification with something greater than race or gender or nation. This "ethics of Love" is *Daughters of the Dust*'s "truth," which can be felt, experienced, and known.

Between Contemplation and Distraction

Cinema, Obsession and Involuntary Memory

Jodi Brooks

In Jane Gallop's essay "Carnal Knowledge" she asks: "How can we admit our resemblance to the twelve-year-old girl who simply loves all pictures of horses, regardless of their formal and aesthetic qualities?"[1] This seemingly throwaway line, with its somewhat melodramatic tone, has always evoked for me both a mode of spectatorship—that which has been theorised as the "too close, lack of distance" variety—and more generally a certain relation to cinema—an obsessive, mono-maniacal attraction to the very idea of cinema which seems less to do with the love of particular films than with an amorous state—the idea of a relation, an (anticipated) encounter.

Gallop's argument is about "charged pleasures"—an erotics of engagement in relation to the artwork. She proposes this erotics of

engagement through a reading of two texts—Freud's "Moses of
Michelangelo," and in a later section, Barthes' *Camera Lucida*. In her
reading of Freud's text, Gallop argues that (good) psychoanalytic art
criticism is not so much about uncovering a latent sexuality in subject
matter but rather about (the sexuality of) a charged attraction, a type
of encounter. Gallop writes:

> I am trying to suggest here that there are two different ways in
> which psychoanalytic criticism can be linked to sex. The more
> familiar and least interesting concerns latent subject matter,
> but the criticism that interests me, which may in fact be one
> that barely exists at all, is concerned with what we may call
> the erotics of engagement, a sexuality that is not in the object,
> however deeply hidden, but in the encounter.[2]

One could claim that a lot of psychoanalytic feminist film theory
has, for some time now, been concerned more with something like the
"erotics of engagement" than with latent subject matter. But what
interests me about Gallop's argument is the idea that such encounters
are "erotic" because they involve what she calls an illegitimate attraction. When the attraction is in some sense "improper" (a status which
produces a sort of pleasurable unease in the one so afflicted), the relation or encounter is charged. In Freud's text this illegitimate attraction
takes the form of an interest in subject matter rather than the work of
art's formal and aesthetic qualities. While Freud claims that such an
interest or attraction is in some sense illegitimate, it is this very interest which he claims as his own. It holds a "stronger attraction" for him
than the aesthetic qualities of the work. For Gallop it is this attraction
and its illegitimacy, rather than the "uncovering" of a latent sexual
content in Michelangelo's work which is the site of sexuality in Freud's
essay—a sexuality which lies in and is produced by an attraction
which is in some sense "not proper." It is then a sexuality which is tied
to the relation between subject and work and the system of values

around such relations. "Subject matter," she claims, "is sexual not because it is about some experience of sexuality but because we experience the relation to subject matter in art as forbidden, powerful, desiring and embarrassing."[3]

It is this idea of an erotics of the encounter and improper, "charged" pleasures that I want to draw on as a way of addressing the forms of pleasure and investment possible in cinema spectatorship and their popular and theoretical evaluation. Cinema as a cultural form is of course radically different to the high art which is the subject of Freud's essay, and these differences cannot be overlooked. In many ways cinema operates as that place where one can, in fact, indulge in such "illegitimate pleasures," but this then begs the question of what are cinema's, or rather film theory's, forbidden—and therefore charged—pleasures and attractions?

When it comes to cinema and certain forms of film theory, there is nothing particularly improper in saying, for instance, "I love all Steve Martin films." Indeed it can even add to one's academic street credibility. The anxiety that Gallop's question induces is rather to do with the possibility of there being a similarity between such cinematic obsessions and those of this hypothetical twelve-year-old girl and her pictures of horses. Indeed, I'd like to push the parallel further by drawing on Benjamin's idea of collecting. To be a little less precious about the figure of the collector, one could regard both this young girl and cinema's amorous subject (the spectator as a sort of melancholic lover) as being involved in forms of collecting. Both, in other words, are involved in an amorous enterprise, and what the cinema's amorous subject collects—both nurtures and hoards—are discarded images (moments, scraps of dialogue, certain poses, whole films ...).

Perhaps in cinema what is illegitimate is a particular type of obsession, a mode of spectatorship which, like the activities of the collector, involves both an intense fascination and a level of daydream—but which more than anything operates as a form of investment and invocation.

While Gallop argues her erotics of engagement through Freud and Barthes' *Camera Lucida*, I'm approaching a cinematic erotics of engagement from a different angle by drawing on the work of Walter Benjamin—in which the seeds of a theory of cinematic spectatorship can be found. I'm primarily interested here in Benjamin's work on Proust and Baudelaire and the concepts of involuntary memory and the correspondences, particularly in terms of how they complicate the contemplation/distraction distinction in relation to cinema.[4] This distinction—which is crucial to his essay, "The Work of Art in the Age of Mechanical Reproduction"—is one which I think continues, in various guises, to inform ideas of spectatorship in relation to film and television. The distinction certainly doesn't originate with Benjamin, and in the "Work of Art" essay he was to radically challenge the meaning and valuing of these terms. What I want to do here is further complicate the distinction by following Benjamin's own complex—and at times ambivalent—proposal of it, an ambivalence which can be charted through the labyrinth of concepts involved in his proposal of these two forms of spectatorship and reception. These concepts are, for my purposes, principally involuntary memory, correspondences, and the aura. By re-reading some of these concepts it is possible to map out a mode of spectatorship which I would place somewhere between contemplation and distraction, and thereby repropose a mode of spectatorship which has been defined in terms of proximity or a lack of distance, as being too close to the image.

This idea of a lack of distance in relation to the image has generally been associated with concepts of female spectatorship both in film theory and in popular discourses. *I Love Lucy* plays out this figure of the female spectator beautifully in "The Publicity Agent" episode. Lucy, trying to get some publicity for Ricky's act at the club, produces a story about a Maharincess of Franistan who has fallen in love with Ricky after hearing one of his records and is flying to the U.S. to hear him. Lucy, of course, is this Maharincess, and Ricky, as usual, cannot recognise her behind her disguise. Lucy and Ethel arrive at the club as the visiting royalty for a private performance for the Maharincess and the press (which Lucy has summoned for the occasion). After the introductions and various rituals, Ricky launches into song, the central lyrics being "when we're dancing and you're dangerously near me". As soon as he reaches the words "dangerously near." Lucy, on cue, wails and pretends to faint. Ricky, somewhat disturbed, turns to the Maharincess' side-kick (Ethel) and asks what's wrong, to which Ethel answers in glorious dead-pan, "You sing, she swoon." Ricky, being the gentleman, suggests that perhaps if the Maharincess is going to faint he should stop singing. Lucy at this point makes the scene by coming to just enough to open one eye and say "I like it," obliging Ricky to return to the song, and the cycle starts all over again.

What Lucy plays out here is a particular image of the female spectator/fan/lover in a sort of state of rapture, unable to take up or maintain a distanced position from the image (here in the form of Ricky). I'd like to shift the focus of what such forms of proximity and their charged nature entail, whilst nevertheless hanging on to this idea of enthrallment. I'd like to deal, then, with a mode of spectatorship which involves a logic of suspension, fascination, and an intense but absent concentration: an intensification of the gaze at the same time as the object contemplated recedes. Benjamin's work addresses such a state or relation: suggesting that it involves not so much a lack of distance in the sense of an experience of a spatial merging with the image, but something closer to a sort of temporal dynamic.

Contemplation, Distraction and the Auratic

Benjamin's explicit references to cinema are few and far between, and yet there is much in his work that is suggestive for cinema—primarily because his attempts at a theory of experience revolve around ideas of the temporality of the image. Benjamin's main and best known references to cinema are in his essay "The Work of Art in the Age of Mechanical Reproduction" where cinema is dealt with in terms of the demise of auratic experience in favour of distracted modes of reception. In the "Work of Art" essay, cinema and its distracted modes of reception are seen as having a radical potential, through which the spectator could be "blasted" into a sort of recognition of the forms of alienation seen as operating in modern life. Contemplation on the other hand is aligned with the aura and social privilege, something which is complicated when we turn to much of Benjamin's other work where his position on the demise of the aura is more markedly ambivalent. According to Benjamin's well-known argument in this text, the demise of the aura and contemplative experience are brought about by the prevalence of shock sensations in modernity and through the changing role and nature of art. The technical reproducibility of the work of art—and the development of new media forms like film and photography in which technical reproducibility is essential—is seen as radically threatening what had historically come to stand for the aura of the work of art: uniqueness, authenticity, singularity in time and place, and with these, social privilege. Film's radicality, for Benjamin, lies primarily in the idea of shock sensations (that result predominantly from editing and framing—things like the fragmentary nature of the film image, changes in scale, rush of sensory stimuli etc.). Film can fragment the apparent givenness and continuity of the social world by isolating and reconfiguring it as fragments, as a series of shocks. In this formulation then, cinema is aligned with a distracted rather than contemplative mode of reception, and therefore also regarded as having an exemplary role in the contemporary demise of the aura. Nevertheless, for Benjamin film treads a fine line between, on the one hand, being able to make sense of contemporary forms of alienation and, on the other, perpetuating them.

When we turn to much of his other work, however, the ambivalence over the decline of the aura which is hinted at in the "Work of Art" essay becomes more evident. By reading this essay in the context of Benjamin's other work, moreover, the argument in the "Work of Art" essay becomes even more complex; for what is potentially lost with the demise of the aura is a mode of experience involving a complex temporality—the field of involuntary memory and the correspondences.

In his essays on Proust and Baudelaire, for example, the auratic, the correspondences and involuntary memory all appear to be intricately connected. In "Some Motifs in Baudelaire" for instance, Benjamin writes that: "To perceive the aura of an object we look at means to invest it with the ability to look at us in return. This experience corresponds to the data of the *mémoire involontaire.*" These data, incidentally, are unique; they are lost to the memory that seeks to retain them. Thus, they lend support to a concept of the aura that comprises the "unique manifestation of a distance."[5] (Earlier in the same essay he writes that "the distinctive feature of the images that rise from the *mémoire involontaire* is seen in their aura.")[6]

Now this is a conception of the aura in many ways at odds with that in the "Work of Art" essay. It is this idea of the aura which I find more useful for film; not so much as a means of redeeming cinema as an auratic form—a project that doesn't really interest me—but more in terms of an idea of a mode of spectatorship which involves a process of investment which has to do with the anticipated return of the gaze. In this concept of the aura, what we are dealing with is a charging or intensification of the viewing relation (something we also find in Barthes' *Camera Lucida*). This investing of the object with an ability to return the gaze, or even more, a charging of looking itself, has less to do with any literal return of the gaze than with a process of activating/animating the field of correspondences. Now in a sense involuntary memory and the correspondences do return something, but as we find in Proust repeatedly, it is not the subject's look that is returned, but those images or that self which we have never known in a waking state.

What we are dealing with here is a sort of invocation, an intensification of the gaze which imbues the object with traces of a past. It both opens a temporal realm between subject and object (a strange mix of temporal proximity and distance) and suggests a physicality—the look that leaves a mark. There are two types of look that are felt as leaving a trace: the look of love and what could perhaps be called the daemonic look or the evil eye—no doubt the two are related. In Miriam Hansen's paper, "Benjamin, Cinema and Experience: 'The Blue Flower in the Land of Technology.' "[7](in which she develops a dynamic reading of his work in terms of cinema), she suggests that such a form of intense gaze in Benjamin's work—the look that leaves a residue—is a memory of the maternal gaze. The source of this auratic gaze has been forgotten and has therefore returned as something "distant and strange";[8] basically it is the idea of the uncanny.

This anticipated return of the gaze thus involves the opening of a distance, but this distance is temporal rather than spatial. Certainly in Benjamin's definition of the aura as "the unique manifestation of a distance, however close it [the object] may be,"[9] we are not dealing with a spatial distance; for what is opened is the field of the involuntary memory and the correspondences, those images and resemblances which are lost to conscious, voluntary memory and rather rise as images of another self, images which fleet past. This opening of a distance must then be seen as a strange mix of proximity and distance: a suspension of the present moment in favour of a sensuous loss of self in a temporal opening. I would argue that an erotics of engagement in cinema often has to do with such an experience of time, with the production of a state of animated suspension in the spectator.

With its privileging of the iconic sign and the persistent unfolding of images, cinema seems far removed from the terrain of involuntary memory. When we relate the idea of charged looking and its components (involuntary memory, the correspondences and the aura) to cinema, there are two questions that have to be addressed. First, in what ways can cinema be conceived of as allowing for and offering the possibility of activating correspondences, and second, what sort of reproposal of the obsessive, intense gaze, does this suggest?

To what extent then does film—or more accurately, particular forms of spectatorship—offer the possibility of activating correspondences? Cinema undoubtedly seems to be more than complicit in the demise of the aura, and with it, therefore, involuntary memory and the correspondences. The iconic nature of the cinematic image can be seen as constantly adding images to voluntary memory, and thereby—for Benjamin—reducing the scope for the play of involuntary memory and the imagination.[10] And the predetermined unfolding of images on the screen would seem to limit or contain any potential reverie. The flow of images and narrative would seem to hold the spectator resolutely in the present of screen time (basically the idea that watching a film would never allow you a chance to go off on the sort of reveries that Proust does with his soggy pastries, or for that matter, that Barthes does on the photograph, because you would simply never get the chance). Neither of these aspects of film preclude the possibility of an activation of involuntary memory. The fact that the cinematic sign is primarily, in Benjamin's terms, to do with sensuous similarity in relation to its referent (a relation of sameness), does not in itself exclude the possibility of non-sensuous similarity (a relation of affinity, basically the field of correspondences). Benjamin frequently—almost despite himself—makes reference to this possibility in cinema, and we find it in a number of concepts. For instance, his reference to what he, following Kracauer, calls "unconscious optics" in film suggests the activation of a peculiar temporality between the spectator and film, and involves a gaze which is both intense (charging the act of looking itself) and absent (the object of the gaze recedes as images arise from involuntary memory).

To this extent I'm not so sure that what is regarded as the compulsory temporality of the apparatus—the flow of images through the projector and across the screen—prohibits such film/spectator relations. In privileging the temporality of frames through the projector, the many temporal forms that can operate in (our experience of) a film are overlooked.

Benjamin deals explicitly with the idea of such a temporal encounter in his essay on Proust, though it can be found in much of his work. The logic of the encounter runs throughout Proust's *Remembrance of Things Past*—it is the force behind what Benjamin calls Proust's "paralyzing, explosive will to happiness."[12] In Proust, the encounter is primarily bound up with sensations, sensations which invoke and yield an ambivalent state in the subject, a pleasure-pain complex of intoxication and loss. The quest for such encounters is the thread running through Proust's work, for instance in the madeleines passage in *Remembrance of Things Past.* No sooner has Proust tasted the tea-soaked cake morsel than a shudder runs through him. The sensation—though not the source—comes in a flash the instant the liquid touches the palate. The self is at once taken over, possessed and relinquished, by this all-encompassing vertigo. The source of the "all-powerful joy" Proust feels, however, does not appear in an instant. It requires attentiveness, it has to be waited for and this waiting too is highly charged:

> I feel something start within me, something that leaves its rest-ing place and attempts to rise, something that has been embed-ded like an anchor at a great depth; I do not know yet what it is, but I can feel it mounting slowly; I can measure the resis-tance, I can hear the echo of great spaces traversed. Undoubtedly what is thus palpitating in the depths of my being must be the image, the visual memory which, being linked to that taste, is trying to follow it into my conscious mind.[12]

What appears through the activation of the involuntary memory is the concealed object—here the memory of Combray where Proust spent part of his childhood. Not simply Combray as it was experienced, but, as Deleuze points out in his book *Proust and Signs,* Combray "in a form in which it was never experienced, in its 'essence' or its eternity."[13] What is recovered is not only what has been lost but also what has perhaps never existed. This "all-encompassing joy" then is not so much in the recovery of a lost time, or an experience of the self as plenitude. It is more like a sort of loss of self in the experience of an open, pure time. Clearly what is of interest here is not so much the discovery of a forgotten moment but the waiting, the search itself. The pleasure is in the activation of the involuntary memory, the relinquishment of the self, and—as is evident in this passage from Proust—an attention to the movement of remembrance and forgetting through the body. The movement not so much of the body through time but rather of time through the body.

This brings me to my second point about such charged relations between film and spectator—the physicality of their relation. In "The Work of Art" essay, Benjamin makes a neat distinction between distracted and contemplative modes of reception in terms of a sort of active/passive distinction:

> Distraction and contemplation form polar opposites which may be stated as follows: a man who concentrates before a work of art is absorbed by it. He enters into this work of art the way legend tells of the Chinese painter when he viewed his finished painting. In contrast, the distracted mass absorbs the work of art.[14]

Benjamin here is privileging the revolutionary potential of the distracted mode of reception, and his example of absorbing the work of art is architecture. Architecture, he claims, is experienced "less through rapt attention than by noticing the object in incidental fashion"[15] and, moreover, through both optical and tactile means. One notices something while engaged in something else. Contemplation on the other hand is for Benjamin purely optical with no tactile counterpart. When we turn to Benjamin's "Moscow Diary," however, we find this distinction complicated:

As I was looking at an extraordinarily beautiful Cézanne, it
suddenly occurred to me that it is even linguistically fallacious
to speak of "empathy." It seemed to me that to the extent that
one grasps a painting, one does not in any way enter into its
space; rather this space thrusts itself forward in various specific
spots. It opens up to us in corners and angles in which we
believe we can localise crucial experiences of the past; there is
something inexplicably familiar about these spots.[16]

In this passage we are dealing with a contemplative relation
between the viewer and the work of art; whilst the viewer intently
ponders or broods over the image, details thrust themselves forward.
Here we find a similar sort of physicality to the one in Proust, an intensification of the relation between the viewer and the work by a compli-
cation of the distance between the two. While the gap between spectator and work is crossed, it at the same time produces another sort of
distance—a temporal one that takes place between the self and an
other self—unknown, forgotten, possible (and melancholic).

It is this relation with the work of art which I think offers most to a
conception of an intense, obsessional mode of cinema spectatorship—
a relation which is charged with a sort of longing, and which, moreover, involves a sort of physicality. Such a mode of spectatorship suggests that the relation between spectator and film is one of imagined
complicity, or what Klossowski—in perhaps not so different a context—calls a daemonic complicity. To an extent—and this maybe goes
for our hypothetical twelve-year-old girl also—this charging has a
relation to subject matter, but it is one in which subject matter (as narrative, as content of the image) recedes with the intensification of the
relation, and in its place a different type of story develops.

Collecting for Benjamin is a process of renewal. If we imagine that
cinema's amorous subject approaches a film, the video shop, or even
the recounting of a film with the same anticipation that Benjamin's
book collector approaches some out-of-the way bookshop or unpacks

his or her library, it is possible to rethink the nature of some of our more intense, obsessive relations to cinema. The collector turns the discarded commodity into a collector's item. It becomes, in Benjamin's terms, a souvenir (the German *Andenken* meaning both reminiscence and keepsake or memento). "The souvenir," he writes in "Central Park," "is the transformation of the commodity into a collector's item and the correspondences are the endless multiple resonances of each souvenir with all the others."[17] Through a mode of spectatorship essentially tied to fascination, a film (and one's memory of it) can become a souvenir, a treasured item. It is in this sense that we also find an amorous relation—and even an erotics of the encounter—being established.

"Every passion borders on the chaotic, but the collector's passion borders on the chaos of memories."[18]

My thanks to Lesley Stern for her assistance in writing this paper.

1   Jane Gallop, "Carnal Knowledge," *Thinking Through the Body* (New York: Columbia University Press, 1988), 138.

2   Ibid.

3   Ibid.

4   Walter Benjamin, "The Image of Proust," *Illuminations*, trans. Harry Zohn, ed. Hannah Arendt (Suffolk: Fontana, 1973); Walter Benjamin, *Charles Baudelaire: A Lyric Poet in the Era of High Capitalism*, trans. Harry Zohn (London: Verso, 1983).

5   Benjamin, *Charles Baudelaire*, 148.

6   Ibid., 148.

7   *New German Critique*, no. 40 (Winter 1987), 179–224.

8   Ibid., 215.

9   Walter Benjamin, "The Work of Art in the Age of Mechanical Reproduction," *Illuminations*, 224.

10 See Benjamin, *Charles Baudelaire*, 146.

11 Benjamin, "The Image of Proust," *Illuminations*, 205.

12 Marcel Proust, *Remembrance of Things Past*, vol. 1, trans. C.K. Scott Moncrieff and Terence Kilmartin (London: Penguin, 1989), 49.

13 Gilles Deleuze, *Proust and Signs* (New York: G. Brazillier, 1972), 12.

14 Benjamin "The Work of Art," 241.

15 Ibid., 242.
16 Walter Benjamin, "Moscow Diary," trans. Richard Sieburth, *October*, no. 35 (Winter 1985), 42.
17 Walter Benjamin, "Central Park," trans. Lloyd Spencer, *New German Critique*, no. 34 (Winter 1985), 54.
18 Walter Benjamin, "Unpacking My Library: A Talk About Book Collecting," *Illuminations*, 60.

"I Wanted to Shoot People"

Genre, Gender and Action in the Films of Kathryn Bigelow

Needeya Islam

The relation between gender and genre, which has provided generous material and insight in the exploration of both terms, bears a particularly pragmatic implication in terms of the Hollywood cinematic model. While there has been a proliferation of genres and sub-genres within this industry in recent times, the number and type which have tacitly been allotted to women directors, proves extremely telling. Although the relative absence of women in the industry makes comparisons difficult,[1] it remains nevertheless significant that "feel-good" movies, teen movies and self promotion vehicles by actor/directors have almost exclusively been their domain. For a complex of reasons, which are in general based on industrial peculiarities, the facility with which male directors shift genres does not usually extend to their female counterparts. As Teresa de Lauretis notes, women have been writing stories "for several hundred years, or telling stories for much longer than that, but they have done so with little or no authority, with severe constraints as to genre, medium and address, and mostly, in someone else's phrase, after great pain."[2] Gender and genre therefore become inextricably linked in terms of authorship in Hollywood cinema, each reflecting the determinants of the other.

The films of Kathryn Bigelow, which all fall under the broad rubric of action film, are notable for venturing into territory generally rendered inaccessible to women filmmakers in Hollywood. In her oeuvre, gender and genre are not categories which provide a safe haven from violence and agency, as genre and industry expectations are always questioned and undermined. Within these terms, her minor position as a female author is reinforced by her consistently unorthodox choice of project. This inflects the dominant 'action' mode with which she is preoccupied, with an element of marginalisation and thus conflates seemingly incompatible discourses. That sub-cultures, the disenfranchised and outsiders populate her work, further substantiates this tendency.

Bigelow's first film, a short made in 1978 as a graduate film at Columbia University, was *Set-Up*, a chronicle of a street-gang fight. This isolated study suggests a critical perspective of the violence which is pervasive in her later films—an inquiry and testing of its workings, rather than an exclusively opportunistic deferral to the exigencies of the industry. Her first feature film, *The Loveless*, which focuses on a motorcycle gang and their confrontation with small town red-necks, was made in 1981. Both these films signal a preoccupation with the marginal, a tendency evidenced with even greater repercussions in her last three features which gained wider release.

Near Dark (1987), *Blue Steel* (1989), and *Point Break* (1991) all belong to the category of action cinema. Gilles Deleuze's analysis of the action-image, while specific and distinct from the industrial sense of action cinema, is nevertheless useful in mapping out some of its coordinates and in turn, the relation of Bigelow's work to these. He writes that realism can include the fantastic, the extraordinary, the heroic and above all melodrama. It can include exaggeration and lack of moderation, as long as these are of its own type. What constitutes realism is simply this: milieux and modes of behaviour, milieux which actualise and modes of behaviour which embody. The action-image is the relation between the two and all the varieties of this relation. It is this model which produced the universal triumph of the American cinema.[3]

Although Bigelow's films test cinematic and generic conventions rather than conform to them, Deleuze's concept of the action-image provides a point of departure from which certain cinematic norms and visual codes can be acknowledged, challenged and transformed. As Deleuze observes of the crisis in the action-image, "the cinema of the action-image had itself engendered a tradition from which it could now only, in the majority of cases, extricate itself negatively. The great genres of this cinema, the psycho-social film, the *film noir*, the Western, the American comedy, collapse and yet maintain their empty frame."[4]

The generic labels used to describe Bigelow's films are invoked not without irony, as within them genres undergo a certain metamorphosis. The tradition of the genre film is one which explicitly informs her work, yet the acknowledgement of generic specificity and codes becomes possible largely because of Bigelow's deviation from and transformation of them. The idea of the genre film is sustained not by necessarily making orthodox genre films but rather, films about genres and generic codes. These are articulated largely through excess, dislocation, and the conjuncture of seemingly incompatible registers. Jacques Derrida's work on genre is useful here. He writes of the designation "novel" that "it does not in whole or in part take part in the corpus whose denomination it nevertheless imparts. Nor is it simply extraneous to the corpus. But this singular topos places within and without the work, along its boundary, an inclusion and exclusion with regard to genre in general."[5] Similarly, in Bigelow's work, the nominations vampire western, cop thriller, and surfie movie function as active marks of each genre, while simultaneously differentiating them. Boundaries can no longer be maintained as absolute, and the discourse of analysis and its object collapse into one another. Bigelow takes this general textual quality and renders it extreme by testing the properties of a given genre, and adapting cinematic and generic conventions, not merely exposing them. Her work thus indicates a critical project, and something beyond a mere clever homage to the Hollywood tradition.

The constitutive equivocacy of the term genre can be said to be borne of the existence of a sense of the concept, and a simultaneous inability to efficiently determine the nature and properties of its composition. It is at once a form of repetition and a study in heterogeneity, with the two in constant flux. A possible way of apprehending this relationship is to perceive it as a requisite and fruitful agonism, which arises from the play between what Tzvetan Todorov distinguishes as semantic and syntactic elements.[6] Of this Rick Altman writes:

> While there is anything but general agreement on the exact frontier separating semantic from syntactic views, we can as a whole distinguish between generic definitions that depend on a list of common traits, attitudes, characteristics, shots, locations, sets, and the like—thus stressing the semantic elements that make up the genre—and definitions that play up instead certain constitutive relationships between undesignated and variable placeholder—relationships that might be called the genre's fundamental syntax. The semantic approach thus stresses the genre's building blocks, while the syntactic view privileges the structures into which they are arranged ... some of the most important questions of genre study can be asked only when they are combined.[7]

The implication of this for film genres is that a common matrix is established through the dynamic practice of communication, but the possible variations and combinations available are so numerous (although not infinite) that any descriptive or prescriptive attempts prove futile. This would account for, in the case of Bigelow, the sense of genre being apparent despite her constant resistance to generic norms.

Derrida's concept of play has interesting repercussions for genre also. He writes:

Henceforth it was necessary to begin thinking that there was no center, that the center could not be thought in the form of a present being, that the center had no natural site, that it was not a fixed locus but a function, a sort of nonlocus in which an infinite number of sign-substitutions came into play. This was the moment when language invaded the universal problematic, the moment when, in the absence of a center or origin, everything became discourse ... that is to say, a system in which the central signified, the original or transcendental signified is never absolutely present outside a system of differences.[8]

What restrains the "infinite" domain of play and thus maintains its usefulness in terms of genre (that is, restores the sense that something is being worked against) is the immanent invocation of what it attempts to challenge, for as Derrida states, "we have no language—no syntax and no lexicon—which is foreign to this history; we can pronounce not a single proposition which has not already had to slip into the form, the logic, and the implicit postulations of precisely what it seeks to contest."[9] The terms of communication must be in some sense commensurable, and the default language is usually that of the dominant. In Bigelow's films, effective critique uses the means and methods of its object of interrogation, so in a sense generic codes are responsible for their own undoing. While infraction of a law can have

the effect of strengthening it, excessive adherence can also throw its
very premise into question.

Instances of reanimating classic Hollywood codes and genres in
contemporary mainstream cinema are rarely naive, indiscriminate, or
perhaps even avoidable. However, they tend to occur within the ambit
of those postmodern determinants such as self-reflexivity, intertextual-
ity and pastiche, which require a certain acknowledgement of their
intent. Robert Altman's *The Player*, for example, engages explicitly
with familiar codes and texts; however, its status as a critical treatment of the industry itself is presumed from the outset. The ubiquity of
self-referential and intertextual critique within mainstream cinema
suggests that the concepts have been divested of their coterminous
ideological weight in themselves. This is not to say that they have lost
this potential but rather, that they most often constitute a sanctioned
form of questioning or criticism within mainstream cinema.

In Bigelow's films, the constant maintenance and confounding of
generic codes and registers facilitates a tacit resistance to simple readings. It is never certain whether her films reside in the domain of reverence or parody, as they acknowledge the seductive qualities of various popular genres, but question them internally, never placing the
inquiry above the cultural complex which produces the films. The
viewer is rarely instructed as to whether or not to take an ironic
stance, although this is a tone which is notably apparent in a general
sense. This ambiguity often makes for uncomfortable viewing, a consequence of questioning how far it is possible to explore the constitutive differences and heterogeneity of genre while still maintaining
some sense of the concept. Derrida writes,

> it were impossible not to mix genres ... if there were lodged in
> the heart of the law itself, a law of impurity or a principle of
> contamination. And suppose the condition for the possibility of
> the law were the a priori of a counter law, an axiom of impossi-
> bility that would confound its sense, order and reason.[10]

Bigelow's insistent disregard for and testing of generic limits engages with the question, "Why is there something rather than nothing at all?"[11]

The issue of female authorship within Hollywood cinema raises a multiplicity of questions and aporias, most of which relate to the paucity of women directors in the industry. The concept of authorship itself, one which had exceptional purchase in the domain of film theory with the articulation and transport of *Cahiers du Cinéma's* auteur theory to Britain and America, is historically encumbered with patriarchal overtones. This renders the term problematical for feminist theory from the outset. As Kaja Silverman notes, in announcing the "death of the author," Roland Barthes sought to elide not only the author as institution, but also as the occupant of an exclusively male position.[12] Female authorship thus invokes a project which is at least twofold: to divest authorship of its definitively masculine implications, and to reinstate a feminine position which considers its specificities.

While the manifold revisions of author theory in cinema have sought to collapse the distinction between the figures of the author "inside" and "outside" the text with the mobilisation of what seems to be a truism, that is, that the latter is nothing more than an effect of discourse, in the instance of female authorship, the interdependence of the two (while diverting questions of origin) has profound repercussions. The persistent questions concerning the female author can perhaps be posed as: how do the authorial positions of being "inside" and "outside" the text reflect each other and acknowledge sexual difference so as to avoid establishing an author, who in its capacity as a neutral designation, becomes for all intents and purposes, male, white and heterosexual? And, how is difference in the author inscribed in the text? Here the tension between "woman" as subject of speech, and "women" as speaking subjects becomes particularly significant. While there is a hesitation in drawing too absolute a correspondence between text and author, in this context, Judith Mayne observes,

the act of discarding the concept of female authorship and of
an attendant female tradition in the cinema as necessarily
compromised by essentialist definitions of woman can be
equally dualistic, in assuming that the only models of connection and influence are unquestionably essentialist ones.[13]

It seems that a shift in the properties of the designation "author"
tends to make itself manifest in some form in the text, although this
does not mean that a rigorously feminine or alternative position can
be prescribed. Rather, because of the co-optation of authorship by the
marginal, the term itself becomes decentered and heterogeneous. The
female author does not necessarily correspond to qualities within the
text which can be posited as feminine; the gaze, for example, is not
rendered feminine because of the author's sex, but a certain difference
is registered.

In her work on Dorothy Arzner, Claire Johnston argues that there
can never be a smooth fit between the female authorial voice and
Hollywood cinema, and that the relationship is characterised by a certain agonism. Following the various critiques of the cinema as apparatus, Johnston suggests that the dominant ideology of the industry
structures films in terms of fixity and binarisms, while authorial desire
annexes other means by which to undermine this ideology.[14] By
deploying other languages with which to speak against it, the female
author has facilitated a certain appropriation of the apparatus and
authorship. This in turn alters the natures of these two structures. In
the words of Gilles Deleuze and Félix Guattari, a certain deterritorialisation occurs. Deterritorialisation does not constitute a definite shift or
usurpation so much as a movement toward heterogeneity and
agency. The demarcation of spaces of language is no longer tenable
and the argument that differences and ruptures are subsumed by
established language also becomes questionable, as the former are
always immanent and thus indicative of a potential instability in the
dominant form.

In their articulation of a minor literature, Deleuze and Guattari write that

> a minor literature doesn't come from a minor language; it is rather that which a minority constructs within a major language. But the first characteristic of minor literature in any case is that in it language is affected with a high coefficient of deterritorialisation.[15]

Using the example of Kafka, they argue that for the Czech writer it was simultaneously impossible to write and to not write in German, a predicament which seems analogous to that of the female author within the Hollywood system. Even when the author is in the position of a minority and disempowered by the phallocentric nature of the apparatus, the metalinguistic status of the latter demands that all texts be produced within its terms: the codes and language of the Hollywood model become ineluctable vehicles. The necessity of writing in a dominant language from which one is also excluded does not indicate mere subjugation however, but a significant degree of infiltration, and thus potency. As Deleuze and Guattari note, "minor no longer designates specific literatures but the revolutionary conditions for every literature within the heart of what is called great (or established) literature."[16] The dominant language—in this instance of Hollywood cinema—is therefore divested of its monolithic status by the concept of female authorship which manifests, in Silverman's words, a type of "localised resistance"[17] whereby the insistence of atypical elements in the narrative, *mise-en-scène*, casting etc., work to confound the machinations of the apparatus and the organisation of the gaze.

Deleuze and Guattari write that:

> precisely because talent isn't abundant in a minor literature,

there are no possibilities for an individual enunciation that would belong to this or that 'master' and that should be separated from a collective enunciation. Indeed, scarcity of talent is in fact beneficial and allows the conception of something other than a literature of masters; what each author says individually already constitutes a common action.[18]

A minor position cannot be reduced to an exclusively female situation and is proper to a more generalised population of the marginal. Yet because of her rarity and the ideological implications of her recognition, the female author acts as a particularly cogent exemplar.[19]

Praying for High Noon, Playing with Genre in *Near Dark*

In her essay on the filmmaker Yvonne Rainer, Teresa de Lauretis writes that "obviously, therefore, much is at stake in narrative, in a poetics of narrative. Our suspicion is more than justified, but so is our attraction."[20] While discussing this in terms of a particular tendency in avant-garde filmmaking as well as in expressly feminist filmmaking and scholarship, the implications are not lost when addressing Hollywood films, for reasons which are clear enough. Perhaps even more so now considering that Lizzie Borden (whose films, as de Lauretis writes, are among those which have shown her "what it is to look at a film as a woman ... they have somehow managed to inscribe in the film my woman's look—next to, side by side, together with, my other (cinematic) look"[21]) has made a mainstream Hollywood film. De Lauretis describes all the properties of the pleasure of the text as mechanisms of coherence, but significantly not necessarily of closure. This pleasure she argues, is the result of those narrative strategies which produce closure not inevitably but because of historically and semiotically specific requirements, as in the case of media, genres and spectatorship. She writes:

> Thus to our contemporary eyes, even the texts of classical nar-
> rative cinema display, as feminist critics have repeatedly
> shown, the very gaps and paradoxes that the operation of nar-
> rative is meant to cover up ... If it can now be said, not only of
> Balzac but also of the classical narrative text *tout court*, that the
> text "opens up an ironic space which articulates the force of
> the question of femininity." it is because of [Shoshana]
> Felman's rereading, Barthes rereading, and the feminist
> rereadings and rewritings (I would like to say remakes) of clas-
> sical narrative films.[22]

This feminist reassessment of narrative seems particularly pertinent in relation to Bigelow's work, because of her specific concern
with film genres, that is, her remaking of certain classical narrative
film forms, in which detectable resistance and ambiguity are inherent.
The historical and ideological encumbrances of narrative forms are
effectively announced and challenged. While the question of the feminine may not be one which is manifestly and self-consciously explored
through this use of narrative, and while Bigelow—like Rainer—does
not posit herself as a feminist filmmaker, her work marks the nexus of
female authorship and the workings of cinematic forms in a mainstream context. This allows feminist film theory some fruitful insights.

In terms of its position within Hollywood cinema, *Near Dark* is
somewhat of an anomaly. It is on the one hand an extreme venture
into horror terrain. Marketed for video release with warnings such as
"pray for daylight," and "not for the squeamish" plastered over the
image of a charred and blood splattered male body, it nevertheless sits
uncomfortably within these generic boundaries. Its climactic scene for
example, is a depiction of hyperbolic and grotesque violence combined
with nervous comedy, yet this seemingly extreme moment of horror
takes place in a roadhouse, and functions like a saloon scene in a

Western. Bigelow states that "*Near Dark* started because we wanted to do a Western. But as no one will finance a western, we thought, 'Okay, how can we subvert the genre? Let's do a Western but disguise it in such a way that it gets sold as something else.' Then we thought, 'Ha, a vampire Western!' "[23] The scene maintains a certain moodiness and restrained menace, which along with the soundtrack ("Fever") recalls the 'youth in peril' films of the 50s such as *The Wild One*, and most significantly, Bigelow's own homage to this genre, *The Loveless*. A scene where an empty diner in a small town is slowly filled by a bikie gang while the Peggy Lee-like waitresses look on, seems an obvious reference. While mainstream and avant-garde cinema have often made reference to popular genres, in this film the distinction between citation and example becomes blurred, and this, coupled with highly stylised formal qualities (such as the play between daylight and darkness) that characterise the film as a whole, problematise its demarcation from 'low' genres. Although the film is saturated with generic signs, it is the way they subtend and complement each other—while remaining historically distinct— which suggests that *Near Dark* is less enlightening as a 'vampire Western' than as a film exploring the machinations of genre itself as an informing constituent of Hollywood narrative cinema.

The film is set in a small country town where an adolescent boy, Caleb encounters a strange girl, Mae whom he offers a lift home. As she alights from his truck, she bites him, leaving him feeling inexplicably ill. He is soon captured by Mae's "family," a vampiric bunch of nomads. Caleb's father and sister search across the state for him and finally find and free him after a transfusion. When the itinerants return and take Caleb's sister, he instigates a showdown in the middle of the town and saves his sister while they burn to death as the sun rises. Mae also escapes and is saved by a transfusion.

Near Dark opens with an extreme close-up of a mosquito on an arm, and then wide angle shots of rural America: deserted sheds, car wrecks, and the landscape itself. This is generic America, the West, a locus which is consolidated by the image of Caleb's boots, complete with spurs, emerging from the back of his pick-up. It is not Monument Valley, the West of John Ford, but a contemporary image of rural America, filled with industrial motifs, grain silos, wheat fields. It is related to and inflected with the mythological West through motifs such as spurs, cowboy hats, lassoes, and Caleb's silver horse. Similarly, a peculiarly American myth, the 50s bikie gang is invoked in *The Loveless*, and in this instance stylised to such a degree that it resists being familiar to the bikie genre and rather self-consciously and insistently refers to its extreme artificiality. As one review noted, "stylish to a fault—no motorcycle movie contains more preening, posturing hard-asses."[24] There are a number of close-ups of boots, buckles, tattoos and other details, some of them so sustained and static that they impress as still shots. These shots disrupt the narrative flow and emphasise a dependence upon generic expectations by drawing attention to other establishing elements of the genre such as the process of fetishisation—not only of objects and women, but of action (most notably the posturing of the protagonist, played by Willem Dafoe). While still succeeding as a classical narrative film, it also makes discrete its very components, and therein creates a critical space which allows for the accommodation of difference. The interdependence of Western and horror elements in *Near Dark* also suggests a canny negotiation of the specificity of certain images and action by welding together two seemingly incommensurate genres, and self-consciously diminishing absolute categories.

The particular pathology of the feral itinerants in *Near Dark* is never clearly articulated. Caleb's father, after saving his children from the gang and seeing that gunshots have no effect on them, demands to know who they are. Caleb replies: "You wouldn't believe me if I told you, I hardly believe it myself." This namelessness of the group, and the absence of iconic and Gothic elements usually required of vampire narratives (castles, bats, silver bullets, crosses, garlic) indicate that it is only specific actions and movements which define them as a group of vampires. This amounts to a distillation of vampirism to its most basic level (which is foregrounded in a sense by the opening image of the mosquito), that is, the life sustaining search for, and the drinking of blood. The aristocratic figure of the vampire in classic texts has given way to an image of the disenfranchised and homeless; a stark contrast to Nosferatu in his castle. The only reference to this precursor, aside from a general invocation of the expressionist fascination with light and dark, is the figure of Homer. An old man trapped in a child's body, he is simultaneously menacing and touching in his pursuit of Caleb's little sister, a tragic figure as he runs after her into the daylight and to his end. As Bigelow observes, "Ours are modern vampires, American vampires on the road. I don't know what they are. They're creatures of the night, who must drink blood to survive. They are ... curious."[25] Like the bikies of *The Loveless*, they are figures of marginality who must keep moving, the road being absolutely essential to their definition. Both films contain repeated images not only of vehicles and movement, but of the road itself. Shots of empty highway are eventually filled with images of bikies riding through. As Caleb struggles home after being bitten, there are sustained close-ups of his boots shuffling along a dusty track. In their van—a hermetically sealed unit of generic horror space immediately available and mobile—the feral gang traverse a mythic landscape. They have the effect, not unlike the surfers of *Point Break*, of deterritorialising, in this case, the West. They upset its boundaries by infiltrating it and making movement their locus.

While many films contrast the generic space of horror with a certain quality of the everyday, or with nature, Bigelow contrasts it in *Near Dark* with another mythologically resonant domain, the Western—one which is seemingly incompatible in tone and competitive in terms of visual and formal qualities. They are brought into harmony however, by the founding of both in the realm of action and the duel. Deleuze writes:

The duel is moreover not a unique and localised moment of the action-image. The duel stakes out the lines of action, always marking the necessary simultaneities. The passage from situation to action is thus accompanied by a dovetailing of duels into one another ... Even in the Western, which presents the duel in its purest state, it is difficult to mark out its boundaries.[26]

Both the Western and the horror genre which *Near Dark* invokes are preoccupied with the protracted duel, which also characterises the relationship between the two genres, a condition which Deleuze states might be external to the film, but is internal to the cinema.[27] Bigelow succeeds in modifying both genres by exploiting this characteristic in each and using it self-consciously, against the generic signifiers themselves. The emphasis on the very codes themselves is once again responsible for their dissolution. This becomes particularly apparent in the roadhouse sequence, which takes place at night. The gang enter with the obvious intention of causing trouble. While the others sit at a booth, Severen (the most active of the gang) and Caleb are at the bar, where Severen begins to antagonise a patron. When he retaliates, Severen begins a process whereby all the customers are one by one ruthlessly killed by the gang. The visceral rendering of the confrontation, the excessive violence and blood, pushes the film towards horror, yet the dramatic structure and rhetoric remains that of the Western. The two genres are imbricated (this becomes particularly apparent with the silhouette of the gang on a hill as they approach) yet the film still exceeds both categories. It becomes an articulation of the workings of genre as an informing category itself and its efficacy as a critical tool.

A preoccupation with light and its absence pervades the entire text and acts as a formal analogue of the film's two most obvious generic domains. It finds its most affirmative instance in a sequence where a shootout occurs in a darkened hotel room. It takes place during the day, and as shots are fired, sharp rays of light pierce the room. The absolute heterogeneity of light and dark, and their agonistic relation throughout the film, is crystallised. After this, the distinctions become more blurred, with Caleb riding into town on a horse at night, his father coming face to face with the nocturnal gang, and Homer running in the daylight. In the film's final scene, where Mae undergoes and survives a blood transfusion, the ruptures and contrasts of earlier scenes are somehow made congruous and the two milieux are able to connect without confrontation. The transfusion takes place at dawn, at the cusp of night and day, in a barn. It ends with a tableau of Caleb and Mae embracing as light streams through the half open barn door, the effect of which, as one reviewer noted, is "perversely life affirming"[28] for a violent horror film. Each genre is signalled in historically specific terms, hyperbolised in its relation to the other, and ultimately rendered fluid. The dichotomies of night/day, and light/dark as generic markers are invoked in their own dissolution as precise properties of particular genres.

Bigelow's flouting of generic norms, the bringing into relation of the seemingly incommensurable and her choice of material that is violent and kinetic, is indicative of a departure from the properties and expectations of Hollywood cinema. While a preoccupation and informed engagement with genre films in *Near Dark* is irrefutable, generic qualities are used to facilitate their own undoing and to establish an ironic and analytical space within and through narrative discourse. This tendency, which I have only touched upon, is apparent in even more detail in *Blue Steel* and *Point Break*—where the traditional hero figure and genre itself are enlisted in their own critical questioning.

Gun Crazy? Gender and the Hero in *Blue Steel*

In *Blue Steel*, through the simple act of placing a woman at the centre of an action film, of requiring her to possess physical skill, anger, and the moral high ground, Bigelow conducts an analysis of the function of the hero itself, and further, of those categories of mainstream cinema which, because of their putative self-evidence, are rarely called into question. Carol J. Clover's writing on women in horror films, and in particular Jamie Lee Curtis' role as an archetypal figure within these is, perhaps ironically, an extremely useful model for mapping the shifting terrain between victim and hero in *Blue Steel*.

In *Blue Steel*, the law, and the 'law of the father' allow Megan Turner (Jamie Lee Curtis) agency only insofar as her difference is obscured and she is efficiently assimilated into the male domain. That this is not an unproblematic tactic is integral to the film; simple inversion is an unsatisfactory possibility. Very early on, Megan's difference becomes evident, and her task is then to negotiate a position which acknowledges the fact and implications of this equivocacy.

Bigelow replaces the jaded macho male detective of the cop thriller with a female rookie cop whose inexperience functions as the narrative catalyst. On her first day on patrol Megan Turner intercepts a store robbery and shoots the gunman dead. This is witnessed by Eugene Hunt, a psychopathic stockbroker with a gun obsession, who steals the hold-up weapon. He becomes obsessed with Megan and sets out to seduce her, committing murders across town and inscribing her name on the bullets. She soon realises who he is, but her attempts to have him arrested are complicated by his lawyer and her involvement with Eugene. He is released and stalks her and her parents; he eventually kills her best friend, Tracy. Megan is intent on recapturing him, but he manages to break into her apartment, to shoot her boss/boyfriend and to rape her. At the hospital she knocks out a guard, steals his uniform, and sets out again to find Eugene, whom she shoots dead after a cross-town chase. The shift between the classic cop character and the specific modifications prompted by a young woman assuming this role are carefully negotiated, so that a more nuanced reading is necessary.

The scene of Megan's ritual dressing, in which her body and thus essential difference is systematically obscured, places her within an institutional and symbolic framework. Her gestures are militaristic and Bigelow's attention to each separate action (putting on gloves and tying shoelaces in particular) establish that Megan does not take her occupation lightly. She is marginalised by her choice of work and because of her sex, yet her individual commitment to her profession remains unequivocal. It is only after she is suspended that her problems begin. Her uniform is treated with reverence as it connotes power and is a licence for both gender and social mobility. In an establishing sequence, Megan and her male African-American partner discuss why they decided to become cops. She says "Ever since I was a kid," and her partner concurs: "Yeah, nobody fucks with a cop!" She also announces that she wanted to shoot people, which stated deadpan, when in uniform and on the beat, obviously worries her partner until he senses that she is joking. The police force offers them both the possibility of empowerment.

For Megan, the uniform inspires confidence; in an early scene, she swaggers and grins as she walks home in it, apparently pleased by the attention she receives from her neighbour and girls on the street. At the end of the film, when she regains control of the events around her by punching out a police guard and stealing his uniform, she takes the same care dressing as she had the opening scenes, paying particular attention to the shoelaces of her sneakers, and tightening her tie (which later serves a directly practical purpose when she uses it as a tourniquet). Jude Schwendenwien notes that "the image of Curtis in uniform is both awe-inspiring and scary, for she embodies all the sexual connotations of a person cast in the role of authority and power."[29] The two elements of which she becomes representative and which are in a sense at odds, that is, the law and women, are conflated. This is palpable in a close-up of her buttoning her uniform over a lacy bra. Bringing together the traditionally disparate, however, functions most evidently only to emphasise her singularity.

The suggestion of the transvestism of the uniform is complicated by the questions of transvestite spectatorship it inspires—particularly in relation to the identification with the active hero, which is the focus

of the film. Mary Ann Doane argues that female transvestism is characterised by a certain ease and acceptability, in contradistinction to
the male transvestite, who is traditionally represented in terms of
farce: "Male transvestism is an occasion for laughter; female transvestism only another occasion for desire."[30] Doane maintains that
transvestism is recuperable by the dominant ideology, while the masquerade—which recognises femininity as a construct, and thus exacerbates it—is not so amenable. In terms of spectatorship, Laura
Mulvey asserts that "for women (from childhood onwards) trans-sex
identification is a habit that very easily becomes second Nature. This
nature does not, however, sit easily and shifts restlessly in its borrowed
transvestite clothes."[31] While still somehow confirming these distinctions, Megan manages to counter the recuperability of transvestism. It
is a sign of her narrative status rather than of desire, thus disencum-
bers female spectators of their historical alternatives. Here they are
able to identify with the female character without surrendering to an
exclusively masochistic position; they can identify with a female hero,
and obviate the need for uneasy transvestite identification. Megan in
uniform is an acknowledgment of the usual limitations placed on
female spectatorship; she gives the problematic nature of identification
a tactile presence.

The film opens with and is framed by a scene of domestic violence
(albeit a fabricated one), where Megan 'shoots' the aggressor, only to
be 'shot' by the victim. As it progresses, a sub-plot emerges: Megan's
father physically abuses her mother, for which Megan handcuffs and
arrests him as he insists that "you can't arrest me, I'm your father!"
The locus of the law radically shifts from the father to the institution in
a general sense, and she is able to redress a power imbalance in a sym-
bolically potent act. She eventually releases her father, but it is only
after he breaks down and her authority over him has been asserted.
This marks a point at which both the personal and wider implications
of Megan as a female cop crystallise at the juncture of her private and
public worlds. Later, when her boss asks her why she became a cop,

she replies ambiguously, "Him"—an oblique reference perhaps to her father, to Eugene, or to the "law of the father." All three are not successfully exorcised until the final scene when she shoots Eugene dead, signalling an overcoming of the question of complicity raised by the opening sequence. In the final tableau, Megan sits slumped and alone in a car and lets the gun drop out of her hand and on to the seat. In killing Eugene, there is a sense that, as B. Ruby Rich observed of Clarice Starling in the climactic infra-red scene in *Silence of the Lambs,* she could avenge an entire decade's genre sins in a single act.[32] By being in uniform, her act is sanctioned; she has simultaneously conquered patriarchal obstacles in the form of Eugene, while employing one of these, the law itself, to carry out an instance of its own demise.

The casting of Jamie Lee Curtis as Megan is crucial to this analysis of hero function for a number of reasons. First, she is often described as an androgynous actress. In the most simplistic terms, her lanky body and short hair contribute to a resistance to conventional signs of femininity within mainstream Hollywood and facilitate her move into the male world. This is a quality common to all of Bigelow's central female characters. David Kehr writes (and this is in 1985 before *Blue Steel* was released) that:

> Curtis' gestures too, have a masculine force and plainness. The touch of sexual ambiguity in her stance suggests something of the Hawksian woman—she can, when she wants, be one of the boys. But Curtis would be too private a personality to ever join the Hawksian group. The sadness which lurks just below the surface sets her apart, and in most of her films she has been an outsider ... Curtis has mastered the technique of holding back ... In American movies, it's a technique that has traditionally been the property of male stars (like Wayne, Stewart, Bogart and Eastwood); we expect our actresses to be openly demonstrative.[33]

The attendant vulnerability of Curtis' character suggests a repudiation of binary opposites and simple transformations. She is an ambiguous female figure because she cannot be codified. She clearly enjoys the power of being a cop, as she constantly jokes that she "likes slamming heads against walls" and scares a man she meets socially about his out of date car registration sticker. Yet her manner is not stereotypically "tough" like Sarah Connor in *Terminator 2*, or Ripley in the *Alien* films; she is only so in terms of her actions, mainly those relating to her job. The generic boundaries which Bigelow tests in this film pivot on identification with this figure, who remains fallible and sympathetic, while possessing the requisite male hero traits to carry the film. Like the character of Clarice in *The Silence of the Lambs*, Megan simultaneously embodies, as Elizabeth Young writes, "deconstructive theories of identity that seek to destabilize the conceptual boundaries of gender, and approaches to feminist praxis that, in addressing issues like sexual violence, seek to preserve the strategic force of identity politics."[34]

Jamie Lee Curtis' history as "slasher bait" in horror movies offers an intriguing connection and perspective on the function of the female hero in mainstream Hollywood cinema. Clover, who has paid considerable attention to this phenomenon, argues that:

Fans of horror recognize the "tough-girl heroes" of films like *Thelma and Louise*, *Silence of the Lambs*, *Sleeping with the Enemy*, and *Mortal Thoughts* as upscale immigrants from slasher and rape revenge movies of the 80s—forms that reveal in no uncertain terms the willingness, not to say desire, of the male viewer to feel not just *at* but *through* female figures on the screen. Perhaps the mainstreaming of that operation, in films like *Thelma and Louise*, will call it to the attention of theory, which has not done full justice to "wrong-direction" cross gender imaginings.[35]

Clover identifies a character in the slasher film she designates as

the "Final Girl," the survivor who "perceives the full extent of the preceding horror and of her own peril."[36] Laurie in *Halloween* (Jamie Lee
Curtis) is an original example of this figure. Clover observes that "it is
no surprise that the films following *Halloween* present Final Girls who
not only fight back but do so with ferocity and even kill the killer on
their own, without help from the outside."[37] Bigelow's use of Curtis,
who did not act in the occasional horror film but rather was typecast
in these Final Girl roles, is particularly relevant in light of this, and signals perhaps another generic shift or play: the use of B movie elements
and tactics in a mainstream film. Clover writes that "as any horror fan
knows, much of what reviewers tout as mainstream innovation is not
new at all, but has flourished for years, even decades in the world of
movies that lies beyond the world of reviews ... the direction of the
trickle here is up not down."[38] What sets Bigelow apart in this
instance is her use of Curtis, the Final Girl *par excellence*, and having
her reprise this role in a mainstream milieu. Megan's promise to
Eugene that she will "blow his head into the next state" echoes B-
movie sentiments.

The reduction of character motivations to the most basic level pervades Bigelow's work. Eugene does not kill for personal gain, but
because he has a psychotic fascination with guns. The gun is the very
instrument of the cop thriller—its ubiquity means that it is generally
taken for granted and results in audience desensitisation—that preoc-
cupies the narrative. Much of the narrative in *Blue Steel* concerns the
relentless search for a gun. The film's opening credit sequence renders
this explicit: a .44 calibre Smith and Wesson handgun, made famous
by Dirty Harry no less, is bathed in a blue light and explored from
every possible angle by the camera. The camera looks down the barrel
and maintains its gaze as bullets are loaded—the gun is hyperbolised
and fetishised, and the fascination with guns within the genre and its
audiences is laid bare. But the detail and hesitation in the initial shooting scene reveals a consideration—rather than glorification—of violence. It is significant that within this action film, at constitutive

moments, everything slows down; every movement, noise, and expression is reflective and precise. In contrast to the jokes she cracks, when placed in a confrontational situation, Megan is the very opposite of "trigger happy"; rather she is "gun-shy" and a close-up of her face acts as an index of the gravity of the situation. The very premise of the film is the consequence of a shooting, that is, a reflection upon violence. A paring down of the genre thus occurs, which allows for the problematising of its most basic tenets.

The constant negotiation of the familiar and the unfamiliar, in establishing and disregarding gender codes, bears a significant relation to Bigelow's project in the domain of genre, where her heterodoxy makes definite, clear-cut readings impossible. This resistance to being either a faithful cop thriller or a straightforward feminist revision (which is the film's most potent critical property) exposes the difficulty of critically challenging generic expectations when to be effective requires the maintenance of some of the genre's most problematic terms.

Boys' Own Adventure? The Engendering of Space and Action in *Point Break*

The surfie movie—which for lack of an authoritative definition, generally signals any film which features that sub-culture of people for whom surfing is a lifestyle and includes surfing sequences—can perhaps be considered the action film *par excellence*. In its classic documentary form it is largely comprised of action sequences with a soundtrack, and the occasional interview with surfers; it rarely adopts any of the qualities of narrative cinema.[39] In *Point Break*, Bigelow conflates it with the conventional Hollywood action film, specifically the cop/buddy movie, thus relocating a modified sub-cultural form into the mainstream.[40] The pure action quality of the surfie film inflects *Point Break* significantly, not so much at a diegetic level, but in terms of the extremes to which the film takes the Hollywood model. It is consonant with the distillation of action film codes evident in the film and the reduction of the thematic qualities to a most unabstracted level.

The film's advertising pitch, a quotation describing the rush of sky-diving—"It's 100% pure adrenalin"—succeeds in defining not only the fundamental premise of the film, but also the logic of action films in general. The thrill of agency and danger, which is a theme common to all such films, is neither relegated to the sub-text nor diverted by narratives which endeavour to offer a rationale for the action sequences. Rather, it is the seductive potential of energy and move-ment itself which overtly determines the narrative, thematic and spa-tial structures of the film. That the central characters are "adrenalin junkies" means that other motivations (social, moral or avaricious) are relatively absent. This paring down of the model—rendering its essential qualities *in extremis*—allows for an exploration of the generic qualities of the "boys' own adventure," the characteristically hetero-geneous nature of sub-cultures, and the more abstract question of space and how it is negotiated between these two structures.

Johnny Utah is a rookie cop who arrives in Los Angeles to investi-gate bank robberies. His much maligned partner, Pappas, believes that a group of robbers known as the ex-Presidents are surfers, so Utah goes undercover. To learn how to surf and to find a way into the sub-culture, he befriends Tyler, who is aligned with one of the suspected groups, and becomes involved with her. He also meets Bohdi, who leads the group of "adrenaline junkies" and soon realises that Bohdi and his gang are responsible for the robberies—but his loyalties have become confused. When Johnny's cover is blown, Bohdi kidnaps Tyler in return for safe passage for himself and his gang to Mexico. Johnny goes along with this to ensure Tyler's safety, and during the last rob-bery which they have coerced him into taking part in, a number of people including Pappas are shot dead. Johnny and Bohdi both finally land in Mexico, where Bohdi disappears and Tyler and Johnny are reunited. After tracking him for years he finds Bohdi at a beach during the "fifty-year storm" and, rather than arrest him, allows him to swim into the storm and presumably to drown.

Point Break, opens with a series of surfing images which are gradually intercut with scenes of an FBI shooting range where Johnny Utah is being assessed. The training scenes recall the openings of *Silence of the Lambs* and *Blue Steel*, which also deal with rookies, but whereas Clarice Starling is interrupted and Megan Turner falters, Johnny is congratulated for his perfect score, "100% Utah!" By remaining faithful to the cop film formula, a type of parody is effected in this scene: of male rapport and communication through gestures, of the shooting skill of the hero, and of the hero himself as pin-up, soaking wet and wielding a gun.

The figuring of the male star offers another means of testing of the properties of the genre. Miriam Hansen explores the question of how a man occupying the place of erotic object effects the organisation of vision and the conception of visual pleasure. She writes that:

> the figure of the male as erotic object undeniably sets into play fetishistic and voyeuristic mechanisms, accompanied—most strikingly in the case of Valentino—by a feminisation of the actor's persona ... it seems more promising, tentatively, to approach the textual difference of a male erotic object as a figure of overdetermination, an unstable composite figure that connotes "the simultaneous presence of two positionalities of desire" ... and thus calls into question the very idea of polarity rather than simply reversing its terms.[41]

Johnny is recurrently figured as an erotic object, and a certain tension is created between this and his position as hero. Like Megan in *Blue Steel*, his narrative status as hero is definitive, yet the constituents of this figure itself are fundamentally challenged. As Stephen Cohan observes of William Holden, "such unabashed erotic attention to the body of a major male movie star prevents the films closure from easily serving as an affirmation of traditional masculinity. In response to this

problematic marking of Holden as active hero/passive pin-up, the film
tends to deny its own terms of visual representation."[42] The criticism
that *Point Break*'s preoccupation with the masculine in general[43] is a
regression for Bigelow, after the female hero in *Blue Steel*, is qualified
by this exaggerated "to-be-looked-at-ness" of Johnny and most of the
other male characters. The film is not simply recuperable as a "boys'
own adventure," since the status of the active agents as the locus of
identification is tempered by their position as the locus of desire. It
repudiates Laura Mulvey's observation that the buddy movie dispens-
es with the problem of integrating the alien presence of the spectacle
(usually woman)[44] by making her the catalyst of the narrative. Cohan
notes that the spectacle of the male body on film epitomises the potential problems of apparatus theory for the masculinity of the Hollywood
movie hero by making him an object of vision on the screen. He writes
that "since the camera always subjects him to its gaze, placing him in
the position of exhibitionist and focussing on his body with the kind of
look supposedly reserved for the female star, his masculinity can all
too easily turn out to be the effect of a masquerade."[45] There are
repeated uninterrupted close-ups of Johnny, usually occupying the
centre of the frame. This becomes hyperbolised in the most heightened
suspense sequence in the film when a rival gang member pushes
Johnny's face perilously close to the blade of an upturned lawn-
mower. The scene brings pure action, with its emphasis on the hero
function in the form of the duel, together with a feminisation of the
hero—whose face becomes the site of vulnerability and the horror of
potential disfigurement. It is perhaps this modification of the hero
which facilitates a crisis in the normativity of apparatus theory, and
raises the question of the effect of female authorship on visual regimes
in the cinema.

Point Break is less a film about a sub-culture than one about its
perspective on the usually conservative and urban cop/buddy genre.[46]
Bohdi's discussion of the spiritual aspect of surfing and his statement
that he hates violence—while somewhat ironic in light of his actions,

and unintentionally comic—puts thought in the domain of the action film and addresses the issue of violence directly. It signals a definite shift in a genre that usually portrays violence as merely one of many examples of activity.

The counter-cultural values of the Ex-Presidents also signal a departure from the usual characterisation of action film villains; their motives for the robberies are fundamentally non-materialistic, instead, they are the result of a rebellion against mainstream lifestyles. Their seductive lifestyle is crucial when Johnny's loyalties are tested, for the criminal environment in action films is rarely endowed with any ultimately positive or desirable attributes. When one of the gang voices fears of being caught after they are chased by Johnny and Angelo, Bohdi observes that the robberies "were never about money anyway. It's about us against the system. Against those people inching down the freeway in their metal boxes." While perhaps banal, his comment goes against the grain of traditional criminal motivations in the Hollywood action model, which tend to be financial, drug related, or nationalistic. The Ex-Presidents steal from the cash drawers but never go into bank vaults; as Pappas notes, they "never get greedy," they rob in order to "find the next wave, to finance their endless summer." Their actions are thus co-ordinated by the terrain, by nature, and not by the society in a broad sense. This also sheds light on the way in which violence is addressed in the film; as a primal, base, and asocial act—and something which, perhaps because of this, is constantly reflected upon.

The relation between narrative and movement, which Michel de Certeau describes as inextricable, is played out lucidly in the film, where the traversing of different spaces and activity determine the diegesis. The surfers "go where the waves go," they are itinerants and have no proper place. De Certeau distinguishes between place and space, and writes that

the law of the "proper" rules in the place: the elements taken into consideration are beside each other, each situated in its own "proper" and distinct location, a location it defines. A place is thus an instantaneous configuration of positions. It implies an indication of stability ... A space exists when one takes into consideration vectors of direction, velocities and time variables. Thus space is composed of intersections of mobile elements. It is in a sense actuated by the ensemble of movements deployed within it.[47]

The surfers live at the interstices and create their own space through action. By traversing the sea, desert, and sky, they invoke the road ethos of the Beat generation, another marginal group. But the exclusively male and genealogical tradition of that genre has become altered. Deleuze and Guattari write that "everything important that has happened or is happening takes the route of the American rhizome: the beatniks, the underground, bands and gangs, successive lateral offshoots in immediate connection with an outside."[48] The American landscape is in a sense deterritorialised while a contemporaneous destabilising of the surfie genre occurs. It is no longer figured as place, but as movement. Rather than valorising the locus itself or attempting to annex it, the nomadic group, according to Deleuze and Guattari, can be called the deterritorialised *par excellence* because reterritorialisation does not take place. Deleuze and Guattari observe that "it is the earth that deterritorialises itself, in a way that provides the nomad with a territory. The land ceases to be land, tending to become simply ground (sol) or support."[49]

Similarly in *Point Break*, the various locations are in a dynamic relationship with the activities which map them; in the domain of generic specificity the action images are parasitic on the landscapes. The surfers' nomadic existence, their lack of property and social space, emphasises their narrative position as tacticians.[50] As opposed to strategists who, de Certeau argues, require a place which can be delimited of their own power and will from an environment,[51] the agent of a tactic

> must play on and with a terrain imposed on it and organised
> by the law of a foreign power. It operates in isolated actions,
> blow by blow. It takes advantage of "opportunities" and
> depends on them, being without any base where it could stock-
> pile its winnings. What it wins it cannot keep. This nowhere
> gives a tactic mobility ... but a mobility that must accept the
> chance offerings of the moment.[52]

While taking the action sequence to new limits, the skydiving
scenes seem to have an intent beyond irony and hyperbole, although
given that in the second scene Johnny chases Bohdi out of the plane
without a parachute, these elements are not inconsiderable. These
scenes open up a new space for the action film, one which exacerbates
the temporal dimension of space itself, and one which cannot effectively become place. From them an indomitable space emerges; it is the
apotheosis of the action locus, as one can only ever move through it; it
can never be appropriated by the body. The first skydiving sequence is
part of the surfers end-of-season ritual. It occasions another instance
of male bonding—Johnny and Bohdi's gang join hands and form a
chain in the air, shouting to each other that "this is unbelievable" and
"I love this brown rice bullshit." Johnny is once again drawn in by the
adrenalin rush of danger and infinite space. That this extreme gesture
of male bonding takes place in the sky, in a space which cannot be
possessed, suggests that here the male buddy movie narrative is not
efficiently colonised by men. In short, the "boys' own adventure" is
divested of its exclusivity and ownership. Similarly the sequence
where Johnny chases "Reagan" on foot introduces domestic and private space as action terrain, but again it cannot be possessed—it
becomes a transit zone, a mere support for activity. The length and
incredible pace of the sequence again privileges movement as the
"space" of the surfers: their existence is predicated on activity.

Skydiving, which Bohdi uses to test Johnny's loyalty and mettle, destabilises the generic codes by allowing the most significant index of the
genre to occur in a highly ambivalent site.[53] Although the space is no
more appropriable by women, it does imply a certain, if not neutrality,
then inexclusivity. Meaghan Morris writes that

> these days a rather dismissive generic term for any bland all-
> male adventure, the phrase "boys' *own*" points to the formal
> constraints that not only define the "place" of the genre in
> Western action cinema—a relative or absolute exclusion of
> women, the isolation of (white) males as "proper" subjects of
> action, and the exteriorization of Nature (and Natives) as
> "other" to Man—but that may also now frame in advance our
> expectations of any film in which ... a young man *does* have an
> adventure, and survives against the odds.[54]

As a "boys' own adventure," *Point Break* is seriously challenged
despite conforming to a significant number of its co-ordinates' specifi-
cations. The first challenge is its female author who immediately contradicts the exclusivity of the boys' club. In this instance the boys are
her agents; the generic tradition becomes altered, whatever the ramifi-
cations of that may be. It is also significant that the women in the film
(particularly Tyler but also those from the rival surfer gang)—while
peripheral—are formidable when they do appear. The surfers are figured as martial arts experts and body builders, and they prove to be a
considerable match for the FBI agents. Tyler equals Bohdi and his
gang in terms of surfing skills, teaches Johnny to surf, saves his life in
the water and even challenges his right to be there. While doing so she
also questions their more extreme tendencies, announcing with dis-
dain at one point that "there's too much testosterone around here."
This acknowledges the film's preoccupation with male bonding rituals; and it suggests that while she can play the game, she chooses
not to. Even when she is reduced to the role of victim after being

kidnapped, she expresses extreme anger rather than fear, and her release is predicated on Johnny's passivity. For her to be released, he cannot act, and this, Bohdi seems to surmise, is the ultimate frustration for someone like Johnny or himself.

Many of the problematic elements of the film thus contain subtle but potent differences from generic expectations; not an overturning but an indication that generic codes and visual regimes are not necessarily as homogenous or limiting as they might seem. *Point Break* acts, in a sense, to reiterate Morris, as a tactical use of the 'boys' own' genre rather than a critique from the genres outside: it uses the "place" of the genre for purposes alien to it.[55]

Conclusion

Near Dark, Blue Steel and *Point Break* all digress from generic norms, but register the seductive potential of genre films and signal a need to maintain their terms for an effective challenge to be undertaken. A sense of a genre remains despite a series of insistent departures from generic expectations. By invoking the workings of genre, Bigelow's films can be considered not so much genre films as films concerned with the way in which genres function. They are broken down and distilled through subtle and complex processes so that the intrinsic properties of each genre and film can be revealed and engaged with.

By conflating and contemporising two established genres in *Near Dark*, Bigelow uses the idea of generic codes to bring about their own undoing. While the Western and horror genres have a common support in action, the two become somehow collapsed and indeterminate almost because of this. The positing of a female hero in *Blue Steel* fundamentally challenges the construction of hero function as necessarily masculine. It requires and facilitates cross gender identification which transforms a requisite property of the genre, the action hero. In doing so, it elucidates the manifold implications of difference and sexual difference and therefore does not reduce this shift to a simple transposition. In *Point Break*, the cop/buddy film is modified through an excessive rendering of generic codes; by literally taking the genre further than it has gone before, and thereby effecting a questioning of its basic premise. The sub-cultural element and the figuring of the hero as spectacle also register a testing of the genre's limits.

Genre itself in mainstream Hollywood cinema is traditionally a gendered concept, with all the hierarchical implications which that entails. While male directors are generally able to traverse the entire generic domain with few obstacles, women directors have been limited in terms of the types of films offered to them and expectations of the nature of their own projects. The significance of Kathryn Bigelow's work is not only that it resides in the realm of action cinema—confounding the notion that women do not and cannot make hyperkinetic films (or perhaps more significantly, aren't interested in this type of material)—but in so doing, it also divests the foundations of action cinema of its masculine privilege. In breaking with the traditions of the industry in an empirical sense, Bigelow has been able to transgress the very limits which are responsible for the gendering of these genres from the outset.

1   Barbara Koenig Quart, *Women Directors: The Emergence of a New Cinema* (New York: Praeger, 1987), 90. According to a 1980 survey conducted by the Directors Guild of America, of the 7,332 feature films released by major distributors during the last thirty years, only fourteen, or two tenths of 1%, were directed by women. Although the disparity has become less marked over the past fifteen years, the statistics are indicative of the general absence of a tradition of female authorship in Hollywood, disrupted only by the occasional mavericks such as the much cited Dorothy Arzner, and Ida Lupino.

2   Teresa de Lauretis, "Rethinking Women's Cinema," *Technologies of Gender: Essays on Theory, Film and Fiction* (Bloomington: Indiana University Press, 1987), 113.

3   Gilles Deleuze, *Cinema 1: The Movement-Image* (Minneapolis: University of Minnesota Press, 1986), 141.

4   Deleuze, *Cinema 1*, 211.

5   Jacques Derrida, "The Law of Genre," ed. W.T.J. Mitchell, *On Narrative* (Baltimore: The Johns Hopkins University Press, 1981), 61.

6   Tzvetan Todorov, *The Fantastic: A Structural Approach to a Literary Genre*, trans. Richard Howard (Ithaca: Cornell University Press, 1973).

7   Altman, "A Semantic/Syntactic Approach to Film Genre," in *Cinema Journal*, Vol. 23, Spring 1984, 33.

8   Jacques Derrida, "Structure, Sign and Play in the Discourse of the Human Sciences," *Modern Criticism and Theory*, ed. David Lodge, (London: Methuen, 1988), 110.

9   Ibid.

10 Derrida, "The Law of Genre," 53.

11 Samuel Weber, "The Blindness of the Seeing Eye," in *Institution and Interpretation* (Minneapolis: Minnesota University Press, 1987), 80.

12 Kaja Silverman, "The Female Authorial Voice," in *The Acoustic Mirror: The Female Voice in Psychoanalysis and Cinema* (Bloomington: Indiana University Press, 1988), 191.

13 Judith Mayne, *The Woman at the Keyhole: Feminism and Women's Cinema* (Bloomington: Indiana University Press, 1990), 94.

14 Silverman, "The Female Authorial Voice," 105.

15 Gilles Deleuze and Felix Guattari, *Kafka: Toward a Minor Literature* (Minneapolis: University of Minnesota Press), 16.

16 Ibid., 18.

17 Silverman, "The Female Authorial Voice," 108.

18 Deleuze and Guattari, *Kafka*, 17.

19 This is particularly resonant in terms of women working in mainstream Hollywood cinema, who are almost without exception discussed in terms of a group, despite significantly different approaches and projects.

20 Teresa de Lauretis, "Strategies of Coherence: Narrative Cinema, Feminist Poetics, and Yvonne Rainer," in *Technologies of Gender*, 107.

21 Ibid., 113–4.

22 Ibid., 108–9.

23 Ana Maria Bahiana, "Interview with Kathryn Bigelow," *Cinema Papers*, (January 1992), 33.

24 John Powers, "Pressing Ahead", in *American Film* vol. XIII no. 6, April 1988, 49.

25 Bahiana, "Interview: Kathryn Bigelow," 34.

26 Deleuze, *Cinema 1*, 153–54.

27 Ibid., 153.

28 Mitchell, "Interview with Kathryn Bigelow."

29 See Jude Schwendenwien, "Review: Blue Steel," in *Cinéaste*, vol. XVII, no. 1, (1990), 51.

30 Mary Ann Doane, "Film and the Masquerade: Theorising the Female

Spectator," in *Femme Fatales: Feminism, Film Theory and Psychoanalysis* (New York: Routledge, 1991), 25.

31 Laura Mulvey, "Afterthoughts on 'Visual Pleasure and Narrative Cinema' Inspired by *Duel in the Sun*," *Framework*, no. 6 (Summer 1981), 13.

32 B. Ruby Rich, "Nobody's Handmaid," *Sight and Sound* (December 1991), 7.

33 David Kehr, "Defiant Gravity: Jamie Lee Curtis," *Film Comment*, vol. 21 no. 2 (March/April 1985), 37–8.

34 Elizabeth Young, "The Silence of the Lambs and the Flaying of Feminist Theory," in *Camera Obscura* 27, September 1991, 17.

35 Carol J. Clover, "Crossing Over," *Film Quarterly*, vol. 45 no. 2 (Winter 1991–92), 22.

36 Carol J. Clover, "Her Body, Himself," in *Fantasy and Cinema* (ed) James McDonald (London: BFI, 1989), 104.

37 Clover, "Her Body Himself," 105.

38 Carol J. Clover, "Getting Even," *Sight and Sound* (May 1992), 18.

39 *Endless Summer* (1962–64), produced by Bruce Brown (no director cited) is perhaps the classic example of this model.

40 Although John Milius' *Big Wednesday* (1977) set a precedent as a main-stream surfie movie, action sequences play a very small part.

41 Miriam Hansen, *Babel and Babylon: Spectatorship in American Silent Film* (Cambridge: Harvard University Press, 1991), 252.

42 Stephen Cohan, "Masquerading as the American Male of the Fifties: Picnic, William Holden, and the Spectacle of Masculinity in Hollywood Film," *Camera Obscura*, no. 25–26 (January–May 1991), 45.

43 See Strick, "Review: Point Break," 48.

44 Laura Mulvey, "Visual Pleasure and Narrative Cinema," ed. Bill Nichols, *Movies and Methods*, vol. 2 (Berkeley: University of California Press, 1985), 309.

45 Cohan, "Masquerading as the American Male," 45.

46 Robert Philip Kolker, "Woman as Genre," ed. Janet Todd, *Women and Film* (New York: Holmes and Meier, 1988), 137.

47 de Certeau, *The Practice of Everyday Life*, 117.

48 Deleuze and Guattari, *A Thousand Plateaus*, 19.

49 Ibid., 381.

50 While Meaghan Morris argues that the strategy/tactics distinction is per-haps not as elucidating as it appears given the rich implications of contin-gent circumstances, the structure of the film with its opposition of main-stream and counter-culture seems to lend itself to readings through such a dyad. See Meaghan Morris, "Great Moments in Social Climbing: King Kong and the Human Fly," ed. Beatriz Colomina, *Sexuality and Space* (New Jersey: Princeton Architectural Press, 1992), 37.

51 de Certeau, *The Practice of Everyday Life*, 36.

52 Ibid., 37.
53 The latent homosexuality and narcissism of male buddy movies is parodied by excess also. Aside from Johnny's general fascination with Bohdi, with whom he shares a "killer instinct," the two are literally intertwined in the air in the final skydiving sequence, and Bohdi says to Johnny as he jumps from the plane, "You want me so bad it's like acid in your mouth."
54 Morris, "Great Moments in Social Climbing," 34–5.
55 Ibid., 35.

"Fourth Person Singular"

Becoming Ordinary and the Void in the Critical Body Filmic

Melissa McMahon

Introduction

This paper grew out of a fascination with particular films and perfor-
mances: Robert Bresson's *Mouchette*, the work of Chantal Akerman in
film, and Pina Bausch in dance. What fascinated me was the way these
works problematised, in various ways, the attribution of meaning to
the body; or rather, perhaps, the ways they debunked attempts to hol-
low this body out, to make it a more or less transparent container con-
veying a subjectivity or driving a tight narrative. The bodies in these
works seemed to unfold themselves around a void, a space that was not
meaningless, but rather where the *what* of meaning—the "what does it
mean?"—was effaced under a *how*, under the modalities and modula-
tions of gestures, objects, desire, the schema of the everyday.

The "fourth person singular" (a term used by Jean Narboni in an article on Akerman's film *Je tu il elle*[1]) refers I think to this undecidable space of the body and its involvements—qualities of the person that are neither attributable to the subject of action nor to an impersonal object of observation, devolving upon the notion of singularity.

In this paper I want to trace the contours of some theoretical texts that address this space and that could be helpful in developing theoretical approaches to this cinema—a category which I assume not to be exhausted by the films I mention, but which could perhaps be called a cinema of "sublime banality." What is also in question here is the relation between "theory" and "cinema" itself—because if the point of contention is the way in which a body can be subordinated to a transcendent concept, in the form of a subject, a meaning, or a narrative, then this problematic extends to the body of cinema as a whole, and its relationship to the critical subject and spectator.

The scene—de Certeau and Modernity

In Michel de Certeau's book, *The Practices of Everyday Life*, there is a chapter called "The Arts of Theory,"[2] which examines in detail a recurring configuration of the relationship between discursive and non-discursive practices that sets the scene, in a general way, for my concerns in this paper. In this configuration, where non-discursive practices are "located far away from knowledge and yet possessing its secret," de Certeau sees a "figure of modernity."[3]

The recurring pattern, covering a variety of disciplines and their objects, is that practices are presumed by theoretical discourses to be the bearers of a more complex knowledge than the discourse, but this knowledge is unconscious, unreflective—it awaits the enlightenment of theory which perforce characterises itself as totally conscious of itself and self-reflective. Practices bear an "improper" knowledge which will become, in time, "proper" in, and the property of, discourse. The *presence* of knowledge in practices is both assumed and deemed inadequate—it must be mediated and absolved, filled in by the process of *re*-presentation. Assuming that there *is* knowledge in practices, locating it elsewhere, at a distance, enables the discourse to seem to be *discovering* what was already *there*, *recovering* what was already *theirs*. Projecting knowledge into the "unknowing" subject enables it to be appropriated by theory without there seeming to be any "impropriety."

This configuration of modernity has lent itself to the shadowy outlines of a figure of woman, or perhaps the hysteric rather—unable to speak, the locus of an unspeakable secret, a knowledge of which she is unconscious, enabling "truth" to be projected onto or into her and then recovered, the focus of so many fantasies. From the outside she will be transformed by the magic wand of language. As de Certeau says: "Science will make princesses out of all these Cinderellas."

Also around this configuration of modernity is the myth of Zobeïdes,[4] the dream of the naked woman running away through the city streets, subtracting herself from the knowing subject yet by this very subtraction enabling knowledge's fantasy, its future, always just a little further down the track—the glimpse simply being the promise of a future encounter. Her flight is not a vision of a non-capture by, or an exceeding of, knowledge, but precisely that which ensures her capture in this myth—lack of presence being required for the process of re-presentation. Her elusiveness is both a sign of mystery and its effacement. It is her flight that enables the pursuit, the progress, of knowledge, and her disappearance will entail the construction of great edifices, metropolises, of theory. In the dream she disappears and the dreamer builds a duplicate city with a trap at the place of her disappearance.

What then could be an exit from this myth when the very activity of flight and the moment of exit is its condition of possibility? Where apparent elusiveness is but the precursor to capture, or is itself a form of capture? And I thought: maybe she could just stop, turn around and face her pursuers and say: "OK here I am what's all the fuss about?"

And—call it wishful thinking—I could not but imagine her pursuers being totally dumbfounded, at a loss, perhaps saying: "Oh sorry we thought you were someone else—perhaps if you could just turn around and run again—ah yes! there she is!" The myth becomes undone by the sheer obviousness, the banality of the gesture of showing oneself, which paradoxically marks a point of total uncapturability, the break in or the rendering meaningless of the pursuit.

If I seem to have cast my net wide by invoking an entire history of modern disciplinary practices, it has only been in order to catch this one fish: the politics of hiding versus showing, the meaningful secret versus the ingenuousness of presence. It forms my mythical entry point into the exiting movement of materiality in performance and spectatorship.

Deleuze and Guattari, Brecht

This politics of representation is at issue in what Deleuze and Guattari would call, among other things, a sedentary philosophy, a philosophy of capture precisely because it posits itself as a centre of meaning, projecting knowledge into objects (and constituting objects in this process), the better to recall them back to itself and recoup them without ever seeming to leave its ground (the pursuit is thus a false pursuit, merely a *projection*). Vincent Descombes, writing on Deleuze, describes this representational philosophy as one revolving around the principle of identity: "Every present must be re-presented, in order that it may be re-discovered as the same; it follows that in this philosophy the unknown is only ever a not-yet-recognised known, that to learn is to remember, that to encounter is to meet again, that to leave is to return, etc."[5]

It is this process that Bertolt Brecht critiques in the practices of production and reception in Western naturalistic theatre. The success of the naturalistic play, according to Brecht, depends on its ability to con-

vey an already-known, an already-seen, its ability to instill a sense of
familiarity in its audience: "If the seance is successful, it ends up with
nobody seeing any further, nobody learning any lessons, at best everyone *recollecting*."[6] At the level of the actor this is a process of identification and empathy, both the interior conversion of the actor into the
character, and the audience's recognition of themselves in the character. At the level of the spectacle as a whole, Brecht suggests that the
process of recognition is about an even broader assimilation of the
events and characters to the generalised sameness of what Brecht calls
"Man with a capital M": "All its [the play's] incidents are just one
enormous cue, and this cue is followed by the 'eternal' response: the
inevitable, usual, natural, purely human response."[7]

Roland Barthes reinscribes the Brechtian polemic against naturalistic theatre in his texts on Japanese Bunraku theatre.[8] He claims that
naturalistic methods of presentation and their reading involve organising the spectacle into a unity that relies on a series of dualisms, the
main ones being interior/exterior and animate/inanimate. The body of
the actor and the play are invested with an *organic unity* that enables
them to function as vehicles for an assumed unity of the soul or of life.
The body and narrative become projections of the identity of the character, exterior signs of an interior that justifies and elucidates them.
Voices, gestures, and actions are subjected, that is, made instrumental
to an inferred *subjectivity* of the character, maintaining only a
metaphorical or metonymic status as bearers, but not owners, of the
play's "meanings," they are made to *signify*.

It is these processes of *organisation, subjectification,* and *signification*
that Deleuze and Guattari identify with the operations of the sedentary
philosophy of capture—together they constitute a "plane of organisation."[9] This plane is defined by the requirement that any given material be submitted to a process of supplementation, that a "given," as
immanent, be submitted to a transcendence which can take the form
of a function (organisation), a subject (subjectification), or a meaning
(signification).

Challenging this model, Deleuze and Guattari dis-organise the body in a way that I find particularly useful in considering the body in and of the cinematic image. Their work amounts to a radical ontological upheaval in the way they renegotiate relations between presence, representation, desire and absence. The constitutive mechanism of this ontology is desire, conceived as a self-consistent multiplicity of productive force that forms the plane of consistency: "a process of production without reference to any exterior agency, whether it be a lack that hollows it out or a pleasure that fills it."[10] Desire has no privileged site, it is not in the place of subject or object, or a bridge between these two points, but is the process of activity: "Do you realise how simple a desire is? Sleeping is a desire. Walking is a desire. Listening to music, or making music, or writing are desires. A spring, a winter, are desires. Old age is also a desire. Even death. Desire never needs interpreting, it is it which experiments."[11]

The productivity of desire is what necessitates and effectuates, what *is*, in fact, a body's "connectivity"—its propensity to connect with heterogeneous elements in the process of its becoming.[12] "A body" here is not only a physiological body, but can be any entity or operation (the entity considered as operation) that forms connections with other things or events—a book, a group of people, a discourse, a sentence, a film. Desire is what provides, again what *is*, the travelling movement of this body as opposed to the re-couping operations of representation. This body is not brought back to an interior or anterior state or structure in order to be provided with meaning: its relations are always exterior and heterogeneous, it cannot be separated from a moving on, a moving further, a going beyond.

Deleuze's notion of *repetition*, in contrast to the process of representation, could be alluded to here in relation to this operation. The structure of re-presentation requires a hierarchical distinction between two terms (model/copy, signifier/signified, presence/representation), that enables the difference between these two terms to cancel itself out (the formal difference between the terms is compensated by an identity in content). The movement from one term to the other thus recoups itself, folds back upon itself and presents only a "false" movement. Repetition, by presenting two identical terms, produces a real movement that has no basis for its return (neither term can establish authority over the other, or can be said to represent the other), and a non-localisable, and thus insubordinatable, difference. This idea of repetition will be connected to certain filmic features to be looked at later: the long take in film as persistence/repetition of the image; repetition of gestures; absence of highs and lows (and thus hierarchy) in narrative structure.

On this model, then, where the propensity to connect is the body's only *a priori*, activities like using utensils, reading, watching a film, walking down the street, are not *extensions* of the body or the *incorporation* of the environment into the body, both of which presuppose a boundary, a division between inside and outside, but are rather the forming of a "machine" around the points of connection. The relations of forces constitute a new "body," an assemblage that disassembles the unity of subject and object. The action, the process, becomes the "subject": a modal, non–personal subject, a "how," rather than a "what." This form of individuation, "very different from that of a person, subject, thing or substance,"[13] Deleuze and Guattari call a *haecceity*, an event, the intersection of particular times, spaces and bodies, animals and/or objects.

The becoming of a body is its becoming-*molecular*, its dissipation into particles in relations of movement and rest, speed or slowness—forming fields of intensity, collections of affects, a transitive assemblage of desire in relations of proximity or co-presence with other assemblages. It is at the level of the molecular that oppositions between the interior and exterior, content and form, animate and inanimate, subject and object, disperse, become unattributable though not abolished: difference remains but not identity. This is because becoming is not a relation of one point to another, but the undoing of the unit or point of reference to become the operation of the middle, the between.

The process of becoming replaces *intentionality* and its *extensions* with *intensionality*—intensities, involvement. If it sounds a little abstract, indeed the ultimate abstraction, to talk about the real (for this is the real according to Deleuze and Guattari, and no metaphor) in terms of particles and intensities, I think it is rather the point where the extremes of formalism meet up with the concrete—"the plane of consistency is the intersection of all concrete forms."[14] The particularity of a body, in the sense of the *molecular*, is also the particularity of a body in the sense of the *singular*.[15] The becomings of molecular bodies that constitute the real also seems to elude the spectre of essentialism that hovers close whenever one wants to talk about the body or the real—it is precisely the real that lacks essence because it is what is in constant displacement, it is never in its place or identical to itself, but always forming assemblages with other things, times, being part of an event.[16]

In one text, and not in his books on cinema, Deleuze writes: "there are no more forms but cinematic relations between unformed elements."[17] Even before looking at Deleuze's specific writings on cinema one can make connections with the operations of the cinematic apparatus, or rather, see how Deleuze's understanding of the body is itself informed by the cinema. The film image is always in movement, even when what it represents remains quite still; the continuity of the image comes through the middle of the frames of the film reel. Particles of black and white or colour disperse themselves across the plane of the screen, differentiating people, places and objects only by differing thresholds of intensity. We can understand individuation within the image not only in terms of character and narrative but in terms of gestural assemblages, space-time-body assemblages, eye-object-assemblages, hand-object-assemblages, colour assemblages, etc., and of course, spectator-image assemblages.

In relation to this sort of inorganic and unorthodox promiscuity of the film experience, I was reminded of an article by Felicity Collins on the film *Patterns*: "Should a Feminist Knit?"[18] She writes, among other things, about the difficult issues surrounding the "reproduction" of a film, whether in text, image or memory, and it becomes clear that there can be no question here of the film's *representation* as such, but rather of the *intersections* at certain remarkable points and moments (between writer and spectator and film and itself and sound and image and ...) which together make up "the other film." This is not the film as it was organised and developed in the process of its narration and projection, but one more like the overlappings of the film reel, composed of unholy alliances, connections between heterogeneous elements taken out of the evolutionary time of the projected film. The subject-spectator and object-film are not discrete variables, but between themselves form an event, or a number of events—commenting on a critic who was particularly moved by a sentence in a book, Deleuze writes: "would he be moved if he was not himself a haecceity which runs through the sentence?"[19]

The time-image

The aim of what has been said above is to argue for a certain *fullness* of cinematic and other bodies, which, while it involves heterogeneity, repels the *lack* which is introduced into a body as soon as it is subordinated to a *higher* concept or *inner* principle of organisation (subject, object, meaning ...). Why then have I referred above (in the title, in the introduction) to the *void?* "Fullness" cannot refer here to something that has simply been "filled-in"—"filling-in," after all, is simply what representation *does*, after having posited a deficiency in presence, a lack in the object (or between subject and object). Fullness is what *absolutely* cannot be filled-in or added to—not now, not before, not in the future—and in this absolute form it meets up with absolute emptiness, which, being also what cannot be filled in, is the opposite of a lack, which calls to be filled. The disorganisation of the body is only possible by virtue of this cut or rupture with the narrative of representation that relies on lack. It is this tendency towards an absolute form that is essential to my concern with the disarming quality of the act of showing, which ruptures any secrecy of the image (a hidden *content* that fills the "lack" of form), and confronts a certain intolerable/pleasurable indeterminacy.

It is this tendency, this "limit," which, as the form of *time*, is the focus of Deleuze's volume on the "time-image" in cinema,[20] the second of a two-part "natural history" of film which begins with an account of a "movement-image." The relation of the time-image to the movement-image is one of disruption, and what is at issue is the relation of the image to time, or the different temporalities that are invoked by the film image. The cinema of the movement-image is one in which movement proceeds by regular connections between "sensory-motor" situations: "actions link themselves to perceptions, perceptions prolong themselves into action."[21] Montage provides the link between action and perception, it synthesises and measures movement. Because time is measured out by this regular movement, it is only indirectly perceived, it is a function of movement's regularity (as on a clock). In the case of the time-image, the regularity of the sensory-motor links is broken, producing an irregular or aberrant movement which no longer defers or displaces our perception of time by providing its measure. The situation of action is replaced by a pure optical and sound image, and a direct perception of time. Montage loses its synthetic capacity, its ability to link, and becomes *montrage*, the ability to show (from the French verb *montrer*—to show).

The many aspects of the notion of aberrant movement need to be drawn out. The cut in sensory-motor links not only implies a not knowing what to *do*, but also a not knowing what to *say* or what to *think*—the whole sphere of action-reaction connections. This applies not only to what may go on within a film but also to our ability to react to the image, the whole filmic event. As models for these different reactions, Deleuze (following Bergson) distinguishes two types of recognition—*habitual* recognition and *attentive* recognition.[22] In the case of habitual recognition, aligned with the sensory-motor situation, the object is recognised as *for* something, as linked with certain activities. We organise the object according to characteristics that are pertinent to our or its situation, to its past or future, we *determine* the object in a particular way, this organisation being, and ensuring, our ability to react to or act upon it. This process can also be understood as an abstraction or generalisation of the object/image—the abstraction of characteristics that link or liken it to a group or category. A similar process is involved in treating the object/image as metaphorical, or regarding it in terms of (narrative) function. The object is extended, supplemented, certain features are emphasised that enable it to link up with another object, an idea or an action in a determining way: "even metaphors are sensory-motor evasions, and furnish us with something to say when we no longer know what to do."[23]

Attentive recognition, the attention to the singular, arises when the sensory-motor link is cut. In this case, aligned with the time-image and the optical-sound situation, we are unable to extend the object upon recognising it, to refer it outside of itself, but are forced to revert and return to it, that is, to *repeat* the object. We can note particular features in a particular way but are forced to erase them and start again in a recurrent process of erasure and recreation that forms the object's indeterminability. There is a certain correspondence here between habitual and attentive recognition and the distinction Deleuze and Guattari make between the use of the definite article "the" and the indefinite article "a."[24] *The* is a determinate mode of the object, implying a foreknowledge or an extraction of certain characteristics— "the chair I sat on last night"—while *a* is the indefinite mode of the object, bringing out a singularity.

A simple example would be the case of a long take of a largely immobile object or situation, what happens when we look at something for a long time. The time it takes to attribute an identity or purpose to the image is exceeded by its persistence in time, forcing a return to the object and a destabilisation of its initial determination.

To say that a long shot "labours a point" detracts from the way persistence in time brings the "point" into question and becomes itself a factor in the determination or rather the indetermination of the image (fragmentary shots can achieve this effect through a different or opposite process—the truncation of the image or partial representation of the object rather than its persistence or elaboration): "the restraint of this image, the thinness of what it retains, line or simple point, 'slight fragment without importance,' brings the thing each time to an essential singularity, and describes the inexhaustible, endlessly referring to other descriptions."[25]

The time-image's break with sensory-motor links, modes of organisation, is what produces its singularity and its *literalness*—its non-metaphorical or non-figurative aspect. It is the literalness of the image, its ability to give rise to heterogeneous descriptions that succeed and erase each other without settling upon a determinate meaning, that leads Deleuze to characterise it as *readable*. This term does not set up an analogy between the film image and language, but refers to the way the time-image perpetually sheds its different determinations, separates and differentiates (I want to say "dis-parates") its components, and precludes their convergence or *decision* upon the image, which would make it no longer readable as such, but simply "transparent," a lead for the sensory-motor links to follow up: "Readable designates here the independence of the parameters (of the image) and the constitution of divergent series ... it is as though, instead of the model of the window, an opaque plane, horizontal or at an incline, was substituted, upon which givens inscribe themselves."[26]

The literal image, the most clear, obvious and emphatic—a simple act of showing—is also inextricably opaque because it refuses the sensory-motor link of abstraction, explanation, or generalisation. The image and the body is uncertain because it maintains itself in a space outside its determination in action, a space of infinite possibility, of the forces of grace or chance. This is not the "secrecy" of a dark interior, hidden so that it can all the better be inferred or perceived, the secret of a content within form, but a sort of unfolding or unravelling of the opposition between interior and exterior across a surface plane, across time, defying the depths of secrecy to create an impenetrability of the surface: "an infinite form of secrecy that no longer even requires a content and that has conquered the imperceptible. ... Some people can talk, hide nothing, not lie: they are secret by transparency, as impenetrable as water, in truth incomprehensible."[27]

This notion of the act of *showing* destabilising and transforming itself is Narboni's concern in his article on Akerman's *Je tu il elle*, which is mostly composed of long takes depicting everyday postures and gestures (lying down, dressing, undressing, eating), the telling of everyday stories, as well as explicit sexual scenes. He is interested in getting away from, or getting between, a dichotomy that consists in, on the one hand, an order of *production* which denotes the obscenity of visual evidence, and on the other the order of *seduction* denoting a secrecy, a slipping away.[28] He suggests that the obscene can be undone by its multiplication—not an exacerbation that transforms it into its other, seduction, but a sort of implosion of the obscene by a persistence that defies the grip of meaning. In *Je tu il elle* we are shown and told everything, but in such an indeterminate way: its space, time and sounds are those of passage, of passing away, of brushing against people and situations without any grasp—the sites and rites of *passage*. There is the voice-over that confronts and diverges from the image in the first section, showing and telling actions of indecision and boredom that travel through an ambiguous time and setting. Then there is the hitchhiking sequence with its inconclusive encounters between bodies and stories, and the banal spaces of the roadside bar and diner; and the hesitant and finally violent collision of bodies in the last section's sexual episode. I'm not trying to make it sound all sad and empty—this is a rich and intense film, with all the pleasure of a touch without a grip.[29] This indecisive tactility is chiefly conveyed for Narboni through sound-effects (who says you can't touch with your ear?), which he describes at length:

It is a matter ... of marking the frontier of the body and language, a sonorous turbulence at the limit of the formation of
words, the tangency, in a way, of a background noise (linked
to anal-oral voracity) to articulated speech: cracklings, crin-
klings, sucking noises, rustlings of sheets, audible scratchings
on letter paper, cry-breaths, cooings, foghorns hooting from
the depths of the body, silky murmurings of skins rubbed
against each other or shock of colliding limbs.[30]

I want to say something about the hand-job sequence in *Je tu il
elle*, whose impact insists itself whenever I think about this film, an
eroticism certainly not accounted for by its content (erotic is not
what first comes to mind at the *idea* of masturbating a truckie, and
his eroticism is not exclusively connected with this scene—
although it is dynamised in a particular way within it). It is something to do with a collusion of the body and language, a disturbance of the frontiers that Narboni talks about, their turbulence. If
we can objectively distinguish different levels of his enunciative
position in this scene—imperative subject when he directs the girl's
movements, subject to/object of the emotive/physical sensations
that he experiences, his description again as subject/observer of
these sensations—its impact seems to be something to do with their
undoing, their de-stratification, the contagion of their intensity. He
is part of what he is describing, his descriptions and directions
become *part* of the sensations, in no way "meta" to, i.e., above,
them, and these perverse collaborations and overlappings, these
indiscretions (in both senses) form some sort of loop or spiral (a
Moebius strip?) that feeds itself and accumulates affects, and we too
become part of what we are observing, we feed into this loop. This
effect is no doubt partly a result of the fact that we never actually
see the area of his body in question (in hand)—its indeterminacy
enables it to become diffuse and dispersed over all the perceptible
elements of the scene. When he says *"Je bande"* ("I'm getting hard"),

his *sentence* is what is filled with sexual energy, as part of his body, and we also tense up, as part of the film.

Brecht and Bausch

The notion of the cut in sensory-motor links, the displacement of interiority, and the disruption of habitual recognition can be compared to Brecht's "distance" as a challenge to naturalistic theatre. This distance designates as much a distancing or detachment of theatrical codes as a desired intellectual position to be taken up by the actor or spectator. Most notably Brecht detached the character from the actor, the voice from its origin; he also introduced non-traditional elements into the spectacle—song, written text, film, etc.—in order to produce a texture of different codes. The aim was to defamiliarise, to make strange, the characters and narrative of the play, to produce them as singular instances affected by particular social and political circumstances: "If I choose to see Richard III I don't want to feel myself to be Richard III, but to glimpse this phenomenon in all its strangeness and incomprehensibility."[31]

Brecht has a particular agenda here, in explicitly linking the reflective action of the spectator to that of the scientist.[32] The scientist must not take for granted the phenomena of the world, but must perceive them as strange in order to better penetrate their secrets. In this Brecht retains the sensory-motor link by retaining the positions and reactions of the controlling and self-possessed subject at the two poles of theatrical production in the roles of the actor and spectator.

Pina Bausch's performance work situates itself within the Brechtian tradition, extending and transforming this tradition in so far as she does away with this residual humanism of the rational and critical subject, and displaces Brecht's preoccupation with the "strangeness" of a socio-political context onto a foreignness of the body. The bodies of Bausch's performers are traversed by and immersed in a montage of disjunctive codes (dress, gender, music, gesture ...). The minimal unity that the body presents is disturbed by repetition and ritualisation, by the mechanisation of its movements, and by its displacement from any coherent context. In this way Bausch truncates or shatters the possibility of a Brechtian "overall attitude" as manifested by the *gestus* or fable. She cuts the remaining Brechtian link. The unfamiliar is not the precursor of a greater understanding; rather the opposite: the minimal extent to which one can identify a gesture or posture leads only to a greater unease when its distortion or exacerbation confounds the easy attribution of meaning. The effect, nevertheless, is of a violent polemic, its near-intolerability the product of its indeterminability. Deleuze talks about extracting from the event "the part that cannot be reduced to what happens"[33] i.e., the part of the body or image that is not related to extensions into action or reaction but remains a point of intension, intensity: "that part of inexhaustible possibility that constitutes the unbearable, the intolerable."[34] Bausch's work is almost a study in the shattering of narrative and subject into irreducible fragments of intense affect.

The Everyday

Everyday gestures receive particular attention in the cinema of the time-image, in part because they are non-extensive or non-narrative actions: their automatic quality puts them outside the decision-making realm of the sensory-motor situations. It is also by virtue of this automatic, indecisive quality of the everyday gesture that it lends itself to aberrations in movement, the rupture in regularity that produces the singularity of the time-image: "watch someone walking down the street and see what little inventions he introduces into it ... what little inventions he puts there."[35] The distinction between the banal and the exceptional tends to become indiscernible around this point of singularity that brings the one out in the other. They form two poles between which there is constant passage: the exceptional is the extra-ordinary. The automatic movement is implicated, and continued, in the catastrophic moment that is its aberration or disintegration:

> [I]f everyday banality is so important, it is because, being sub-ject to sensory-motor schemata which are automatic and pre-established, it is all the more liable, on the least disturbance between stimulus and response ... suddenly to free itself from the laws of this schema and reveal itself in a visual and sound nakedness.[36]

All of the films considered in this essay produce, in various ways, this travelling between the poles of the everyday and the exceptional or ceremonial, and the disintegration of the subject into the events of the body and the objects and codes with which it is connected. Chantal Akerman's film, *Jeanne Dielman, 23 Quai de Commerce, 1080 Bruxelles*, involves about three-and-a-half hours of a highly ordered household routine of a Belgian woman who practises prostitution in the after-noon with the same orderly indifference as when she cleans her son's shoes. Over the course of the film, Jeanne's personal individuality dis-perses and melds with her actions, the rooms, the routine. She does not individuate the film but rather the events and spaces do—washing dishes, eating lunch and cooking dinner, minding a friend's baby, bathing: rooms and times of the day take on the force of characters. This is an experience of the spectator: as with the scene in *Je tu il elle* analysed above, there is a sharing of affect at the limit of the spectator and the film, referring in my own case at least to the trance-like state induced by the film and its time that is so like Jeanne "herself," herself being one with her diffusion. The spectator's most intense involve-ment is not that of personal identification but is rather a physical tak-ing-on of her time, particularly the times when she does nothing.

The automatic is the site of rupture in this film; intense moments are when she drops a spoon or forgets to replace a lid. Her omitting to put a pair of scissors back in their place becomes a murder whose impact and modality is little different from the precision and automatism that regulates all her gestures.

Bresson's *Mouchette* also is a film where characterisation and plot is elaborated around everyday gestures and spaces, aggregations and collisions of bodies, textiles and fluids. Gestures accumulate and contradict each other without cancelling each other out. They are evocative while maintaining their status as fragments, as parts of a texture, without coalescing into moral messages or unambiguous determinations of motive or psychology, even in the event of Mouchette's suicide which, like the murder in Jeanne Dielman, so closely approximates a banal gesture. Its restraint is shocking, but it leaves us with nothing to say. Bresson's is eminently a cinema of the cut; he explicitly seeks to truncate the shot before it yields a definite interpretation in order to create the "non-significant image"[37] that is able to be "transformed on contact with other images,"[38] creating a rhythm where the image or form acts as a substitute for (rather than vehicle of) thought: "Forms that resemble ideas. Treat them as actual ideas."[39] In *Mouchette* in particular we get a sense of strong physical presence, the "fullness" of the physical, which immediately flips over into a certain ineffability, the "void". This perhaps accounts for the "spiritual" sense in Bresson. The suppression of will in Bresson's films, at both the level of the actor and the image, suggests a sort of cinematographic erotics in the way they focus on sensual form and its discipline, its submission to a technique and a technology, its connections and frictions, its alienation from a finality, its achievement of impact through restraint, a cinematic courtly love.[40] As Bresson says, his systematic approach is not an attempt to totally regulate things but a "bait for something, a transformation, a seduction between the images."[41]

Conclusion

I'll begin the end with a quote from Samuel Butler's *The Way of all Flesh* describing one of the many ways that flesh has, pertaining to the disorder of the properties and primacy of the visual order in becoming, the visceral processes of presence. In the novel it comes as a prescription from a doctor as a remedy for various sicknesses of capture, by a course in "crossing":

> Seeing is a mode of touching, touching is a mode of feeding, feeding is a mode of assimilation, assimilation is a mode of re–creation and reproduction and this is crossing—shaking yourself into something else and something else into you.[42]

The situation of the practices and states of the body between meaningfulness and meaninglessness seems to make them particularly vulnerable or subject to a double exclusion—either a throwing up of hands at the ineffable, or the crunching pursuit of a transcendent discourse, both of which play into the myth of the "secret" of presence which is put on a pedestal, and differing only in their level of ambition. Although it could be said that this whole essay is an attempt to reforge the sensory-motor link to meaning (it certainly has the function of giving myself something to say in this context), I've tried to carve a critical passage between the exclusions: not a passage of pursuit I hope, but more like a passing-by, or passing-over a palm, a tangential relation or connection, like brushing up against a film in the dark.

1   Jean Narboni, "La quatrième personne du singulier (Je tu il elle)," *Cahiers du Cinéma*, no. 276 (May 1977). It was after writing this piece that I discovered that Narboni himself had borrowed the term "fourth person singular" from Deleuze's *Logique du Sens*. My understanding of the term in this context, however, is derived wholly from Narboni's use of it in the above article.

2   Michel de Certeau, *The Practices of Everyday Life*, trans. S. Rendall (Berkeley,Los Angeles, London: University of California Press, 1988).

3 Ibid., 64.

4 This myth is told by Italo Calvino in *Invisible Cities* (Picador, London, 1979), p. 39, and seems to have captured the imagination of several theorists of women's relation to modernity—see, among others, Patricia Mellencamp, "Last Scene in the Streets of Modernism," *Indiscretions: avant-garde film, video, and feminism* (Bloomington: Indiana University Press, 1990) and Moira Gatens, "Corporeal representation in/and the body politic," eds. R. Diprose and R. Ferrell, *Cartographies: Poststructuralism and the Mapping of Bodies and Spaces* (Sydney: Allen & Unwin, 1991).

5 Vincent Descombes, *Modern French Philosophy*, trans. L. Scott–Fox and J. M. Harding (Cambridge: Cambridge University Press, 1980), 154.

6 Bertolt Brecht, "A Dialogue about Acting," ed. and trans. J. Willet, *Brecht on Theatre: The Development of an Aesthetic*, (New York: Hill and Wang, 1964), 26, my italics.

7 Brecht, "Alienation Effects in Chinese Acting, *Brecht on Theatre*, 96–97.

8 Roland Barthes, "Les Trois Écritures," "Animé/inanimé," "Dedans/dehors," *L'empire des signes* (Geneva: Éditions Albert Skira, 1970). These texts are reproduced, in an abridged form, as "Lessons in Writing," *Image, Music, Text*, trans. S. Heath (Glasgow: Fontana/Collins, 1977).

9 Gilles Deleuze and Félix Guattari, "November 28, 1947: How Do You Make Yourself a Body without Organs?" *A Thousand Plateaus*, trans. B. Massumi (London: Athlone Press, 1988), 159.

10 Ibid., 154.

11 Gilles Deleuze (interviewed by Christine Parnet), "Dead Psychoanalysis: Analyse," *Dialogues*, trans. H. Tomlinson and B. Habberjam (New York: Columbia University Press, 1987), 95.

12 see "Rhizome," *A Thousand Plateaus*.

13 "1730: Becoming-Intense, Becoming-Animal, Becoming-Imperceptible...," ibid., 261.

14 Ibid., 251.

15 There is in fact an important technical distinction (which is elided in the connotative senses I am relying on here) that Deleuze makes between the "particular" (as adjunct to the "general") and the "singular"—it is hard to find a synonym for "singular" that does not run into philosophical problems in the context of Deleuze's work ("specificity" would have been even worse, implying the arborescent "species-genus" dyad), perhaps precisely because the singular is the *irreplaceable*.

16 Barthes makes a similar point about formalism and materialism (as historical or artistic movements)—that they address the displacement of the real rather than its fixation under the proper names of Form and Matter—see "Digressions" in *Le bruissement de la langue: Essais critiques IV* (Paris: Éditions du Seuil, 1984), and "Réquichot et son corps," *L'obvie et l'obtus: Essais critiques III* (Paris: Éditions du Seuil, 1982).

17 *Dialogues*, 93.

18 Felicity Collins: " 'Should a feminist knit?': Narcissistic Narratives and the Other Woman,"*Flesh, Intervention*, no. 21/22 (Sydney: Intervention

Publications, 1988).

19 *Dialogues*, 93.

20 Gilles Deleuze: *Cinema 2: The Time-Image*, trans. H. Tomlinson and R. Galeta (Minneapolis: University of Minnesota Press, 1989).

21 "La photographie est déjà tirée dans les choses." Interview with Gilles Deleuze by Pascal Bonitzer and Jean Narboni, *Cahiers du Cinéma*, no. 352 (October 1983), 38.

22 *Cinema 2*, 44–47.

23 Ibid., 20.

24 *A Thousand Plateaus*, 164, 264–265.

25 *Cinéma 2*, 45.

26 Ibid., 12–13.

27 *A Thousand Plateaus*, 290.

28 He is referring to, or abbreviating, a distinction of Jean Baudrillard's.

29 Deleuze develops this notion in *Cinema 2* in the idea of the "tacti–sign," with reference to Bresson's films.

30 "La quatrième personne du singulier," p. 7. In relation to this, and the constitution of the divergent and independent parameters of the "readable" image outlined above, I am reminded of Barthes' text on the painter Requichot, where he constructs an alternative to the visual model of representation, the instantaneous capturing of and reproducing an image in vision, as structuring the history of painting, aligning it rather with the activity of *cooking* or *writing* (as in calligraphy)—a tactile and material process of assembling fluids and solids and flavours, the bubblings of their integrity and interaction in the case of cooking, or the manual activity of scratching and scraping, the modulation of lines and curves in time, inscribing and erasing and reinscribing, effacing the code under the illegibility of the scribble.

31 *Brecht on Theatre*, 27.

32 Ibid., 96.

33 *Cinema 2*, 19. This expression is actually one used by Blanchot, who draws it from Hölderlin.

34 Ibid., 19–20.

35 Deleuze, *Dialogues*, 128.

36 *Cinema 2*, 3.

37 Robert Bresson: *Notes on the Cinematographer*, trans. J. Griffin (London/New York: Quartet Books, 1986), 11.

38 Ibid., 10.

39 Ibid., 30.

40 Deleuze and Guattari discuss 'courtly love' in this sense in various places, eg. *A Thousand Plateaus*, 156–157, *Dialogues*, 100–101.

41 Bresson, *Notes*, 10.

42 *The Way of all Flesh* (London: A. C. Fifield, 1920), 360.

Film Figures

Rainer Werner Fassbinder's *The Marriage of Maria Braun* and Alexander Kluge's *The Female Patriot*

Michelle Langford

> *Roswitha feels an enormous power*
> *within her, and films have taught*
> *her that this power really exists.*[1]

In an article published in 1982 Miriam Hansen remarked on the challenge presented by the New German Cinema to a foreign film critic. This challenge, writes Hansen, "consists in the particular way in which these films relate to their primary context of reception, that is to the historically determined public sphere of West Germany."[2] The challenge was taken up at great length by Anton Kaes in his book, *From Hitler to Heimat: The Return of History as Film*.[3] Kaes' book situates several films of the New German Cinema in the context of the "cultural, social, and political ambience from which they issue and within which they function."[4] The films which are discussed in detail include Rainer Werner Fassbinder's *The Marriage of Maria Braun* (1978), Alexander Kluge's *The Female Patriot* (1979), Helma Sanders-Brahms' *Germany, Pale Mother* (1980), Hans Jürgen Syberberg's *Hitler, a Film From Germany* (1977) and Edgar Reitz's *Heimat* (1984). What they have in common is the way in which they prefigure the ambiguities that surrounded the subsequent revisionist attempts by Germans to come to terms with their past. Kaes' study follows one path of a polarity that has characterised many commentaries of the New German Cinema and its films. On the opposing track lies a pre-dominantly American predilection for elevating certain directors to the status of stars. Populated mostly by film critics writing for newspa-pers and magazines, it was they who helped to secure a popular appeal for such proper names as Fassbinder, Wenders and Schlöndorff. Their bias filtered through to some of the initial commentaries on New German Cinema. These include James Franklin's *New German Cinema: From Oberhausen to Hamburg* and *The New German Cinema* by John Sandford.[5] As Thomas Elsaesser points out in the introduction of his book, *New German Cinema: A History*, the emphasis of these studies falls either on the side of auteurist concerns or else concentrates on a thematic-generic approach.[6] The fact is that all of these studies, with their diverse offerings, have themselves constructed around the New German Cinema a body of criticism and theoretical work which has shaped its "history." Ironically, while forming part of a history, these studies are concerned with films which are often attempts at decon-structing the dominant perspective of "official" discourse.

Between the dominant trajectories of literature on the New German Cinema lie such works as Richard McCormick's *Politics of the Self: Feminism and The Postmodern in West German Literature and Film*, and Julia Knight's *Women and the New German Cinema*.[7] The first situ-ates various works of German literature and film within the context of the emerging women's movement in Germany through the 1960s and 70s, and the latter is an attempt to fill a gap in the "dominant" lit-erature on New German Cinema. Knight constructs a history of women filmmakers through the 1960s, 70s and 80s in Germany, "whose work," she contends, "—although excluded from many accounts—equally forms a part of the New German Cinema."[8]

I too am concerned with women and the New German Cinema, but not from a historical or thematic perspective, nor from an auteurist one. I am interested in two women in particular; Maria Braun played by Hanna Schygulla in Rainer Werner Fassbinder's 1978 film *The Marriage of Maria Braun* (*Die Ehe der Maria Braun*) and Gabi Teichert, played by Hannelore Hoger in Alexander Kluge's 1979 film *The Female Patriot* (*Die Patriotin*). These films have been widely discussed from various perspectives and both characters have been subject to criticism from feminist writers, especially Gabi Teichert. I will look specifically at their roles within particular contexts—the stylistic, structural and strategic aspects of each film—in order to show how Maria and Gabi interact with and are integral parts of the filmic process and mirror, or figure, each film's own mode of production. In doing so I would like to displace some of the criticisms of the films and their makers, not to displace these films from their "primary context of reception" but to show how secondary contexts shift the mode of reception and along with it the mode of analysis. These contexts are never static—especially when they concern films that depend upon a degree of investment by the spectator in the production of meaning. Both of these films form part of a history, but they also alert us to the fact that films also produce history, ideas about history, and various ways of conceiving history, not only through film, but other media as well. At the same time, these films offer different ways of presenting the roles of women in cinema, roles that cannot be adequately appraised from feminist perspectives alone.

The Marriage of Maria Braun

Towards the beginning of *The Marriage of Maria Braun* there is a moment when a pack of cigarettes appears in extreme close-up, so close in fact that it occupies the entire screen. Anton Kaes has read this and other uses of the close-up in the film as a device emphasising "people's greed for simple pleasures like cigarettes or coffee" in post Second World War Germany, where the film is set.[9] Kaes may offer a valid and accurate reading of the function of the frequent and, in his words, "often obtrusive" close-ups used throughout the film. However, his reading of them as purely historical signifiers is limiting in that they are prevented from functioning on other levels—as methods of filmic expression and as modes of exchange within the terms of the film itself. By this I mean that they contribute to the network of exchanges which, on the level of narrative, work as catalysts for Maria's rise to success and fortune and, at the level of filmic techniques, signal the film's ability to transform such techniques to suit the particular circumstances of the film. The shot of the packet in extreme close-up comprises part of a chain which drives both the narrative and the signifying strategies of the film.

Throughout *The Marriage of Maria Braun* Fassbinder films his elaborate sets with a clear, crisp, deep focus, bringing all elements, near, mid and far into a direct relationship with each other.

Gilles Deleuze distinguishes between two types of depth in an image. The first he calls a depth *in* the field or image. Using the example of sixteenth century painting, he explains that "each plane, especially the first, performs its own task and stands only for itself in the grand business of painting which harmonizes them."[10] In the cinema this type of depth, according to Deleuze, "was produced by a simple juxtaposition of independent shots, a succession of parallel planes."[11] The second, which marked a crucial change in painting in the seventeenth century, is created when elements and characters of different planes refer directly to one another and the picture is organised "along the diagonal, or through a gap"—thus privileging the background and bringing it "into immediate touch with the foreground."[12] At this moment, writes Deleuze,

> depth becomes depth *of* field, whilst the dimensions of the foreground take on an abnormal size, and those of the background are reduced, in a violent perspective which does even more to unite the near and the faraway.[13]

It is the invention of this type of depth in the cinema that Deleuze attributes to Orson Welles. It is also this type of depth *of* field which is used extensively in conjunction with the close-up—with far reaching implications for Fassbinder in *The Marriage of Maria Braun*.

Depth of field is a common device used in film for bringing together people or objects for the purpose of suggesting a comparison, contrast or juxtaposition between them. Fassbinder's striking use of it in *The Marriage of Maria Braun* helps to scale the film within its own terms and should be thought of not only in visual terms but also figuratively in terms of the way in which the film opens up a field, or scope within which objects and people collide and traverse a variety of images and sequences. The objects and devices which weave their way through the film function less as leitmotif—which would merely suggest associations between objects and characters—than as catalysts that actually move the film and its characters to action. Particularly striking are several sequences that take place in the interior of the house where Maria and her mother live during the earlier part of the film.

One example of how a close-up may figuratively expand the film's depth of field occurs during a sequence where Maria and her mother barter over a pack of cigarettes. Maria has just returned from a Red Cross soup kitchen where an encounter with some American GIs has earned her several packs of cigarettes. On her arrival home, Maria throws one of the packs down on the kitchen table, her mother quickly snatches them up and rushes to the sink to find a match. Maria blows out the match. After a short bartering session, Maria's mother agrees to trade her brooch (which she tells Maria is "very valuable") for the three packs of cigarettes that Maria has brought home. It is at this point that one of these packs is shown in extreme close-up. As Maria's mother runs off to fetch the brooch, a single pack fills the entire screen, effectively dwarfing Maria's mother who is shot predominantly in long or medium shots throughout the film. In their enormous disproportion, the packs become a standard or scale by which many other things may be measured in the network of exchange woven throughout the film.

As catalysts sustaining the momentum of Maria's story, the cigarettes carry a weighty significance. In the sequence in the soup kitchen—where they are given to her by an American GI—it is not through bartering that she acquires them but through her own assertiveness. After a short, somewhat comical moment when a cigarette butt is thrown to the ground by one of the GIs and a dozen men dive for it as it hits the ground, Maria is whistled at and a comment is made to her by another GI. He says: "You should see mine honey, you'd love it." To this Maria responds by walking over to him and, standing tall and proud, saying; (in English) "Mister" (then in German) "I don't know what you said, but you don't have any right." She returns to her seat and the GI promptly walks over and places three packs of cigarettes on the table in front of her saying "I'm sorry ma'am, I apologize." As the GI returns to his seat Maria starts to laugh, the GIs follow suit and with this laughter the scene closes.

During this scene the exchange value of the cigarettes begins to increase and circulate, but this value extends beyond that of their shortage and consequently high exchange value in post-war Germany. By first showing a dozen men scramble for a single cigarette butt, and then in the same sequence suggesting another scramble which we do not see but hear, Fassbinder gradually compounds their worth. In the following sequence a single pack has become gigantic in comparison to Maria's mother and has attained the worth of a "very valuable" brooch. It is with this brooch that Maria procures the sleek black dress she wears when she acquires not only her first, but also her second job. And it is Fassbinder himself, playing a black-market dealer, who trades the dress for the brooch. Here again we can see the interaction between various levels of the film: Maria's and the film's appearance are inherently linked. Fassbinder applies the "cosmetic" touches without which neither Maria nor the film could operate.

The importance of "cosmetics" to various levels of the film is high-lighted during a sequence in which Maria and Betti (Maria's sister-in-law) are doing each other's hair in front of a mirror. On the dressing table in front of them—amidst hair curlers and makeup—lies a photo-graph of Maria's husband, Hermann Braun. The scene suggests that Hermann, and by extension Maria's marriage to him, share a similar function to the make-up, curlers and new dress. All function as adorn-ments with which Maria may "make up" and propel her own story. This is further emphasised when Betti says, "Willi would definitely not approve" and Maria answers, "Hermann would." Due to their separa-tion after only one night and half a day, Hermann is largely a con-struct of Maria's memory and imagination. Hermann is quite literally *her* man. For instance, a photograph of Hermann is able to provoke outbursts of emotion in Maria, whereas Hermann the man cannot. We see an example of such displaced emotion during the scene when Willi first returns after the war. Maria takes one look at Hermann's photograph and begins to weep. At the end of the film we view Hermann on his return from Canada; for the most part the sequence is shot from behind, his face reflected in and framed by a mirror that he holds in his hand. For Maria, Hermann is an image and is used by her as a distancing device, an excuse for her not to become involved with other men—even though Bill and Oswald become involved with *her*[14]—and a way of maintaining her autonomy, even if that too is a construct of the same imagination. The "depth" of this sequence is fur-ther complicated because it is shot entirely as a reflection in the mir-ror. Maria sees herself as we see her, as a reflection, as an image made up for effect, but significantly it is she who is most able to utilise that image, making that image work for her. Maria treats her own image as an object with exchange value, but it is not to *herself* that she ascribes this value: it is quite literally her image. Each time we see her dressing up, applying make-up or fixing her hair we come to understand that it is because there is something that she wants.

It is useful to think of Maria as Peter Märthesheimer, the film's scriptwriter, describes her: Maria is "not a realistic character, but something that is usually called a 'film figure.'" By this he means "a figure that embodies in a very condensed form the wishes, characteristics, and desires of the viewers."[15] I would, however slightly reformulate this definition by saying that she is a "film figure" in the sense of the figurative. But rather than a figure of speech, Maria is a "figure of film" and as such embodies "in a very condensed form the wishes, characteristics, and desires" of the film itself. In the context of the film, Maria Braun figures in a similar way to the objects that surround her, she is dependent on them in the same way the narrative progressions are dependent upon her. It would be wrong to simply suggest, however, that Maria is presented as a woman objectified or simply an "object of exchange ... between two men" because throughout the film, Maria proficiently engages in all manner of exchange contracts. In a sense she engages in what Fassbinder has called the use of women's own "'oppression' as terrorisation."[16] This is not to say that Fassbinder was proposing any kind of "feminist text" with *Maria Braun*, but that he wanted the figure of Maria Braun to participate intelligently in the filmic process. Maria is able to make use of the objects in her environment rather than be suffocated by them.

The emphasis on the relationship between characters and their environment throughout *The Marriage of Maria Braun* signals the way in which the film simultaneously depends upon and dismantles the genre of melodrama. In the areas of style and technique *The Marriage of Maria Braun* conforms to the standards of Hollywood melodrama; the use of elements such as lighting, composition, and attention to decor "become functional and integral elements in the construction of meaning".[17] It is also here where it literally blasts open the genre and allows its female protagonist to enter into a different kind of relationship with her environment. *The Marriage of Maria Braun* still conforms to the melodramatic mode when it is conceived, as it is by Thomas Elsaesser, strictly in terms of *mise-en-scène*. It too is an enclosed, self-referential environment, but one which is for the most part of the film more liberating than constricting.[18]

With the *Marriage of Maria Braun*, Fassbinder takes literally the notion of domestic conflict and disruption of the 50s melodrama. According to Christine Gledhill, this type of melodrama "focused on upper-middle-class homes crammed with lavish furnishings and consumer goods."[19] *Maria Braun* embodies conflict and disruption within the home itself. Not only has the family disintegrated, but the building in which they live is literally falling to pieces, crumbling beyond repair. The walls gape with holes (which are used to move from one room to another), there is little wood for warmth, little food and, due to the war, a conspicuous absence of men. At one point Maria remarks to Grandpa Berger how nice it is to come home and see a man in the house. Grandpa Berger, old and frail, is however far from the ideal father figure of the American melodramas, and Maria's remark points to the fact that they must make do with what they can get. The details of Maria's environment mark a striking contrast to "the middle-class home" of Hollywood melodramas, "filled with objects, which ... surround the heroine in a hierarchy of apparent order that becomes increasingly suffocating."[20] The situation of crumbling buildings, social disorder and lonely hearts forces Maria to make the most of the few objects she can acquire.

In order to sustain herself and her story, Maria must go out to work, and in order to do so she must adopt a ruthless manner. Having neither the time nor the energy to be emotional, she displaces the emotional torment expected of a melodramatic woman onto her mother. But in order for her mother to cope, Maria supplies her with alcohol "to help her forget the troubles she has with her daughter and drown her sorrows." (So it is said to Fassbinder, playing the black market dealer in the scene where Maria obtains, along with her black dress, a bottle of gin.) The following scene opens with a collision of these two items, a collision which assists in locating Maria's place in the melodrama: Maria's foot is seen in a high-heeled shoe on the kitchen table as her Mother's hand pours a drink. The clink of the bottle on the glass rings out obtrusively as we view Maria's shoe and her mother's bottle in a close-up which dominates the deep-focused view of the kitchen. Maria's mother drowns the domestic sphere in a bottle of gin while Maria prepares herself for a life beyond. This moment further illuminates the importance of various "cosmetic" touches used to enhance both Maria's and the film's appearance and the use of depth of field as a device not only within but also between images. The exchange value of the cigarettes may now be gauged, since they allow Maria to buy the brooch, which buys the dress and the gin. These objects not only exchange value among themselves but also help to define a character's relationship to the domestic sphere and to the genre of melodrama. In a comment to her doctor Maria enumerates the terms of this relationship: she says of her mother, "She nibbles at my rations, cries my tears, lies my lies, but she leaves all the thinking to me so I don't have time to be sad."

In a review of *The Marriage of Maria Braun*, Tom Noonan remarks on the film's relationship with Hollywood melodrama and the "woman's film." He says: "It's a story line straight out of the forties, from Hollywood's "women's films." Fassbinder is knowingly trading on old clichés, and it's a risky venture that sometimes falters."[21] I would argue that it is the moments when the film falters in generic terms that it takes, in Noonan's own words, "the woman's film and [stands] it on its head."[22] Fassbinder's film does not, however, simply invert the "woman's film," rather it breaks it at the seams and opens a space within which the genre may become relevant to the particular circumstances of the film. According to Laura Mulvey, "the 1950s are marked by the particular resurgence of the family melodrama, the Hollywood genre associated with the dramas of domesticity, woman, love and sexuality."[23] Thus it is not surprising that Fassbinder, remembering his reverence for German ex-patriot filmmaker Douglas Sirk, should choose the melodramatic genre to tell a story set in post-war Germany. With the Allied occupation it is likely that characters such as Maria Braun would have been exposed to such films. Although she never actually goes to the cinema during the film, *Maria Braun* (the character and the film) seems to be aware of the difference between family life, the domestic sphere, and the possibility of romantic love in 40s and 50s America, and post-war Germany. Fassbinder highlights this difference both visually and through characterisation.

Maria's distance from emotions and from the domestic sphere of the family melodrama mirrors the distance between herself and Hermann. Ironically it is only because of this distance from Hermann that she can seek the ideal of romantic love. This distance is maintained throughout the film—Hermann only occupies the same space as Maria in three short sequences. In the first, at the wedding ceremony, the final shot shows Hermann caught in freeze-frame, imprisoned by the film. The second is when he returns from the army to find Maria and Bill making love. Maria hits Bill over the head with a bottle, killing him, but Maria and Hermann do not make physical contact. The standard melodramatic reconciliatory embrace is notably absent. The following sequence shows Hermann like a shadow in the rear of the make-shift court room and it is here that he takes the blame for Bill's death. This time Hermann is literally imprisoned. Until the final scene, Hermann and Maria see each other only in jail where the presence of bars, keys and guards is omnipresent. In the final scene—Hermann has returned from Canada—the couple are reunited, but Maria withholds her passions, saying to Hermann that she must get to know him first; after all, they have only been married one night and half a day. It is now time for their marriage to continue; however, it continues as it always had—in separation. In what seems like a half-conscious gesture, Maria, having blown out the flame on the stove but left the gas running, goes to the kitchen to light a cigarette. The result kills them both. Parallels with the opening sequence—the white dress, the explosion and the scream are obvious. In it, a baby is heard crying amidst the sounds of the air raid and machine-gun fire. In the penultimate, a woman's scream accompanies the sound of the explosion. Both effectively liberate Maria from the confines of the domestic sphere and assist her to maintain the ideal love she has for an ideal husband as simply that—ideal. Recalling the cigarettes which served as the catalyst for her initial liberation, leading to her success, it is significant that by the end of the film she has taken up smoking—cigarettes are the vehicle once again for her final, irreversible liberation. Maria shows herself throughout to make no compromises; for her it is all or nothing.

Anton Kaes has read the "disastrous" end of the film as the effect of Maria's half-conscious realisation that her success came at the price of being "a mere object of exchange in a business transaction between two men"—Oswald and Hermann. "The illusion that gave her life meaning shatters completely."[24] This reading does not, however, take into account the fact that if it were not for her assertive behaviour, first toward the GI, then toward the proprietor of the "off limits" bar who gives her the the job where she meets Bill (to whom she falls pregnant—the pregnancy which prompts her to visit her doctor but which results in a still-birth), she would not have been alone on the train where she makes the acquaintance of Oswald, the French industrialist who speaks no English. On the train and in the presence of Oswald, she swears at an American soldier, in the English that she learnt "in bed"; consequently she is employed by Oswald as a "personal advisor," the position in which she earns her wealth. Hermann, as I have already pointed out, is an object of Maria's imagination, an image of a husband rather than a person, and Oswald occupies a similar place. It is Maria who sets the terms of their relationship. Ironically, they are seen less and less frequently together after Hermann's release from jail and departure for Canada. This suggests that Oswald has paid dearly for a contract he is powerless to control. It is true that the discovery of the contract between Oswald and Hermann may have shattered her illusions, however this does not give reason to discount the assertions *she* has made, the deals *she* has contracted and the men *she* has manipulated throughout the film. It is not fair for Kaes to say that "she was *never* in control of her own destiny."[25] This is a simplistic, pessimistic reading, a reading that Fassbinder wishes an intelligent audience to think beyond.

It is never made clear whether Maria intentionally sparked the film's explosive conclusion. The ambiguity allows the audience to make up their own minds, and gain from the film what they will. That Fassbinder originally intended Maria to bring about the deaths of herself and Hermann deliberately is evident when we refer to the notes on the shooting script.[26] Maria and Hermann would take a drive into the country; on a bend, Maria would continue to drive straight ahead. The car would race over an embankment, disappear and after a few moments of silence an explosion would be heard. To end the film in this way—with little ambiguity—would certainly not have been as potent or thought-provoking as the ending we have. The film seems to complete a circle, ending virtually where it began: but at the end it is a woman rather than a baby who screams, suggesting that Maria has learnt something from her experience. To end Maria's story through the simple, almost mundane act of lighting a cigarette directly links this "end" with the beginning and makes it possible, for the audience at least, to begin again.

Fassbinder responded to the criticisms that his films are pessimistic by saying that "revolution doesn't belong in the cinema screen, but outside, in the world ... my aim is to warn them that that's the way things *will* go if they don't change their lives. ... My goal is to reveal such mechanisms in a way that makes people realise the necessity of changing their own reality."[27] When viewed in light of this statement, Anton Kaes' reading of the ending of the film as hopeless, as Germany's missed chance of making a radically new beginning from

the "Zero Hour" of 1945, is itself pessimistic and takes the film only at
face value as a recreation or reconstruction of post-war Germany and
as an allegory for the rise and demise of Germany's "economic miracle" during the 1950s. Kaes, I believe, misses the film's powerful use of
fiction and devices of figuration. These are not means to reconstruct,
but, borrowing a phrase from Deleuze, invitations to recollect.

Beyond the innovation of depth of field as a technical procedure,
Deleuze views its importance for the cinema "as a function of remembering, a figure of temporalisation."[28] For Deleuze, this figure becomes
manifest in what he calls the "coexistence of sheets of past" and the
"simultaneity of peaks of present."[29] The connection between depth of
field and memory is not like that between psychological memory and
the flashback, nor is it "a case of a succession of presents according to
chronological time."[30] The emphasis must be placed upon coexistence
and simultaneity "...to show how spatially distant and chronologically
separate regions were in touch with each other."[31]

To think the structure of *The Marriage of Maria Braun* in terms of
"virtual regions of past" is appropriate if we see the film's relationship
to history as other than simply historical reconstruction. Similarly, the
film is related to the genre of melodrama not as nostalgic recreation. It
functions on a different level from the Hollywood melodramas of the
1940s and 50s and consists of several levels. These different levels, or
strata, would be inherently linked in an archaeological sense: *Maria
Braun* simultaneously builds on and demolishes old clichés that evoke
referential recollections.

The first region or sheet of past which enters the film is what could
be called "official history." This enters the film in the opening shot by
way of an image heavily laden with associations. This image is a close-
up of a portrait of Hitler. But "Hitler" crashes to the ground, figuring
the fall of the Third Reich and signaling a departure from that region
of past. But this region is shattered, as the opening shot suggests,
into an infinite number of connected but distinct regions. These
enter the film at various points: through radio broadcasts of the

names of missing soldiers, Chancellor Konrad Adenauer's post-war speeches and the broadcast of the 1954 World Soccer Championship. The characters, who occupy yet another plane, are oblivious to these ghosts attempting to haunt their space. Here depth of field is at work between two separate but interdependent technical procedures— sound and image. A frequent sound heard at various points throughout the film is that of a jackhammer, but it remains unheard by the characters of the film. It is as though history is hammering on the door, attempting to enter the fictional space of the film but never quite managing to break through. It is the spectator who may see the collision between these sheets of past and for whom a recollection may be evoked. The images with which the film closes illustrate this more evocatively. These are portraits of Germany's post-war Chancellors from Adenauer to Helmut Schmidt. They appear as transparent sheets, negatives dissolving into one another, superimposed for a few fleeting moments. They constitute the only moments of the film which do not belong to the diegetic space of the film, but even these are overlapped, haunted by the soundtrack continuing from the previous sequence.

The impression left by the film is not one of a reconstruction of historical reality, but a reminder of the "official history," no less fictional, occupying a different plane to the virtual space constituted by the film. It is thus that the film invites the viewer to recollect; not to nostalgically remember the past, but to enlist one's imagination, one's intellectual capacities in order to view history from other perspectives, perspectives which may lead beyond the apparent pessimism of the end of the film.

The strategic moves made by the film in terms of melodrama also invite the the audience to engage in a form of intelligent recollection of a highly nostalgic genre. At the end of the film, when Maria has become wealthy, she owns a house crammed with lavish furnishings which are closing in on her. We watch her falter as she absent-mindedly places her handbag amongst the roses in a vase. The apparent order of her large house has rendered her life chaotic. The camera partakes of this chaos as it follows Maria around her house. The climax of the film builds contiguously with the radio broadcast of the 1954 World Soccer Championship, the announcer's voice intermittently rising up between Maria's conversation with her husband. Neither seem to be aware of the rising intonation of the announcer's voice nor of the chaos mounting around them. But Maria answers these chaotic moments as if by intuition. With the simple act of lighting a cigarette she returns her world to its former liberating state. Rather than leave his viewers suspended in the realm of the virtual, Fassbinder once again blasts open the historical continuum. In a reverse move, the blast at the end of the film helps to reinsert the audience into a space in which to function. The portrait of Schmidt dissolves from negative to positive then fades to black. The sound of the radio also fades and the murmur of the audience in the cinema begins to fade in, as do the lights. It is now time to negotiate the depths of our own stories, our own "sheets of past."

The Female Patriot

Image: Framed by a black iris, a man is seen in the distance standing on a snow-covered hill, a match flares as he lights a cigarette. The camera pans left following the contour of the hill and pauses momentarily on a leafless tree. The camera then pans right to bring the man with the cigarette back into view.

Voice-over: Documentary: A man lights a cigarette in the distance, I cannot know his history.

Image: The iris that frames the man closes, the final fragment of him we see is the glow of his cigarette.

This short sequence, a mere fragment inserted at a point close to the beginning of Alexander Kluge's film *The Female Patriot* (1979), is not, despite its banality, unremarkable. This fragment is not simply remarkable but itself marks, or punctuates, a point at which to enter discussion about the film. As both image and device this fragment sparks a number of associations which not only collide with the film itself but also suggest ways of bringing together various aspects of Kluge's theoretical writing and filmmaking practice—specifically his theories of montage and what he has called the "film in the head of the spectator," and his use of the German word "Zusammenhang." These notions will be used as ways to refigure the presentation of the female protagonist of The Female Patriot, Gabi Teichert, and to displace a range of feminist criticisms that have been levelled at her and at other female protagonists in Kluge's films. I shall focus particularly upon Gabi Teichert's position as a figure who must make her way through the film while negotiating the peculiar nature of the film itself.

The figure of the man who lights a cigarette in the distance suggests both literally and metaphorically one technique of montage: ellipsis. The iris-in/out structure of this sequence is a common device used to indicate omission or digression; a leap in time or space. Ellipsis nonetheless maintains continuity despite excluding sequences deemed superfluous to the preservation of continuity. But in relation to The Female Patriot and Kluge's theory of montage, the notions of ellipsis and montage must be thought of as promoting discontinuity rather than continuity. As Stuart Liebman has noted, Kluge's theory of montage

> pivots around the break in the flow of images, the cut between
> shots, or the cut to a title ... Linear narratives ... must ... be
> abandoned, though narrative elements, punctuated by leaps
> and reversals of time and circumscribed by reflection-inducing
> montage sequences [ellipsis], could still be retained.[32]

However, the images between which there is a cut are not presented as if there is a preconceived association between them. A common means of presenting intentional comparisons or juxtapositions is through "matching" shots on either side of a cut, highlighting the similarity of the composition of the two images and consequently making a comparison between the content of each. Contrary to this, Kluge's formulation of montage requires that each image have no obvious relation to any other. Kluge edits together a multitude of vastly disparate images, including archival footage, illustrations from children's books, still photographs, paintings, drawings, and fictional dramatic episodes—all of which are punctuated by intertitles variously quoting and misquoting known and anonymous sources. These are arranged in illogical juxtaposition not in order to construct meaning, but to conjure up a limitless variety of associations in the spectator's mind. "Editing opens a space in which 'distracted' spectators can invest their imagination, or, as Kluge puts it, their 'fantasy.' "[33] Kluge's theories of montage are inextricably linked to his notion of the role of the spectator.

Speaking of the role of the filmmaker in relation to that of the spectator, Kluge has said:

> At the present time there are enough cultivated entertainment and issue-oriented films, as if cinema were a stroll on walkways in a park ... One need not duplicate the cultivated. In fact, children prefer the bushes; they play in the sand or in scrap heaps.[34]

According to Kluge, it's not the job of the filmmaker to lull the spectator into complacency, or go down a single path. Spectators should be encouraged to activate their own imagination and create meaning from the disparate elements of the film; just as a child will make use of the discarded items on a scrap-heap to make something new. Kluge's wish is to tempt the audience from the well-known paths of dominant cinema so that they may become co-authors in the construction of the film. His films are often puzzling, even baffling. They are puzzles, but each fragment forms part of a different puzzle. The spectator should not worry, therefore, about piecing *everything* together, for, as Kluge says, "If I have understood everything then something has been emptied out."[35]

In *The Female Patriot* the role of the spectator is figured during the sequence introduced by the title *"DER SPANNER"* (the voyeur). In this sequence a man defines his occupation as a *"Verfassungsschützer"* (an Officer for the Protection of the Constitution). He works for the State Intelligence Service "observing politically suspect individuals."[36] Nocturnally he continues his voyeuristic activities as a peeping tom, but complains that he is unable to relax, and is left by night as little fulfilled as by day. In a later sequence he spies on a woman in a nearby apartment block. She turns out to be Gabi herself: "I'm down here now," she says. A conversation between them ensues where he again complains of his inability to relax. Gabi instructs him on eye-blinking exercises for relaxation.

The figure of the voyeur has often been used, especially in psychoanalytic film theory, to describe the position of the spectator of film. Miriam Hansen reads the sequence of the voyeur as providing a response to the psychoanalytically perceived nature of voyeurism in the cinema. She writes that the "foregrounding of looking as a legitimate activity ... raises the question as to whether there can be a fetishistic mode of scopophilia, an alternative to the voyeurism that governs the fiction film and its spectator."[37] On another level this sequence also suggests a method for the viewer to engage with a film actively, rather than passively. In the case of *The Female Patriot* and Kluge's emphasis on the cut—the "break in the flow of images"—in his theory of montage, these eye-blinking exercises would also serve as an approach to relaxation for the audience. In the published script of *The Female Patriot*, Kluge writes of the imperative of relaxation for the spectator and stresses the fact that not every fragment of his films is to be understood:

I encounter something in film which still surprises me and which I can perceive without devouring it. I cannot understand a puddle on which the rain is falling—I can only see it; to say that I understand the puddle is meaningless. Relaxation means that I myself become alive for a moment, allowing my senses to run wild: for once not to be on guard with the police-like intention of letting nothing escape me.[38]

Gabi's advice to the peeping tom also suggests that it is not necessary to see everything. A relief from images may inevitably be as inspiring for the imagination as the images themselves. The momentary lapse of vision functions not unlike Kluge's use of intertitles or his notion of the cut, the empty imageless space where spectators may engage in the production of meaning. Spectators capable of responding to the gaps in *The Female Patriot* are similarly capable of creating their own gaps. Kluge speaks of his wish to "bring the thoughts of others into the world spontaneously, that is Socrates' method. This is what I like, too."[39] And as Socrates drew upon the myths of his culture as a means of teaching about life, so too Kluge, in *The Female Patriot*, draws upon the stories, legends and fairytales as well as so-called historical events of his native country Germany, in order to evoke the limitless complexity of that world. Through montage, Kluge wants each spectator to become imaginatively engaged with the material, and to be involved in the production of meaning and in the filmmaking process itself. The spectator's engagement with the film should, however, not be thought of as a peaceful or untroubled relationship. This is where the term *Zusammenhang* may be brought into play.

The notion of engagement summons to mind such ideas as joining or binding together—interconnection. At the same time the phrase "engaged in conflict" also springs to mind. It is between these conflicting associations that Kluge's use of the German word *Zusammenhang* may be situated. *Zusammenhang* translates roughly into English as "connection" or "context." However, the English translation does little to summon up the complexity with which Kluge employs this word. When in English we say that we wish to place something into context—to contextualise something—we mean to fix its meaning within a given set of coordinates. When the narrator of *The Female Patriot* utters the words "Most of the time Gabi Teichert is confused. That is all a matter of context (*Zusammenhang*)," it is precisely the friction caused by fragments colliding—as in montage—that Kluge wishes to emphasise—while at the same time pointing to Gabi's position within a film based upon such friction. The friction created through montage and *Zusammenhang*, according to Stuart Liebman, "produces a shock to the spectator's memory" facilitating "a more comprehensive grasp of ... history," that is, of the particular history referred to by each of the colliding fragments.[40]

The role of Gabi Teichert in *The Female Patriot* must be seen in the context of such collision and friction—turbulence which she both creates and is subject to. Gabi is introduced into the film in the opening scene. An image shows a close-up of her face. On the soundtrack we hear the following words; "Gabi Teichert, history teacher from Hesse, a patriot, she therefore takes an interest in all the dead of the Reich."

Following traditional narrative conventions, one would expect to be presented with this character's story, or, given that she is a history teacher, her history. The film does not, however, pursue Gabi Teichert's history, nor even her story immediately, but diverges from it at the very point of introduction. The images which follow her introduction consist of grainy documentary footage. The camera pans over dead and wounded soldiers, victims of an unidentified war, at an unidentified moment in time, accompanied by an appropriately slow, melancholic music, string instruments weeping for the dead. Any sentimentality evoked by such a sequence is brought to an abrupt end with the intrusion of a title that breaks the flow. The title reads; "THE KNEE."

The voice-over introduces Gabi as a history teacher from Hesse. This at once introduces her as part of a mutually exclusive situation. As Hansen has noted, the "topical urgency behind" the question of history that was "crucial to the whole film" was "the decision of the Hessian government to abolish history as an obligatory part of the curricula," a decision upon which Gabi's attempt to "render German history in a patriotic version" is hinged.[41] Gabi as a history teacher in the region of Hesse makes her a f(r)ictional element disturbing the boundaries between documentary and fiction, history and story. She is situated in the space between rather than within any one particular category and thus must develop her own ways of functioning within each situation—just as the spectator of a film by Kluge is supposed to invest their own imagination in the cut, the gap between images. Hansen sees this device of genre-crossing as "the most interesting yet also problematic device" in Kluge's films.[42] Hansen's reference is to sequences where Gabi attends an actual SPD (Social Democratic Party) conference in order to question the delegates on the issue of the quality of the text books used to teach history in schools. Her ironic catch-phrase throughout the conference is "I'm here to change history." But which "history?" As a history teacher in Hesse, Gabi occupies a virtually impossible position, similar to that of a fictional character interacting within a situation usually reserved for the cameras of documentary films. The problematic nature of Gabi's position allows Kluge to pose questions about not only the crossing of genre boundaries, but also those of traditional historical discourse, mainstream filmmaking and gender stereotypes.

Gabi is presented as a history teacher who wants to break down the grand and impenetrable texts that constitute history within the school curriculum. The metaphor of the impenetrable and indigestible nature of history text books is played out literally by Gabi in a scene which takes place in the basement of the apartment building where she lives. In this scene, Gabi, surrounded by test tubes, beakers, and tools of all shapes and sizes, sets to work on one of the text books. First she uses a sickle, but to no avail—the cover of the book is barely scarred by the experience. Next she uses an ice-pick, but this too is able to penetrate little more than the superficial layers of "history." The third tool, a hand-saw, has little hope against the monolithic document. Gabi's fourth attempt is with a drill, but with it she only manages to drill a tiny hole. Her entry into this book will certainly be no easy task. She then attempts to dissolve the pages in orange juice, and to drink the mixture, but these books are literally so upsetting that she makes it her task to gather other resources from disparate sources with which to teach an entirely different approach to history.

The second time we meet Gabi is when she is preparing for a nocturnal journey of excavation, walking off into the night with a pick and shovel balanced on her shoulder. (Later in the film a similar image is shown of two men sporting picks and shovels; the voice-over tells of the Brothers Grimm who "went digging into German history, and found fairytales.") What is Gabi digging for? Although she is later shown digging illegally at an archaeological excavation site in the middle of the night, the suggestion arises that it may not be only actual historical artefacts in which she is interested. Gabi's interests go far beyond what is traditionally conceived as history. In a lecture on the human foot, that Gabi attends, the lecturer argues that the human foot has been severely underrated in the history of the human body. So Gabi sets to work on her flat-mate's foot, in order, I imagine, to draw out the complexities of this underrated limb. But she does not limit herself to the features of her immediate surroundings, she also looks toward the stars. When she visits an observatory, the camera pans around the inside of the domed roof of the building as it rotates, aligns itself and opens up to allow Gabi to take a view through the telescope. The opening of the observatory's dome metaphorically links Gabi's project with the role of the spectator. The film opens spaces for the spectators to invest their own imagination in the way that Gabi invests her own.

Although she spends much time and effort, and even risks her job participating in illegal excavations, to collect new materials for use at school, her students are as unable to digest this new approach to history as Gabi is to digest the text books. As one of her students says, "You're hitting us with either too much or too little." Perhaps the problem lies not only within the text books but, as Gabi's apparent lack of communication suggests, within the codes and structures of

the education system itself. Gabi first needs to find a way of communi-
cating her new methods so that they may be understood by students
who have already been taught the "historical" process in history texts.
As one of the teachers at a staff meeting points out: "history is written
in certain ways for historical reasons." Of course history has a history.
But the film suggests that it has in the past only been written *within*
and *for* itself, and that its value also may not extend beyond its own
borders, may not reach out into other realms, other disciplines or
indeed into people's own experience. Another comment by one of the
teachers spells this out precisely: "we have to keep the term 'history'
limited." Sitting comfortably in their hermetically sealed history
department, Gabi's fellow teachers don't have the language with
which to communicate outside of their realm. The department head
says to Gabi: "You've talked our ear off, yet you haven't said a word."
The problem facing Gabi is similar to the filmmaker's, whose task is,
according to Kluge, to "bridge the gap" so that the spectator can
become engaged with the material from the beginning of the film.

Gabi, like her approach to history, is similarly a character who
lacks codes with which to operate in a similarly uncodified film. At
times she appears silly and clumsy—leading some critics to criticise
Kluge for his treatment of women in his films. Of *Occasional Work of a
Female Slave* (1973) Marlies Kallweit wrote: "Here we see, once again,
how Kluge purports to side with women while at the same time trivial-
izing their most important problems."[43] The problem here is abortion,
and while this issue is not directly relevant to *The Female Patriot*, the
criticism is characteristic of those directed against Kluge's female
characters in general. Helke Sander claims that he chooses "excellent
actresses who can feign an independence they are not really allowed
to possess, let alone to act upon, within the context of his films."[44] Her
criticism is that Gabi Teichert is denied her own voice and lacks coherence, a voice and coherence that is given to the male-voiced narrator.
The narrator, Sander writes, "frequently expresses itself during the
film in extraordinarily long, uninterrupted passages. The protagonist

Gabi Teichert, however is pieced together through commentaries and only rarely gets a chance to speak herself."[45] This is a criticism based on dichotomies (male/female, active/passive, spoken/spoken for) which the film itself wishes to break down.

Just as Gabi's students and fellow teachers are unable to understand her reformulation of history because the dominant historical language has no space to accommodate anything different, so too must Gabi inevitably trip, stumble and lack the words to speak in a film which places her in situations unlike any other in the history of film. As she traverses such "alien" spaces as an actual SPD convention with the intention of changing history, it is the ability for a fictional character to enter such a space that should first and foremost be noted. Gabi's catch-phrase, "I'm here to change history," refers as much to the history of school texts books as it does to film history, complicating the so-called boundaries between documentary and fiction film. Gabi is not subordinated by the film, but, like Maria Braun, is a "film figure," figuring both Kluge's ideal spectator and his mode of filmic production based on montage. Gabi is a figure who is open to suggestion, open to new experiences, and while she does not possess a predetermined code with which to confront each new situation, it is her ability to adapt, even if she stumbles; that is her strength. Kluge does not provide an easy passage through the film for the audience, nor does he—nor, indeed, *should* he—provide one for Gabi.

In his book *Gelegenheitsarbeit einer Sklavin: Zur Realistischen Methode*,[46] Kluge addresses the question of women in his films. In the section entitled "The Interest in Women's Films: The Interrelationship (*Zusammenhang*) Between Modes of Production in Society," Kluge comments upon a question that is often asked of him: why are women given the roles of "characters that are, as people, substantially diminished." He answers by clarifying his conception of such roles: "Often these roles do not portray women in terms of gender differences, but are ciphers of characteristics attributable not only to women."[47] In "Roswitha's Programme" he speaks of the principle of "antagonistic realism" that shifts the mode of discourse away from the principle of reality through which dominant masculine discourse is organised.[48] The result is to provide no codes by which a viewer's attention may be structured. In female characters such "antagonistic realism" can cause them to "appear to a certain extent unsuccessful, naïve and, under the circumstances, dumb."[49] But, as Kluge writes, "the film must run the risk of being misunderstood by some of the viewers otherwise a genre from which viewers may actually learn might never be developed."[50] With the principle of antagonistic realism Kluge wants to provoke and to upset the hierarchy of modes of production in society. Through his female characters Kluge figures the confusion inherent in an attempt to assert the social validity of what he calls "the female modes of production."

In *The Female Patriot*, Kluge mixes various spheres, just as he mixes and creates friction between the modes of documentary and fiction. If we imagine Gabi Teichert as a figure of the female mode of production we can see the difficulty inherent in any attempt to place it in a sphere that is foreign to it. Kluge does not see the benefit in presenting women in film who manage everything easily because that does not identify their method of working. It is necessary, according to Kluge, for a film to be provocative; in order to be so it must remain somewhat implausible.[51] This is why Kluge's female protagonists appear, in Laleen Jayamanne's words, as "utopian screwballs". The comic, or the "madness of retardation," as Kluge puts it, is a way of making visible the productive force of women even while they continue to be suppressed.[52] Gabi Teichert may appear silly or naïve, but this is in order to provoke the friction through which her actions may become visible. In the manner of a screwball, Gabi must remain unaware of the apparent silliness of her actions so that the spectator may become aware of her different ways of working, different ways of engaging in the medium that is film. In her utopian aspect, Gabi possesses the imagination to look beyond her current circumstances with a positive attitude. As we are told at the end of the film, Gabi Teichert, at the beginning of each new year, looks forward to the next 365 days with the hope of improving the raw materials for use in history lessons. So too, Kluge wishes to bring about new relations between films and their spectators, this is his utopian conception of film: film's capacity to bring about new contexts and situations. As Kluge himself has said, "Even if everything has been said, it has not yet been realized."[53] And film, for Kluge, is a means toward producing many, various and antagonistic realisations.

Viewing the role of Gabi Teichert in light of Kluge's statements about his conception of female protagonists it becomes clear that preconceived codes of analysis are inappropriate for understanding such roles. If Gabi lacks speech—and this is deemed a subordinate position by feminist critics—it is only due to the codes of criticism which have evolved around feminism and film theory: silent woman equals subordinate woman. *The Female Patriot* does not proceed by a readily supplied set of codes, and encourages spectators to read the film in an uncodified way.

The fact that Gabi is described as a (female) patriot is, as Helke Sander has indicated, ironic. This is another point in her criticism of Kluge's representation of women. Sander writes, "the very term 'woman patriot' is already a joke. Realistically, a woman patriot doesn't even exist, because a patriot is really a male who does something for his country."[54]

Kluge does not, however, use this term as innocently as Sander suggests. It is used, rather, to present a role for a woman that lacks the codes and conventions that such a term holds for a man. Because of the "impossibility" of a woman taking up such a role, new definitions and connotations rise up within a term which is already highly coded. To pair such heavily loaded and differentiated terms as "woman" and "patriot" is to use a kind of montage—a new *Zusammenhang* that engages them in direct conflict to produce friction. When Gabi is assigned the role of patriot she is playing a part not usually played by a woman, she therefore has to invent the terms in which she is to play that role. In redefining a designated masculine word (*patriot*) in terms of a woman, Kluge does not attempt a simple subversion. He does not call her a "matriot," precisely because such a coined term would lack the heavily laden associations of the patriot. He adds the feminine suffix -*in* (*Patriotin*) so that the contradictions may arise *within* a single term, thus blasting apart and fragmenting its formerly coherent, non-contradictory and unquestioned status. Kluge uses *Die Patriotin*—the film, the character and the word—as sites within which to raise contradictions and pose questions.

The male-voiced narrator in *The Female Patriot* has also been criticised in terms of the "gender specific division of labour."[55] Kluge's own voice is heard providing fragmentary commentary—often illustrating (rather than explaining) the images with sometimes unacknowledged quotations, thoughts, or literal and ironic descriptions of events. Sander similarly subjects the voice-over narration of *The Female Patriot* to condemnation by the same logic. Sander explains that Gabi Teichert's role is "not defined by her, but for her by the voice-over commentary."[56] She compares the frequency with which this narrator is allowed to "express itself ... in extraordinarily long, uninterrupted passages" with Gabi, who "only rarely gets a chance to speak herself."[57] Such criticism, as Hansen has argued, "hinges, in part at least, on the dimension of authority and closure traditionally associated with voice-over narration, especially in its documentary usage."[58] Hansen goes on to point out how, in the case of *Germany in Autumn* (the film in which Kluge introduces the character of Gabi Teichert), the voice-over "consistently shifts its stance and mode of articulation, deconstructing itself as it goes along."[59] The implicit deconstruction of voice-over which occurs in *Germany in Autumn* becomes explicit in *The Female Patriot*. Helke Sander, in her criticism of the male-voiced narrator ironically uses the pronoun "itself" rather than "himself" to describe that narrator, for that narrator happens to be a knee. I say ironically because although Sander acknowledges Kluge's use of the knee she fails to recognise the implications of such an articulation.

And so I return to the title which interrupted my description of the earliest fragments of the film. This title reads "THE KNEE." Following this a male voice introduces itself as a knee, providing commentary accompanying the images. This knee is not just any knee, it is the knee of a particular corporal Wieland who, we are told, died at the battle of Stalingrad. The idea of the talking knee came, Kluge reports, from a discussion with the film's editor, Beate Mainka-Jellinghaus: "She said you need a metaphor of something that has to do with the body and with Stalingrad."[60] Kluge then thought of a poem by Christian Morgenstern, "*Ein Knie geht einsam um die Welt*" (A knee travels the world alone) and from there the idea found its way into the film.

The voice of the knee is male, in fact it is Kluge's own, but there the position of "male superiority" must end. Contrary to the various criticisms of the film's use of a male voice-over commentary—that it functions as a patriarchal, omnipresent force over the images and Gabi Teichert—the knee obstructs such a dominant, all-knowing perspective from the point of its introduction. As we are told, "It is a knee, nothing else." The knee believes it has a duty to speak. It has a right to. But it does not demand that we believe what it says or that what it says has any meaning. All that we must understand is that it is a knee which is speaking to us, and nothing more than that. In contrast to Kluge's use of voice-over commentary in his other films, the knee of *The Female Patriot* breaks down the authoritative position of traditional, disembodied narration. Hansen writes: "Separated from the body, a voice is more likely to resume functions of authority and closure proper to traditional documentary and narrative genres."[61] It is precisely in terms of the body that the talking knee is able to disrupt the effect of authority. The voice is, in a sense, re-embodied in the body of corporal Wieland but is explicitly only a fragment and thus may only express authority in terms of its fragmentary nature. Kaes has noted that the knee is "nothing more than a joint that makes movement possible." and that it functions as an allegory for montage, a point of "articulation."[62] It also must be seen from its own point of view: the point of

view of a knee is certainly not that of a grand perspective. The only
things over which it claims authority relate to itself. For example, it
tells us that it is a "German knee and is therefore interested in German
history." Furthermore, it is a dead knee (that is, the knee of a dead soldier) and it therefore speaks on behalf of the dead, but dead who are
not simply dead but "full of protest and energy." Late in the film—over
footage of Nazi soldiers marching stiff-legged in a parade—the knee
says: "knees are not supposed to walk like that, they're supposed to
bend and stretch." The figure of the knee also requires viewers to
maintain a certain flexibility. To accuse a knee of maintaining a position of patriarchal dominance is as ridiculous as the very thought of a
talking knee. The knee may have a male voice, but one cannot accuse
it of this, for it only wants to speak to us and to help us think through
the vast and multifarious text which is *The Female Patriot*. Like Gabi
Teichert, the knee both engages in and figures the film's mode of production. They are essential and integral figures in a film which calls
into question the very nature of the divisions of labour and modes of
production of film, and by extension those of society itself.

The New German Cinema is marked by a vast diversity of styles
and approaches. *The Marriage of Maria Braun* and *The Female Patriot*
are no exception. Their common ground is the attempt both films
make to redefine the nature of German filmmaking at the end of the
1970s. They both form a part of the move to invigorate a film culture
that had been subsumed by American industrial cinema from the
1950s onward. *The Marriage of Maria Braun* reflects this situation most
dramatically, as I have demonstrated, by taking melodrama to task.
Rather than simply reconstructing or resurrecting this genre, otherwise known as the "woman's film," Fassbinder deconstructs it via its
own vocabulary—through stylistic, technical and structural strategies
as well as through characterisation. *Maria Braun* masquerades as
melodrama, and despite the banality of her name (Braun is as common in German as Jones, Smith or Brown are in English), Maria Braun
is, in the history of film, a unique and powerful female figure.

Unique also is Gabi Teichert. She lies at the heart of *The Female Patriot* guiding the spectator through the sand and the scrap-heaps—the playgrounds of the film. Like Fassbinder, Alexander Kluge wishes to deconstruct the formulas of filmmaking that characterise the "cultivated entertainment and issue-oriented film." But Kluge takes this further and removes the codes and structures upon which narrative cinema is based. Kluge returns to the prehistory and early history of the cinema through the use of intertitles. But as a counterpart to this return he moves forward with the desire to invent a type of spectator-cinema in opposition to the auteur film. Gabi is our guide in territory as unfamiliar to her as it is to us. In this respect she figures the film's ideal spectator but at the same time she is also a figure of the film's own mode of production. Gabi's work is inevitably the work of the film itself.

Both Maria Braun and Gabi Teichert—like Roswitha—embody an enormous and powerful potential, a power, as Kluge might say, that really exists in film.

1   Commentary accompanying the opening image of Alexander Kluge's film *Occasional Work of a Female Slave* (New York: Zoetrope, 1977), 2.
2   Miriam Hansen, "Alexander Kluge, Cinema and the Public Sphere: The Construction Site of Counter History", *Discourse*, no. 4 (Winter 1981/82), 54.
3   (Cambridge, Massachusetts & London England: Harvard University Press, 1989).
4   Ibid., xi.
5   Boston: Twayne, 1983, and London: Oswald Wolff, 1980, respectively.
6   (London: BFI Publishing, 1989), 1–2.
7   Princeton: Princeton University Press, 1991, and London & New York, Verso, 1992, respectively.
8   Knight, 2.
9   Kaes, *From Hitler to Heimat*, 83.
10 Gilles Deleuze, *Cinema 2: The Time Image*, trans. Hugh Tomlinson and Robert Galeta (Minneapolis: University of Minnesota Press, 1989), 107.
11 Ibid., 107.
12 Ibid.
13 Ibid.
14 Throughout the film, Maria likes to assert control over her affairs. She does this both through action and language. At times she remarks to both Bill

and Oswald that she will never marry them because she loves Hermann. Maria at one point uses a technicality of language to explain her relationship to Oswald. She says; "And I don't want you to think 'you're having an affair with me.' The truth is, I'm having one with you." It may only be a technicality of language, but this speech indicates both the image Maria has of herself and posits the relationship she wishes to have to language. She insists on being the subject of both her relationships and her speech. In Hermann's absence, Bill and Oswald in turn become *her* man.

15 "Strong Emotions: An Interview with Scriptwriter Peter Märthesheimer," in *The Marriage of Maria Braun*, ed., Joyce Rheuban, (New Jersey: Rutgers University Press, 1986), 185.

16 R.W. Fassbinder, "Five Interviews with Fassbinder," Christian Braad Thomsen, in Tony Rayns, ed., *Fassbinder* (London: BFI, 1979), 89.

17 Thomas Elsaesser, "Tales of Sound and Fury: Observations on the Family Melodrama," in *Film Genre Reader*, ed. Barry Kieth Grant (Austin: University of Texas Press, 1986), 288.

18 Thomas Elsaesser writes of the characters of melodrama; "The characters are, so to speak, each others' sole referent; there is no world outside to be acted on, no reality that could be defined or assumed unambiguously." Ibid., 293.

19 Christine Gledhill (ed.), *Home is Where the Heart Is: Studies in Melodrama and the Woman's Film* (London: BFI Publishing,1987), 11.

20 Elsaesser, "Tales of Sound and Fury," 299.

21 Tom Noonan, Review of *The Marriage of Maria Braun* in *Film Quarterly*, vol. 33 no. 3 (Spring 1980).

22 Ibid.

23 Laura Mulvey, "Melodrama Inside and Outside the Home", *Visual and Other Pleasures* (Bloomington: Indiana University Press, 1981), 65.

24 Kaes, *From Hitler to Heimat*, 86.

25 Ibid., my emphasis.

26 "Notes on the Shooting Script," in *The Marriage of Maria Braun*, 180.

27 Fassbinder, "Five Interviews with Fassbinder," 93.

28 Deleuze, *Cinema 2*, 110.

29 Ibid., 101.

30 Ibid., 109.

31 Ibid., 114.

32 Stuart Liebman, "Why Kluge?" *October*, no. 46 (1988), 14.

33 Ibid.

34 Alexander Kluge, *Die Patriotin: Texte/Bilder*, 1–6, quoted in Theodore Fiedler, "Alexander Kluge, Mediating History and Consciousness," ed. Klaus Philips, *New West German Filmmakers: From Oberhausen Through the 1970s* (Frederick Ungar, 1984), 225.

35 Alexander Kluge, "On Film and the Public Sphere," *New German Critique*, no. 25/26, (Fall/Winter, 1981–1982), 211.

36 Hansen, "Alexander Kluge," 69.

37 Ibid.

38 Kluge, "On Film and the Public Sphere," 211.

39 Alexander Kluge, "Interview" with Stuart Liebman, *October*, no. 46 (Fall 1988), 55.

40 Liebman, "Why Kluge?" 11.

41 Hansen, "Alexander Kluge," 68 and 74 note 38.

42 Ibid., 66.

43 Quoted in Heide Schlüpmann, "'What is Different is Good': Women and Femininity in the Films of Alexander Kluge," *October*, no. 46 (Fall 1988), 130.

44 Helke Sander, "'You Can't Always Get What You Want:' The Films of Alexander Kluge," *New German Critique*, no. 49 (Winter, 1990), 65.

45 Ibid., 64.

46 (Surkamp Verlag, 1975). Translation my own. It should be noted that with this book Kluge directly links his concerns as a film-maker with his continuing work in Critical Theory. The book was written in the context of feminist criticisms of his film *Occasional Work of a Female Slave* (1973) with which it shares its name. Feminist film-makers and writers denounced it for its graphic depiction of abortion which, they claimed, hindered the fight of the women's movement in Germany against paragraph 218 of the Basic Law which outlawed abortion. Ironically, the book became a canonical text for reading and discussion in feminist groups.

47 Ibid., 223.

48 Ibid., 179–186.

49 Ibid., 185.

50 Ibid., 186.

51 Ibid., 185.

52 Ibid., 186.

53 Kluge, Interview with Liebman, 59.

54 Sander, " 'You Can't Always Get What You Want,' " 64–65.

55 Hansen, "Alexander Kluge," 66.

56 Sander, " 'You Can't Always Get What You Want,' " 64.

57 Ibid.

58 Hansen, "Alexander Kluge," 66–67.

59 Ibid., 67.

60 Kluge, Interview with Liebman, 52.

61 Miriam Hansen "Cooperative Auteur Cinema and Oppositional Public Sphere: Alexander Kluge's Contribution to *Germany in Autumn*," *New German Critique*, no. 24/25 (Fall/Winter 1981–82), 55.

62 Kaes, *From Hitler to Heimat*, 113.

Nicolas Roeg's
Bad Timing
Fabulising the Author Among the Ruins of Romance

Toni Ross

Introductory Fragments

At the time of its release in 1980 *Bad Timing/A Sensual Obsession*[1] gen-erated a flurry of controversy within the institutions of art cinema and film criticism. Responses to the film were sharply divergent. Some adjudged the portrayal of Milena Flaherty (Theresa Russell) and the imaging of her pain to be violently misogynist. Others praised the film for its surgical desecration of the gendered stereotypes and fairy-tale resolutions of Hollywood romance.[2] I remember the overwhelming pungency of *Bad Timing* most, of enduring a visceral, claustrophobic discomfort at Milena's suffering, especially at the hands of her lover/adversary Alex Linden (Art Garfunkel). Then, I wasn't alone in finding an ethics of sexual difference endorsed by late 70s feminist film theory of psychoanalytic and structuralist persuasion validated by the film. This study carries remnants of these initial feelings and heuristic allegiances, although their impact and credence have faded with time. My justification for returning to an art cinema "classic" of the early 80s, that for some of my colleagues looks rather *déclassé* these days, is an interest in the film's articulation of authorship. And because *Bad Timing* tells a tale of sensual love, heterosexual conflict and a failed suicide laced with feminine martyrdom, issues of authorship and artistic identity are largely operated by metaphors of sexual difference. Additionally, it is only now possible to acknowledge Roeg's film as generative for two later, more commercially successful films, similarly preoccupied with the elusive contours of "feminine" desire: these being *Thelma and Louise* (Ridley Scott) and *The Piano* (Jane Campion). The haunting of both films by *Bad Timing* is folded into the differential ways they tap the capacious gift of Harvey Keitel's screen repertoire. In *Bad Timing* Keitel plays Detective Netusil, a knotted figure of intransigent and beleaguered male authority.

While now a commonplace of film studies, invoking "the death of the author" often results in the exchange of one unifying category in the author for another, whether it be the spectator, history, interpretive community, discursive formations or institutional structures. Instead of taking the death of the author as read, I want to address how authorship and human agency are allegorised in *Bad Timing*. This doesn't mean, however, that the film will be treated as a biographical exposé of a life that exists before its representation. I'm more interested in how Roeg's self-configuration as an art cinema auteur is both invented and consolidated by *Bad Timing*. Aspects of this fabricated artistic identity have worked hand in glove with art cinema protocols of exhibition and criticism that normally frame Roeg's films.

Any allegorical articulation of authorship cannot be directly linked to authorial intention. The connotations of publicity and exhibition relayed by the etymology of allegory assume that allegorical narratives are destined for another, in the guise of a spectator, reader or in this case other directors. Moreover, the romantic affiliations of Roeg's films insist on criticism and interpretation as central components of their making, since the critic, whose desire is incited by enigmas intensified at every turn, is invited to an arduous process of decipherment.

This inquiry focuses on how a number of romantic propositions regarding authorship and criticism (reception) are adapted in *Bad Timing*, while accepting Stuart Cunningham's claim that the film bears the institutional and conventional impress of European art cinema.[3] Certainly, the director's stylisation in interviews and film reviews has tended to recycle a romantic cult of *sui generis* originality. Additionally, frequent allusions to *fin-de-siècle* Viennese painting, a serene art gallery setting and literary references ranging from Blake to Pinter, coupled with the overt painterly and colouristic traits of Roeg's idiom, make *Bad Timing*, on one level, a cliché of art cinema tastefulness and high art aspiration. Taking a slightly different path, I want to broach *Bad Timing* via an early German strand of romantic aesthetics, by registering both affinities and points of contrast between Roeg's practice and early romantic theory. This approach has been conditioned by the advent, in literary studies and deconstructive criticism particularly, of a renewed interest in the resilient, but largely unreflected, legacy of early German Romanticism within modern aesthetics and ethics.[4] A recently translated study by Philippe Lacoue-Labarthe and Jean-Luc Nancy, entitled *The Literary Absolute*, establishes the durability of early romantic ideas about art, the artist and criticism, despite art historical tendencies to confine romanticism to the early to mid 19th century.[5] Perhaps the most surprising disclosure of *The Literary Absolute* is that much of what has passed for innovation in postmodern art—self-reflexivity, pastiche, genre-mixing, "deconstruction," the permeation of art by philosophy and vice versa—retrieves some of the main lines of early romantic thinking.

There are a cluster of matters addressed by Lacoue-Labarthe and Nancy that are pertinent to *Bad Timing*, principally a romantic conception of art as both productive and critical that for early romantic theorists underwrote a quest to dialectically surpass classicism. If the regulative idea of classical art involved the reproduction of the rules and examples laid down by art of the past, then the romantico-modern artist was distinguished by *his* non-imitative inventiveness within this logic of undifferentiated repetition. This now familiar thinking of art in terms of difference and critique reveals a substantial debt to Kant's aesthetics, where the artist/genius is set apart by special qualities of autonomy, freedom and prodigious generosity. Other romantic topoi that resound in *Bad Timing* are a privileging of irony, the genre of the fragment and art works that mix heterogeneous and adversarial genres within a single work. Just because *Bad Timing* exposes the sublimated underbelly of an aesthetics of detached contemplation, good taste and beautiful form, this doesn't mean that the film wholly escapes the grip of Kantian and romantic aesthetics.[6]

In his astute early interpretation of *Bad Timing* Stuart Cunningham has observed that Roeg's signature is commonly identified with modernist evaluative categories.[7] Roeg's idiom has been prized for its extremes of stylistic artifice, an excess of signifiers over signifieds, and aberrant, unpredictable narrative economies,[8] hence the attraction of Roeg's films for film theorists mobilising modernist and art cinema standards to challenge the veristic claims of "realist" or "classical" narrative cinema. This approach informs two rare theoretical accounts of *Bad Timing* by David Silverman and Teresa de Lauretis. Both critics investigate the film's allusions to an alterity on the fringes of "classical" representation, not subsumed by meaning, recognition or identity. Silverman accents the brute physical presence of the filmic signifier and de Lauretis' feminist interpretation emphasises a "feminine" absence beyond the resources of positive representation. In both

cases it is the spectacularly feral character of Milena who emblematis-
es the film's exemplary "critique of representation."

Teresa de Lauretis' interpretation exhibits the impact of that amalgam of psychoanalytic, structuralist and poststructuralist theory that
underwrote the political avant-gardism of *Screen* during the 1970s.
Like Silverman, she views *Bad Timing* as a "deconstruction" of narrative and popular pleasures based upon semantic coherence and fixed
gender identities. Latterly David Bordwell has chastised de Lauretis for
mistaking the semantic ambiguities of *Bad Timing* for innovative singularity when this is typical of European art cinema.[9] While
Bordwell's reminder of the institutional matrix of Roeg's films is helpful, I'm more concerned with how de Lauretis sees sexual difference
articulated. She concentrates on the film's exposure of the tragic fate
of Woman within patriarchal representational structures, while drawing attention to Milena's transgression of these repressive frames.
Milena's "femininity" is allied to a non-exchangeable negativity that
exceeds the efforts of Alex and Netusil, and the power/knowledge
(Foucault) nexus they stand for, to hypostasise her irreducible difference. Drawing on the writings of Julia Kristeva and a rhetoric of sublimity, de Lauretis writes of an "unspoken" (unrepresentable) "femininity" that disturbs established codifications of narrative cinema and
gender.[10] While this grasp of Milena's role still seems just about right,
I want to focus on how Milena's sublimity is fashioned and the implications of her sublime status for the film's allegorisation of authorship.

As figures of "masculinity" and "femininity" in conflict Alex and
Milena enact a symbolic power struggle between two paradigms of
authorship. The first may be linked to art cinema auteurism, with the
filmmaker cast as a visionary prophet (an appellation bestowed on
Roeg with monotonous regularity), who stands outside the prevailing
norms of socio-cultural custom. The other coincides with an authorial
stylisation determined by the generic, which for modernist and anti-
Hollywood theories of cinema is encapsulated by the term "classical."
Because *Bad Timing* is internally divided between classical and roman-

tico-modernist aesthetics, the film allegorises a riven authorship, torn between the demands of the aesthetic category of the beautiful (conducive to feelings of harmonious pleasure) on the one hand, and the sublime (feelings of pain, terror and delayed satisfaction) on the other. In this respect *Bad Timing* restages debates that informed emerging aesthetic discourses of the late Eighteenth Century. As Frances Ferguson has argued, the philosophical reflections on aesthetics by Burke and Kant sought to rethink interactions between the epistemological categories of the particular and the general. This problem paralleled the moral question of how to configure relations between the individual and society.[11] According to Ferguson, and despite their differing accounts of the sublime, Burke and Kant associated the beautiful with the communal aspect of social conformity, whereas the sublime was linked to individuals marked by a "heroic distinction that sets them apart from social norms even as they participate in social enterprises."[12] While in *Bad Timing* the distinguishing traits of the beautiful and the sublime appropriate those of late eighteenth-century aesthetics, the metaphors of gender insinuated by both are inverted. Kant, of course, defined the beautiful as a feminine attribute while nominating the sublime as a distinctly masculine criterion.[13] But in *Bad Timing* the absoluteness, heroicism and inscrutability of the sublime is feminised while an investment in the beautiful is associated with male characters. This reversal taps a traditional modernist strategy where Woman figures as the allegorical ruin, rather than the binding symbol, of a Classical paradigm of representation.[14] In this way, a stable ontological link between art and the real, where artistic representation is thought to directly manifest the prior being of worldly things or ideas of the mind, is put into question.

Before addressing the specifics of *Bad Timing* a couple of general observations about Roeg's practice are called for. Roeg-signatured films are invariably situated within a tradition of European montage cinema. For Roeg, a film is principally an assemblage of parts brought together at the editing table.[15] This emphasis on the partitions of mon-

tage finds cinema defined as a creative art where the filmmaker actively choreographs the various elements of the medium. Moreover, this
interventionist image of the filmmaker has historically combined with
an ambition to produce films that jolt, shock and induce extremes of
spectator response. Hence the frenetic energy of the accelerated montage techniques in Roeg's films, prompting one reviewer to describe
those of *Bad Timing* as "gut wrenching and malicious."[16] Carrie Rickey
is no doubt recalling those scenes where the staccato cuts of the editing process beat in time with the violent pummelling and penetration
of Milena's prone body during efforts to revive her in a hospital emer-
gency room. This sequence culminates in an extreme close-up of a tra-
cheotomy incision at Milena's throat with a lurid display of sundered
flesh and flowing blood. While Roeg employs such horrifying
moments sparingly—in *Eureka* (1982) Jack McCann's murder-suicide
is similarly graphic and brutal—the visual rhetoric of these scenes is
reminiscent of that traced by Tom Gunning to an early silent "cinema
of attractions."[17] The effects specific to this cinema and its "aesthetic of
astonishment"—of shock, revulsion, direct audience address and the
close-up that appears to advance towards the viewer—resonate in *Bad
Timing* while simultaneously evoking the gory "realism" of the modern
horror film.

Although Gunning stresses the commercial orientation of the cinema of attractions, his analogy between that cinema and an earlier literary and philosophical tradition of the sublime bears on Roeg's self-
professed aims. By first enthralling, disturbing and astonishing film
audiences he desires to incite reflection upon the *modest* theme of "the
human lot."[18] When defining the sublime as a more respectable high
art version of the popular entertainments of silent cinema Gunning
cites Thomas Weiskel's account of the romantic sublime in literature.
Weiskel's striking portrayal of the reader who inhabits the inventories
of Longinus, "who is scorched, pierced, inundated, blown down, and
generally knocked about by the sublime,"[19] captures well the aggres-
sive spectatorial effects of Roeg's films and the bodily and psychic suf-

fering of their main characters. Weiskel also contends that while the history of the sublime has been discontinuous, the representation of a human relation to a transcendent or superhuman order remains a prime motivation within discourses of sublimity. The locus of transcendence may be, in combination or separately, Nature, a deity or deities, daemonic forces or, in Kantian idealism, Ideas of reason.[20] In the next section I shall extend my hypothesis that *Bad Timing* partakes of an aesthetics of the sublime and discuss how this alignment impinges on the film's allegorisation of authorship.

Bad Timing's Allegory of Divided Authorship

Despite the routine celebration of Nicolas Roeg's experiments with narrative form, a perfectly poised narrative symmetry frames *Bad Timing*. Ends are secreted in beginnings and a series of unveilings close the film. In this respect the expectations of a narrative investigating a suspected crime are more or less met. The narrative structure is organised along "classical" lines where the fate of the film's protagonists is known from the start. Hence the proleptic reference in the opening credits—set in a Vienna art gallery—to Milena's close encounter with death and the violent turn towards necrophilia that Alex's "love" for her will take. The 23rd shot of the credits comes into focus as a detail of a painting by Egon Schiele, entitled *Death Comes to the Maiden*. This painting, itself a romantic allegory of love and death, indirectly discloses later events. As an allusion to a future story action it also, according to David Bordwell's study of art cinema convention, comprises one way of signalling authorial intervention.[21] This is underlined by the registration of Roeg's name and directing role upon the fragment of Death's embrace of the maiden, which identifies the invisible agent ostensibly in command of the fate of the film's protagonists. In fact, it isn't unusual for Roeg's films to downplay the agency of their characters who are submitted to a disorganised but inexorable passage of events. For example, during the credits an "objective" camera which tracks around behind Alex and Milena, settling behind and observing them unseen, activates a non-diegetic undermining of their knowledge and agency in favour of the observing camera and the viewer.

Bad Timing allegorises two temporalities that are intercut so as to constantly threaten each other's integrity. I stress the allegorical representation of time because the whole film, with the crucial exception of the closing sequence, is made up of unexpected cuts into flash-forwards and flash-backs, that deny any direct access to a present moment, producing a temporal rhythm that contaminates past and future tenses. The retrospective temporality traverses a number of months during which a volatile love affair is played out to its bitter end. Here we witness Milena's early overtures to Alex, his initial reticence, followed by the consummation and gradual disintegration of their "romance." The second temporality covers a much shorter period: a matter of hours during which Milena is shown comatose from a drug overdose. These sequences focus on frantic efforts to save Milena's life which are juxtaposed with the police investigation of a suspected crime against her: "Ravishment" ("Article 205"): an ambiguous and, in this case, lethal combination of charm and predation. Inspector Netusil, played with grim stoicism by Keitel, suspects Alex of lying about the time Milena telephoned him for help and deliberately delaying the call for an ambulance. But even worse, he speculates that Alex fucked Milena while she was in a helpless, semi-conscious state. Two enigmas—whether Milena survives and if Alex is guilty of ravishment—are answered affirmatively, if ambiguously, in the final scenes.[22] But, despite his persistence Netusil fails to extract a confession from Alex who escapes prosecution.

The struggle between Alex and Netusil and their obvious mimetic entanglement has been extensively discussed by Stuart Cunningham, who argues that *Bad Timing* imposes a severe moral judgment upon "mimetic desire"—a triadic structuring of desire disguised as love, but animated more by hatred between the three parties of subject (Alex), object (Milena) and mediator (Netusil). Cunningham draws on René Girard's writings, where those grasped by mimetic desire manifest a fearful anxiety towards anomalous difference which may explode into scapegoating and murder. Writing of Alex's "undifferentiated and obsessive need to mediate Milena through the desires of others,"[23] Cunningham argues that Alex displays the potentially violent obsessiveness and paranoia that attend mimetic desire. While Cunningham's interpretation remains convincing, I want to shift attention from the mimetic rivalry of Alex and Netusil to the struggle for ascendancy between a classical model of mimetic behaviour and a romantico-modernist version played out between Alex and Milena. Cunningham only briefly registers the intercession of a performative alternative to a "masculine," Oedipal economy of mimetic desire, when he recognises Milena's pivotal role in its disruption.[24] If only in this respect he emulates the conclusions of Teresa de Lauretis and David Silverman who both align Alex and Netusil to the monologic narrative structures and reified sexual identities of "classical" narrative cinema. However, this fails to acknowledge an incipient mimetism folded within Milena's emblematisation of absolute difference.

Let us turn first to David Silverman's articulation of Milena's difference. Borrowing his terms of praise from structuralism and poststructuralism, he argues that Milena stands for a "playful" self-reflexivity and semantic indeterminacy that resists totalising regimes of interpretation. Yet Silverman's materialist reading of *Bad Timing* as a critique of the idealising schemes of romantic love perpetuates its own version of idealisation. In his account Milena acts as a repository and agent of excess. She personifies a brute, bodily materiality that "interrupts" the telos of interpretation, by occupying a (real) space beyond knowledge, aesthetic convention and analogy.[25] Silverman's reading of Milena as a salvational figure of freedom hints at why her performance has so captivated modernist criticism. Her "character" and the romantico-modernist paradigm of the film are interchangeable.

While Silverman ignores certain metaphysical dimensions of *Bad Timing*, to which I shall return, his stress on formal elements that trip up hermeneutic certainty confirms Roeg's penchant for proliferating loose ends which outrace the demands of plot or story. This proclivity for arbitrary fragmentation and infinitesimal detailing seems to isolate Roeg signatured films from classical axioms. As Naomi Schor has proposed, neo-classical aesthetics sought to sublimate the particular, the fragment and the detail in favour of an aesthetics of linearity, severity and the subsumption of the part by the whole.[26] While *Bad Timing* displays a decadent ornamental profusion, with elusive story strands and a saturated *mise-en-scène*, a feature of classical aesthetics remains in that this ornamental abundance is presented as coterminous with femininity. Milena with her repeated changes in costume, jewellery and personal adornment remains the most vivacious human medium of the extraneous detail. Silverman agrees:

> Unlike Garfunkel, whose gaze is always turned toward symbols and metaphors (the Klimt painting, the symbolic and erotic paintings and statues in his room), Russell displays a practice involved in signifiers without any immediate signified. At the art gallery shown in the opening scene, where Garfunkel is immersed in his Klimt scene of the man enveloping a woman, she is looking at another less retrievable painting. Her gaze can offer no resource to the narrative: her preferred painting plays no further part in the unwinding of the narration...Russell's gaze is mobile and active.[27]

Throughout the film, Milena's point of view, her sexuality and sensibility are certainly contoured according to a rhetoric of libertinism. She is free-spirited, active, initiating, differentiated and rule breaking. In short, she enacts an array of qualities commonly attributed to avant-garde art. Nevertheless, aspects of Silverman's evaluative assumptions beg questioning. First, we need to ask whether the attrib-

utes performed by Milena are so inaugurating, original or lawless?
Couldn't the various strands of her characterisation be said to retrace
a number of deeply sedimented axioms of romantic and modernist art?
Second, the opposition Silverman sets up between practices of "interpretation" represented by Alex, and a more exalted strategy of textual
"interruption," represented by Milena, collapses when Silverman's
interpretation succumbs to precisely those imaginary projections on
the critic's part that devices of "interruption" are supposed to resist.
His contention that Milena "displays a practice involved with signifiers
without any immediate signified" allows us to locate his projections
and also draws attention to the credits of *Bad Timing*, credits that I
shall be interpreting as a signatory device. In *Bad Timing* no clear
demarcation separates the textualisation of the film diegesis and the
framing credits.

Approximately thirty shots make up the opening sequence. The
first shot is a close-up of a painterly surface of textured ground and a
fragmented pattern, on which is superimposed "a Nicolas Roeg film."
Such opening inscriptions of the director's name are now common in
feature films but they are crucial to art cinema since they authenticate
the film as the product and property of an auteur. *Bad Timing* is therefore introduced as a fragment (of a larger story) and plastic work of art
(a painting). Later shots will confirm that the first detail operates
metonymically for a painting: *The Kiss* by the Austrian Symbolist
painter Gustav Klimt. Contrary to Silverman's mapping of the alternative directions of Alex's and Milena's gazes, *The Kiss* is metaphorically
linked to Milena rather than Alex. For example, during the credit
sequence Milena stands contemplating an unidentified painting, severed by the frame of the shot. But further into the sequence, the distinctive decorated frame of the painting, although still obscured, is
recognisably that of *The Kiss*. Additionally, when the opening
sequence with its gallery setting (retrospectively situated as a flash-for-
ward) is repeated later, Milena gestures to *The Kiss* and says to Alex:
"look at them, they look happy don't they?" Alex, ever the skeptic,

replies: "maybe they don't know each other well enough yet." Melina responds: "c'mon you don't really believe that do you?" Three shots later Milena strides past *Death Comes to the Maiden*, without giving it a glance. But, Alex who is following in her wake does catch sight of Schiele's painting and ironises Milena's earlier query, murmuring outside her hearing: "definitely happy. At least I hope so." At no point in the film is Alex shown gazing at *The Kiss* as Silverman claims. And if, according to Silverman, *The Kiss* represents an idealised fiction of romantic love, then Milena, more than Alex, is shown through words and actions to believe in its possibility.

Alex is, however, filmed from behind contemplating another Klimt painting entitled *Judith (and Holofernes)*. Here it is possible to glimpse between Alex's back and the frame of the shot the lower right portion of the painting where Judith grasps Holofernes' head like a trophy. Judith, who dominates the upper section of the picture and appears to hover over Alex, confronts him and us with a self-enclosed and silent expression on her face. Judith is pictured according to a repeated motif in Klimt's paintings—the enigmatic and menacing femme fatale. Also, memories of Judith as a biblical figure of female heroism—a castrating and vengeful woman—vibrate in the final sequence of *Bad Timing* where Alex is again frozen out of the picture by a woman's [Milena's] defiant silence.

By holding the focus on how Klimt's and Schiele's paintings operate we may extract certain attributes of artistic identity allegorised by *Bad Timing*. At times during the credits the only visible sign of Klimt's paintings are sections of their embossed golden frames. The registration of a frame within a frame or a frame internal to the shot comprises one of many instances of ironic reflexivity scattered throughout *Bad Timing*. With the insertion of this privileged romantic trope of "parabasis," the film confronts its audience with the framing mechanisms of its performance. In the process attention is drawn to the intercessions of the film medium and/or the director of the film, the inference being that we are to witness a pictured image of the world, not a natural emanation. But the significance of parabasis in romantic theory may go in at least two directions, even though in both cases the fact that early Romanticism made criticism or reflection an integral component of the "modern" work of art remains central. On the one hand, romantic irony facilitates art's central role in the formation of an ideal, ironic subject absolutely free, because (self)conscious of itself, its thoughts and actions.[28] This definition of irony informs subjectivist translations of Romanticism, which proffer an aesthetic solution to what Lacoue-Labarthe and Nancy nominate as the prime motive of speculative idealisms—"the auto-recognition of the Ideal as the subject's own form."[29] On the other hand, romantic irony insists upon the ineluctable constraint of formal or rhetorical structures of signification. In Samuel Weber's view these differential definitions of irony tell us that Romanticism is open to at least two divergent readings, one of which has been eclipsed by later subjectivist interpretations.[30] Weber asserts that the practice of reflexivity promoted by early romantic theorists, specifically Friedrich Schlegel, was not simply premised upon the actions or thoughts of a constitutive subject, whether an author or a reader. Instead reflection names a "pure thinking" ("a reflection of reflection") detached from any individual being or entity.[31] Absolute reflection does not belong to subjective consciousness but occurs within the individual work of art and its criticism. Hence Weber's claim, after Walter Benjamin: "What the absolute infinitude of art then involves is not the progressive realization of a self-identical ideal or entity, but the articulation of a medium understood to consist of a 'continuum of forms.' "[32]

Benjamin's term "formal irony" names both an objective moment in the work of art and the conditioning of authorship by formal limitation, rather than spontaneous intention. But "formal irony" is a more paradoxical concept than insistence on the author's finitude suggests. For Weber, it involves a structure both critical and productive, that seeks to break down any formal coherence immanent to the work of art without surrendering a commitment to the positivities of structure and form. For the moment I want to delay specifying the mode of irony that prevails in Bad Timing and return to the web of metaphorical and metonymic relations established between Alex, Milena, Roeg's signature and the paintings of Klimt and Schiele.

The parallel between Milena and *The Kiss* is doubled by the inscription of Roeg's signature upon the mosaic surface of this painting in the opening shot of the film. But Roeg's directing role is also registered upon *Death Comes to the Maiden* ensuring that his signature also cohabits with the expressionist paintings of Schiele. If Milena is identified with the Klimt paintings, and if, as I shall argue, Alex is associated with certain paintings by Schiele, then apparently the director's signature straddles both (feminine and masculine; erotic love and death; Symbolism and Expressionism), suggesting a divided, unstable enunciative position.

While Alex is never metaphorically related to Klimt's paintings, he is analogised with Schiele's works. The first link between Alex and *Death Comes to the Maiden* occurs, as noted earlier, in the second art gallery sequence. The second happens in a scene where Alex, while in conversation with Melina, is distractedly browsing through a book. Unbeknownst to Milena, he has hidden between the book's pages photographs of her Czech husband Stephan and her dead brother. As Alex shuffles through these photos an extreme close-up ensures that a reproduction of *Death Comes to the Maiden* in the book is brought to our attention. Alex is again linked to the art of Schiele in a scene where Netusil searches Milena's apartment. As the detective leafs through a stack of Schiele's nude self-portraits, one image is isolated from the others with a close-up that magnifies the gaunt legs of the artist. A subsequent cut into a flash-back reveals, again in close-up, Alex's naked legs pacing around Milena's apartment just prior to his act of ravishment.

The setting of *Bad Timing* in Vienna, and the many references to paintings of the Austrian Secession movement, generates multiple significations. Alex works as a research psychoanalyst at a local university and Freud makes a cameo appearance on his office wall. Vienna also conjures up the ghost of another "woman's film" about a love affair that ends tragically: Max Ophuls' *Letter from an Unknown Woman*. The allusions to Symbolist and Decadent art are significant in other ways. In art historical discourse Symbolism marks a fin-de-siècle shading of Romanticism into Modernism, and Decadence the triumph of ornamentation, the aggrandisement of the self-determined individual over and above social totality, and the sharp descent of established artistic and moral standards.[33] Symbolist doctrine stressed the imaginative fabrications of an artist-seer, and treated art and its timeless epiphanic images as a conduit to a transcendental spiritual realm. Despite the close historical ties between Symbolist and early Expressionist painting, the correspondences forged between Alex, the director, and Schiele's expressionist style, and the implied threat of all three to Milena's survival, make an unqualified attribution of an expressionist ethos to *Bad Timing* difficult to sustain. This is despite the fact that Roeg's emphatic, ravishing style is often defined in these terms. It seems more likely that an expressionist model of the creative subject, whose colonising will to create its own forms or identity disregards all forms or qualities specific to the object or medium of representation, is at least partially renounced in *Bad Timing*. But this renunciation is complicated. A better way of grasping its ambivalence would be to propose that while Alex may figure, *in extremis*, Roeg's desire to impose and arbitrate his artistic identity through his work, Milena allegorises the repeated frustration of this desire.

The appending of Roeg's signature to a detail of *The Kiss* also amplifies the mosaic structure of Klimt's paintings where human figures are besieged by richly coloured, ornamental details. A number of critics have found affinities between Roeg's idiom and the mosaic medium where the *tesserae* are likened to the segmentations of montage. Roeg has also employed the mosaic metaphorically when reflecting upon his films: "One always wants to make another film just to get it better. But like the Islamic mosaic, there's always a little tile to one

side, or crooked. It's an offence against Allah to make it absolutely perfect. Only God is perfect."[34] This statement suggests two commit-
ments. First, Roeg phrases that synecdochal relation between the particular (little tile) and the infinite or Absolute (Allah) introduced by
early Romantic theorists as a distinguishing trait of modern art. If I
may again cite Naomi Schor, this concern with the detail demarcates
romanticism from neo-classical aesthetics, which sought to expel the
fragment in favour of the symmetry and coherence of a larger spiritual
or social totality.[35] Alternatively, romantic theorists set out to incor-
porate rather than excise the profane detail, to desublimate certain
negative connotations—"the everyday, naturalism, prosiness, small-
ness, insignificance and the feminine"—yoked to the part object within neo-classical aesthetics.[36] Romantic art was articulated in dialectical terms—alternatively questing after totality and the infinite, but
just as strongly drawn towards fragmentation and divisiveness. The
individuality of the fragment, divided between itself and a larger totality, not only stood for the individual's relation to democratic political
structures, but also represented an ethical model of human existence
as provisional and partial. Truth and self-knowledge were not already
given but were to be endlessly pursued through fragmentation and
disjunction. Hence the romantic formulation of a subject incessantly
striving for an impossible completion or perfectibility. The second
salient feature of Roeg's portrayal of his practice relates to a prohibition imposed upon the filmmaker by an unapproachable God who pro-
scribes graven images.

Roeg's hints at his aesthetic and theological alignments bring us
nearer to *Bad Timing's* sublime economy. As many have argued, the
negative theologies of Hebraic and Islamic iconoclasm depend upon
notions of the sublime. In them God is revered as a radical and transcendental Otherness beyond the resources of positive representation.
The sublime deity of negative theology can only be presented negatively (what it is not) in a way that exposes the failure of phenomenal
images or empirical objects to emulate its incomparable greatness.

This ban on image making arguably stems from an ancient fear of and insight into artistic mimesis, which stands accused of inventing differential, false and diversionary surrogates for God's true being. In the *Critique of Judgment* Kant draws an analogy between the stricture on graven images in Jewish Law and those objects in nature that generate feelings of the sublime.[37] For Kant it is those vast, chaotic and fearful natural phenomena which, because of their immensity or power, produce paradoxical feelings of unpleasure alloyed with pleasure. This preliminary constriction of pleasure distinguishes the sublime from the harmonious and congenial pleasures of the beautiful. Kant argued that sublime objects of nature blocked the efforts of the imagination to translate their formless or boundless qualities into finite concepts and images. Nevertheless, the initially painful inadequacy of the mind results in more powerful, because delayed, feelings of pleasure. Precisely because sensible representations fail to approximate the infinite we are able to gain an intimation, if only negatively, of the existence and incomparable greatness of the suprasensible realm. The sublime object acts then as that catalyst through which the subject is assured of the ability of concepts of Reason—unrepresentable Ideas of totality—to transcend, tame and objectify the natural world. In this way, humanity's god-like capacity to "judge nature without fear" and "to think of our vocation as being sublimely above nature" is affirmed.[38] Kant's sublime proclaims the end of an aesthetics of the beautiful—where feeling issues from the harmonious overlapping of mind and nature—by sacrificing the presentative, formalising powers of the imagination, for the mind's higher vocation in moral law and freedom.

In *Bad Timing* the graven image is presented as a violent fixity of representation or naming which provokes allergic reactions throughout, especially from Milena. In this way the film prolongs a still prevalent romantic dictum that censures any attempt to represent, type or classify the individual as a form of violent oppression. Roeg articulates this sentiment to his biographer Joseph Lanza when he says: "I realise you're probably going to murder me by assembling my life and career into some kind of neat little order."[39]

One instance of Milena's aversion to and demolition of the stereotype occurs with a moment of wicked humour. Alex and Melina are holidaying in Morocco in the hope of salvaging their sinking romance. Not surprisingly, overt references to film and literary romance increase dramatically during these scenes.[40] Morocco also serves as the site of one of romance's most durable motifs: the secluded and protected bower, safely outside the conflicts of the city, society and culture.[41] In a Moroccan hotel room the fated couple are unusually in tune as Alex begins to recount a memory from his past life in New York. He speaks nostalgically of an old mansion near where he lived which made him feel "good" just knowing that something so "beautiful" was close by. Recalling that for a number of years there were other turn of the century buildings in the area, he had mournfully rued their demolition and gradual replacement by "monstrosities," until only one building was left. This old mansion became a guiding symbol of permanence and beauty for Alex until he went away one Friday and on his return he found that the building had been pulled down.

Alex's autobiographical anecdote affirms certain character traits already cued in the film. His dress and comportment signify a monochromatic severity (tweedy suits and ties), while his mannerisms suggest intellectual asceticism and sobriety. Additionally, the fragment of Alex's life story exposes his amorous attachment to tradition and an aesthetics of measure, clarity and beautiful form. A feminist study by Maria Laplace of selected conventions of romance and melodrama employed in the Hollywood "woman's film" of the 1940s provides a clue to the generic significance of Alex's anecdote. Laplace informs us that in the "woman's film," which Roeg mines repeatedly in *Bad Timing*, relations between the sexes were based on intimate confessions and a sharing of emotions and life stories.[42] The confiding tone and personal content of Alex's story adopts this etiquette. But with a brutal, prosaic intervention Milena completely breaks the mood and erupts through the mutuality and intimacy of romance's dialogue of equality. In typically active fashion, she slaps away an insect, sprays it with repellant, and then sneezes convulsively as though allergic to everything Alex has just vocalised. In this way she prefigures her refusal, a short time later, to accept Alex's plans for marriage. Rather than performing its generic function of drawing the romantic couple together, the hiatus in Morocco further devastates a romance marred by conflicting interests and sensibilities that seem irresolvable.

What are the details of these discordant sensibilities, and how are they composed? If *Bad Timing* inverts and fractures lapidary forms of gender and genre, then on another level, certain traditional constructions of "masculinity" and "femininity" remain intact. Alex represents knowledge and mind, and Milena represents, for the most part, nature, intuition and the senses. In other words she enacts a bodily, affective register that is opposed to knowledge or understanding. However, her proximate relation to a natural, experiential realm is complicated somewhat by her association with an ideal of romance and the decorative confections of Klimt's paintings. Alex's personification of mind, his investment in the authority of preordained rules, place him on the side of a classical model of art and a rationalist model of knowledge, whereas Milena evokes an infinite order of Nature that thwarts all of Alex's efforts to represent, name and control its true being. This is underscored by Netusil's remark to Alex late in the film: "we are not unalike. People who live in this disorder [Milena]—they envy our strength, our capacity to fight, our will to master reality— they drag us into their confusion, their chaos."

The meticulous enhancement of Milena's esoteric qualities contributes markedly to her sublimity. To Alex's chagrin, he cannot constrain her restless, multi-faceted character within the limits of generic and gendered categories. In the process she exposes a potential for violence in others [Alex, Netusil and by implication the critic] when the desire for certainty that animates the imposition of the stereotype is blocked by someone or something that doesn't satisfy expectations. Alex represents—in line with a classical mimeticism pledged to the continuity of tradition and pure forms—the imposition of normative categories incompatible with the unpredictable heterogeneity of the modern work of art. And in this instance the modern work is inter-changeable with the "new woman." While the analogical relation between Milena and the modern work of art (or artist) may never be explicitly stated it is repeatedly imposed metaphorically. Furthermore, the historical moment of the film's making (at the end of a decade of feminism's revival) ensured a far from untimely convergence of its romantico-modernist ethos and the liberationist rhetoric mobilised by sectors of the women's movement.

Melina displays an absence of coherent and stable identity. She oscillates between extremes: from immaculate grooming to excessive dishevelment, from drunken inarticulateness to magniloquence. Exceeding every attempt by Alex to halt her proliferating differences, she informs him at one point that the more rules she makes for herself the less she is able to stick by them. In short, Milena constitutes a defective and, for Alex, monstrous anomaly—a *rogue* of sorts.

Milena's performance of negative but luxuriant excess finds echoes in Neil Hertz's study of the eighteenth-century literary sublime, where the sublime functions as a "blockage" disruptive of the mind's ability to synthesise objects and processes of chaotic, infinitely vast or power-ful dimensions. Hertz observes that a conventional figure of untotalis-able chaos or the "raw heterogeneity" of the world or of nature is "Woman." Specifically, a woman who, because she is dispersed "all over the place," brings interpretation up against its limits.[43] The wild-ness of this feminine figure resonates in Milena's performance of inconsistent extremes. Hertz goes on to argue that such instances of sublime personification may actually serve the desires of both author and critic. He proposes that Kant's category of the mathematical sub-lime (incalculable quantity) may bear on the motives of critics drawn to impose theoretical models. The sublime personification may fulfil:

the scholar's *wish* ... for the moment of blockage, when an indefinite and disarrayed sequence is resolved (at whatever sacrifice) into a one-to-one confrontation, when numerical excess can be converted into that supererogatory identification with the blocking agent that is the guarantor of the self's own integrity as an agent.[44]

Hertz also suggests that "supererogatory" identification may similarly motivate the author who utilises fictional agents of sublime obstruction in order to assimilate the source of their authority: an untotalisable self-identity and a self-contained "fixed relation" to themselves.[45] The enviable power and freedom of sublime agents is demonstrated by their repulsion of all metaphorical and conceptual substitutions for their true being. This suggests in turn that such figures, because they are imagined to exist as verifiable or "real" entities outside of representation, take up a position of power over processes of representation. This assumption also underlies those interpretations of *Bad Timing* that have praised the film simply in terms of its critique of representation.

I want to propose that from Milena's figuration we may infer certain identifications, or better, mimetic assimilations to otherness on Roeg's part. Kaja Silverman approaches the films of art cinema auteur Liliana Cavani similarly, when she singles out an array of film characters as "anthropomorphic" allegories of the filmmaker's desire, represented by human semblances that do not resemble, in any obvious way, the sexual or physical identity of the director.[46] In fact, Nicolas Roeg has hinted that both Alex and Milena could be understood as figures of self or autobiographical presentation.[47] Moreover, his cryptic remarks about the precise locus of his mimetic entanglements, divided between Alex and Milena, duplicate that unstable enunciative structure that I earlier linked to the splitting of the director's signature between *The Kiss* and *Death Comes to the Maiden*. While a number of contemporary accounts of *Bad Timing* argued for Roeg's complicity

with Alex and Netusil and subsequently dismissed the film as misogynist, I want to focus upon Milena as the privileged medium of the
director's self-presentation since she conforms to a romantic motif of
the artist, and so resolves, if only momentarily, the paradox of the
director's speaking position.

Take for example the final skirmish between Alex and Milena
which precipitates her overdose and his act of ravishment. Here
Milena bitterly and definitively repulses Alex's desire to control her
image and identity according to his own interests, which for her stem
from his "greed." In an effort to preserve herself from any determination by Alex she forcefully proclaims:

> I'm not an artist, poet or philosopher. I'm not a fucking revolu-
> tionary. I don't want to be yours or anyone's. You have every-
> thing, you know everything you greedy bastard. I don't want
> to pretend to be anybody. I just want to be allowed to give
> where I can.

Milena's poignant effort to exempt herself from all that may be
taken hold of, named and objectified, is articulated in terms of the
indeterminacy and inscrutability that distinguishes the deity of negative theology. Consequently, the first part of her speech about who she
is occasions only a negative presentation of what she is not: "I'm not
an artist, poet or philosopher. I'm not a fucking revolutionary." But
her negative enunciation of identity is profoundly ironic, for rather
than evading the metaphors of artist, poet, philosopher and revolutionary, Milena has repeatedly performed as though she were that
complex of vocations from which she so forcefully sets herself apart. It
is precisely this vocational ensemble that makes up the figure of the
romantic artist, described in *The Literary Absolute* as that "invasive and
tenacious" motif which in romantic theory stands for the subject in
general.[48] Milena therefore enacts the paradoxical logic of Roeg's
attempt to invoke an alterity beyond or before available representa-

tions which can only be registered through representation.

For Friedrich Schlegel the modern artist occupied a pivotal and elite position as "mediator" and "educator" of humanity. But the artist as pedagogue was not called upon to actually teach correct criteria or moral behaviour. Rather, because the artist's greatness stemmed from an aptitude for exceeding available rules or models, *his* exemplary singularity derived from qualities of freedom, autonomy, spontaneity and abundant generosity. Hence Schlegel's assertion that the artist should find *his* vocation only in "cultivation"—a liberal and benevolent production that abrogated any desire to "rule or serve" others.[49] The exemplarity of the romantic artist, that which makes the artist worthy of imitation by others, is therefore founded on a self-originating productivity or non-imitativeness. This thinking of mimesis and subject formation as a process of auto-constitution in turn appropriates Kant's concept of genius.[50]

The single positive component of Milena's declaration of negative identity, her desire to only give where she can, invokes a pure, "disinterested" and unilateral giving that echoes the liberality of the romantic artist endorsed by Friedrich Schlegel. Milena's moral censuring of Alex's greed also targets, by inference, capitalist economic principles of exchange value and utility (Netusil is an anagram of utensil). If we adopt Kantian terms, Alex and Netusil belong to a "mercenary" category of art or a constrained mode of scientific thinking which is rule governed and exchangeable for money or some other sign substitute. Melina, on the other hand, belongs to a *natural* economy of excessive, boundless energy: a sublime economy organised by the fact that she herself is incomparable—beyond price or any other form of metaphorical substitution.

The educating privileges enjoyed by the artist in romantic doctrine derive from a singular ability to hold *his* identity within himself. The artist acts as mediator because whoever lacks a self-contained identity is compelled to select and "passively" imitate another model from elsewhere, whereas the romantic artist [Milena] doesn't "pretend" to be anyone.[51] She produces her unique identity from within. The artist as genius holds out the possibility of a future perfect humanity forecast by an educator who does not teach or imitate (as Alex does) but who serves as a myth of autonomy in which others may find themselves. But despite the effort to differentiate the freedom of the artist/genius from the limits of a classical model, imitation and exchange return with the traditional function of exemplarity. If the artist's singular nature is itself proffered for identification and appropriation, then the ideal of genius derives from an ethical imperative to be original and self-producing, that is acquired through mimetic identification with another.

For romantic theorists Woman occupied a special place within the aesthetic education of humankind. Why the education of women and the question of the feminine was included in the pedagogical program of early romanticism is linked by Lacoue-Labarthe and Nancy to a fundamental romantic aspiration—the formation of a perfected humanity or "total man." But this striving for an ideal, completed humanity was also compelled to acknowledge the sexual divisions of society.[52] The inclusion of woman in the "cultural revolution" proclaimed by romantic theorists was narrated as a romance of future reconciliation that would overcome all differences and divisions between the sexes.

Romantic theory, following Kant, metaphorised the differences between the sexes as distinct faculties or "suitabilities."[53] The imaginative faculty, which remained in touch with nature despite its generative superiority, was given a feminine profile, while reason, which surpassed sensuous experience, was figured as masculine. Hence Kant's linkage between the beautiful and femininity on the one hand and the sublime with masculinity on the other. Although it was claimed that woman exhibited a "natural" proclivity for "religion" (a sense of divine Truth) this nascent potential could only be fully developed with her initiation by man (source of ideas and hence the synthesising power) into philosophy. This assumed, in turn, that Woman, who was distinguished by her greater proximity to a phenomenal world of appearances, was responsible for satisfying man's need for art. Because of these distinct gendered tendencies a "total man" or completed humanity and a successful religion of art could only be achieved with a reciprocal exchange between the sexes and the fusion of their differential *natures*.[54] If the aesthetic education of humanity was to succeed, the differences between the sexes needed to be reduced with romantic motifs of a "gentle" masculinity and an "autonomous" femininity that would facilitate an erotic inter-penetration of art (woman) and philosophy (man).[55] For Friedrich Schlegel, the *symbol* was the most effective rhetorical vehicle of spousal union between feminine and masculine suitabilities. In the symbol "the appearance of the finite [woman] is placed in relation with the truth of the eternal [man] and, in this manner, precisely dissolved therein."[56] The reconciling power of the symbol doubled that of the romantic artist who was religious, in the specifically romantic sense, because in *him* multiple genres, including poetry and philosophy, woman and man, art and idea were fused together as one.[57] Thus did the symbol come to prevail in romantic aesthetics, despite a parallel and contradictory retrieval of the allegorical fragment and the prosaic breach it imposed between artistic medium and spiritual ideal.

In the concluding moments of *Bad Timing* Milena, having previously served as an allegorical emblem of fragmentation and dispersion, assumes a symbolic function. As a metaphor taken to directly incarnate the Idea, the symbol poses as an individuality foreign to all others and unique in itself. Additionally, the strongest, most persuasive symbols fuse heterogeneous elements into a single organic ensemble. Melina's ascension to symbolic status occurs in the epilogue of *Bad Timing*: a morally charged address to the spectator preceded by news of her recovery and Netusil's failure to draw a confession from Alex.

With a dramatic shift in locale we are transported far away from Vienna to the Waldorf Astoria in New York. Alex has left the hotel and hails a cab from which a barely recognisable Milena emerges. She doesn't notice Alex as she moves towards the hotel entrance with a group of female companions. Alex recognises her and calls her name. She turns towards him, but her expression freezes as she refuses to return his call or utter a single sound. The operation of eye-line matches and point-of-view in these shots is unusual. First, a cut is inserted on Alex's call and look towards Milena which we might expect to yield a reaction shot of Milena's face. But instead Alex's point-of-view is initially magnetised by a livid scar at Milena's throat (that fills the screen), followed by a vertical passage upwards to Milena's face in search of her response. Second, the delayed reaction shot of Milena's face makes a conventional reverse shot or eye-line match untenable since although we may infer that Alex is the object of Milena's accusing and defiant look, she actually stares into the lens of the camera, out towards the non-diegetic space of the spectator. The close-up that frames Milena's face at this moment is so powerful that despite an immobilising speechlessness her silence still speaks volumes.

The cinematic close-up as a human face, when marked by sharply contoured outlines and a powerful sense of isolation, fulfils that pole of the face's film repertoire that Gilles Deleuze links to its function as a "reflecting immobile unity."[58] "Faceification" is the name Deleuze gives to this kind of close-up, which, like its restless and highly mobile polarity in "faceicity," retains historical ties with portrait painting. Faceification occurs when the face is depicted with coherent outlines and sharply drawn features. Both the strong natural lighting and the unadorned plainness of Milena's face in the concluding close-up suggest faceification. This portrayal operates in stark contrast to the shadowed inaccessibility of Milena's face in the opening credits and the multiple transformations of faceicity that seize her features during much of the film. The narrative passage from dark to light, from mobility to stasis, thus inferred, marks a transition from a partial or obstructed view to a glaring transparency.

The advantage of Deleuze's account of the cinematic close-up is that it comes from Béla Balázs and as such has little obvious allegiance with the psychoanalytic treatment of it in terms of castration: that is, a part cut adrift from a larger network of objects, images or actions. Instead the close-up may bring an entity forward, isolating it from all spatio/temporal relations and anointing it with a certain indivisible singularity, as a totality in its own right.[59] For Deleuze, faceification involves the imaging of a thought that takes over the face and transforms it into a surface of reflection. This reflective function operates as long as the variegated details of the face are ruled by a stable, immutable thought that may be "wonderful" or "terrible" but which halts all movement. The stasis of faceification implies an absence of process or temporality that eternalises the thought or pure quality reflected. In such cases the face becomes "phosphorescent, scintillating, brilliant," "a being of light," regaining a resoluteness and unity of outline that invokes the realm of the mind or spirit.[60] By thus obliterating all division and particularity, faceification marks a passage towards the metaphysical and the transcendental. We may recognise something of how faceification operates in critics' responses to the monumental and awe-inspiring architecture of Greta Garbo's face in close-up. As Roland Barthes proposed, the mesmerising power of Garbo's face derives from the sense that her image is inhabited by a spiritual perfection that transcends the limits of situation, character and even sex.[61] When the face acts as a medium of an idea or ideal it loses all specificity, whether that of an individual character or as one part of a determinate set of relations.

Deleuze suggests that faceification may personify a potential quality, thought or proposition which is not yet actualised. He also relates faceification to a type of image classified by C.S. Peirce as "Firstness." Peirce claims that this image category is not easily described since "it is felt, rather than conceived: it concerns what is new in experience, what is fresh, fleeting and nevertheless eternal."[62] Deleuze, therefore, links firstness to the recurrent and historically generated innovation of works of art.[63] These linkages between faceification, firstness, and the virtuality of "new" ideas of art are implicitly assumed by Stuart Cunningham and Teresa de Lauretis who argue that Milena's difference, which I first read in that heroic register prefigured by the early reference to Klimt's *Judith*, gestures to something radically anterior, beyond the laws of an existing order (of "mimetic" desire, of Hollywood romance, of gender-based exclusions). I am suggesting that the concluding close-up of Milena's face and her profound silence allegorise an idea of art that at the film's end remains unspoken, but not necessarily ineffable. Samuel Weber's analysis of a similar moment of potentiality, relayed by the hero's refusal to speak at the conclusion of Greek tragedy, offers one way of interpreting Milena's charged silence.

Through the prism of Walter Benjamin's studies of literature and modernity, Weber has interpreted Greek tragedy, and its reflection on the question of free will, as a founding myth of origin adopted within Christian monotheistic and humanist discourse. Paradoxically, Greek tragedy is here mobilised as a way of supplanting an ancient Greek view of existence governed by the polytheism and chaotic ambivalence of myth. Weber, after Benjamin, interprets tragedy as a mode where a pagan ethos of acquiescence to fate is refuted by the concluding defiance, through silence and death, of the tragic hero.[64]

While *Bad Timing* initially shapes up as a romance the overwrought agonistics dramatised, involving calamity, pathos, crime and punishment, owe more to the pity and terror of tragedy. Here the optimism and beauty of romance is taken over by the pessimism of the tragic myth where, as Friedrich Nietzsche has phrased it, a "craving for the ugly" drawn to an "image of everything underlying existence that is frightful, evil, a riddle, destructive, fatal," prevails.[65]

Although Milena is a tragic *heroine*, at the film's end all signs of femininity and particularity have been dispensed with. Despite many erotic scenes involving Alex and Milena, notions of nakedness and unveiling are most powerfully articulated by the concluding close-up of Milena's face. All ornamental details, including her long blonde hair, have been sheared away. The visual distraction of minutely observed and repeatedly changed costume details which had overtaken and obscured Milena's person have dropped out of sight. If allegorical or rhetorical devices are commonly metaphorised as the frame, ornament or garb of truth, then during these moments any remnants of allegory are discharged, leaving Milena facing us fully exposed. We are left with the fully determined contours of a human face that reflects qualities of defiance, resilience and autonomy. These qualities are fleshed out with the final image of a flowing river where Milena is definitively brought back to an idea of Nature constituted as plenum.[66]

In his discussion of tragic drama Weber draws attention to the dialectical structure of the tragic finale where the ambivalence, incomprehension and powerlessness of the hero is transcended by an act of self-sacrifice. According to Weber, this sacrificial gesture proclaims a new communal foundation and a new world order.[67] The hero's prophetic speech act issues from a refusal to speak the laws of a world that he no longer accepts. The new order thus prophesied is premised on the resistance of an individual to a particular set of circumstances, that stands for the common destiny of an entire people: a people whose origins issue from a "stubborn silence" that bespeaks the "icy solitude" of individual psychology.[68] Weber subsequently claims:

> Tragedy is thus, first of all, a question of a hero whose silence is prophetic, and whose demise announces the triumph of the self: not so much as an individual, but rather in general: as Man and God, and as a People that embodies both in its Community.[69]

The tragic sacrifice therefore inaugurates a founding principle of humanistic thinking: an ideal of a free and self-determining people.

Nevertheless *Bad Timing* deviates from certain aspects of tragic closure singled out by Weber. While cast as prophetically silent, the tragic heroine survives, despite the shadow of mortality cast upon her existence from the opening credits. Milena transcends the negativity of death and so evades the fatefulness that distinguishes tragedy from romance or comedy. Milena is a genuinely romantic character "animated with its own life" who breaks loose from the directives of the author inscribed in the opening credits upon *Death Comes to the Maiden*.[70] I want to acknowledge at this point that Roeg resists converting a prior celebration of Milena's "feminine" difference into a subtle misogyny that would dignify her sacrificial obliteration. In this respect *Bad Timing* rejects the predictable narrative and ethical resolutions offered by *Thelma and Louise*: a film which may be viewed as a revisionist sequel to *Bad Timing's* "feminist" fable.

Generically speaking, *Bad Timing* begins as a romance and concludes in a tragic register. But an added twist accompanies the turn to tragedy in that we are treated to an ironic reversal of one of the laws of the tragic myth. The significance of this inversion may be linked to Walter Benjamin's account of the transmutation of the finishing stroke of the tragic hero's death into the arrival of a pedagogical exemplar: a self-conscious ironising of tragedy's silent finale represented by the dialogues and figure of Socrates. Weber, citing Benjamin, writes:

> The silent prophecy of the self implies an echo that it, as self, cannot supply, and it is the function of Socratic irony to make that echo audible and meaningful. With the raising of this self-consciously ironic voice, death loses the definitiveness that constitutes its specificity in tragedy. In place of the sacrificial death of the hero, Socrates provides the example of the pedagogue.[71]

With the intercession of irony the tragic heroine of *Bad Timing*, whose exemplarity is signaled by her concluding isolation and compelling look of refusal, becomes profoundly pedagogical. Recalling the earlier focus on Milena's status as a figure of sublimity, we could also affirm that the tragic heroine, in this case, is configured as a romantico-modernist subject. Hence the acuity of Walter Benjamin's initially obscure statement: "The paradox of the birth of genius in moral speechlessness, moral infantility, [of the hero] constitutes the sublime in tragedy."[72] Benjamin's insight confirms more recent reflections on the significance of the sublime within modernism by Lacoue-Labarthe who has written that in the context of romantic aesthetics:

> The sublime is probably ... the generalization to the whole of [modern] art of the Greek (Aristotelian) conception of tragedy. This is grounded in a schema of contradiction and in a logic one could qualify as oxymoronic. I refer to the double tragic stage, or the division of the tragic stage into stage and "orchestra" (two irreconcilable spaces), and also to the tragic conflict, the contradiction which inhabits the tragic hero (the oxymoron par excellence being that of Oedipus, both guilty and innocent), and thirdly to the double tragic effect—itself contradictory—of pity and terror, to use Aristotle's terms, i.e. of pleasure and unpleasure. Finally I refer to the properly modern idea that in the tragic there occurs for the first time (and I'll use Lyotard's formulation) the "presentation" that there is (the) "unpresentable." This is what Hölderlin was trying to get at when he said that God is present in tragedy in the figure of death.[73]

This acute précis provides a key to certain implications for authorship inferred by *Bad Timing's* sublime economy and the oxymoronic logic of life and death, suicide and murder, activity and passivity, masculinity and femininity reconciled within Milena as symbol. Roeg's recourse to suicide as a central motif in *Performance, Walkabout, Don't Look Now, The Man Who Fell to Earth, Bad Timing,* and *Eureka* also emulates an early romantic preoccupation with suicide which was considered an exemplary speculative and artistic act.[74] Lacoue-Labarthe has proposed that the romantic motif of suicide is also inhabited by a logic of contradiction where mortality is transcended while a

self is founded who displays its liberty with a willed loss of freedom.[75]
Bad Timing concludes with a presentient silence that promises a "new"
language of art (prefigured by the film), the ascendancy of the subject
as genius and a regulative idea of art different from generic classicism.
This break up of generic purity is imposed by an ironic reflection upon
romance and tragedy that works alongside a heterogeneous mixing of
literary, painterly and filmic genres and categories. However, Milena
emerges as a new principle of identity from this preceding chaos and
confusion. In this way the culturally sanctioned status of the artist as
a privileged and exemplary subject is both ensured and offered for
appropriation.

While the desired symmetry of spousal union between the romantic couple never takes place, the abyss between Alex and Milena and
the different values they allegorise is resolved within Milena herself.
She is finally represented as a singular, isolated, and tragic self who
unlike others manages to combine and contain all differences within
herself. *Bad Timing* therefore adopts a subjectivist, speculative version
of romantic irony that views the work of art as an index of authorial
agency without limits.

This stylisation of the artist is based on a binary division between
two interpretations of art, available since the Nineteenth Century. On
one side is the artist-innovator who strives to produce an absolutely
novel language of art thereby claiming a central pedagogical role in
the formation of a new world. Rather than being cast as a craftsman
imitator of tradition, the fine artist prophesies an ideal society founded
on an aesthetic model of originality.[76] On the other side the artist
assumes a traditional alliance between art and craft and is determined
as a technician and fabricator of works who is trained through
demonstration and imitation rather than exemplary learning. These
two paradigms of the artist are assumed by auteurist criticism when it
distinguishes between the innovative, originary products of the auteur
and the technically inclined professionalism of the *metteur-en-scène*.
While *Bad Timing* narrates a struggle between these two paradigms of

artistic vocation, it appears that the former prevails with Milena's symbolisation as demiurge.

But this isn't the end of the story. There is a catch, or more precisely a cut, still to be addressed. I'm referring to a hesitation that acknowledges the impossible position of the film director fictioned as demiurge. Such a figure is both compelled to survive in a highly technologised and commercialised industry and driven by a desire to deny these circumstances. The cut I mentioned may be taken as a sign of this impasse: the close-up of the disfiguring scar at Milena's throat during her final encounter with Alex.[77] Obviously the scar may be interpreted as a mark of the hysterical woman, who is compelled to aphasia because impossibly torn between refusing her castration and becoming the passive object of masculine desire. But it begs a number of related interpretations: as a visible reminder of Milena's suffering, a bodily particular, and a profane mark of mortality. The cicatrice invokes the past, the temporal and an intervention from the outside which hollows out Milena's silent proclamation of singular originality. In the process it destabilises the rhetoric of resolution and synthesis carried by the symbol. In other words, the scissional function of the scar ruins the epiphanic power of the facial close-up which directly follows it.

I wish to conclude by introducing an alternative account of the avant-garde artist, which existed alongside that more familiar modernism drawn to strategies of negation and artistic self-origination, where the past and artistic tradition are configured as a *tabula rasa*. Thierry de Duve has argued that this more familiar avant-gardism is based on a "paradigm of rejection," where the artist is assumed to occupy a space outside tradition and the socially sanctioned institutions of art.[78] But de Duve identifies another European avant-gardism derivative of a paradigm of *secession* rather than refusal. As a differential current within early modernism, secession informed the avant-gardes of Central Europe and Germany more than France. And, of course, it was a secessionist paradigm of art and artist that prevailed in

the Viennese Secession founded by Gustav Klimt in 1897, with Egon
Schiele as an active participant. It is also worth noting with regard to
the signs of aesthetic traditions that inhabit *Bad Timing*'s *mise-en-scène*,
that it was Art Nouveau with its early ties to the British Arts and
Crafts Movement that functioned as the basis of the Viennese
Secession. There are aspects of both these movements that bear on
certain artistic and social principles advocated in *Bad Timing*. For
example, Art Nouveau was promoted as a free and vigorous stylistic
that broke away from academic historicism of the late nineteenth century. It was a self-consciously artificial style distinguished by the
amplification of asymmetrical design elements and ornamental profusion, while the Arts and Crafts Movement, associated in Britain with
the writings of Ruskin and the design practices of William Morris,
sought, in direct opposition to industrial and mass production, to
retrieve a vernacular tradition of artist-craftsmen harking back to the
medieval times. This movement endorsed principles of the hand-made,
of traditional craft practices and individualism.

According to de Duve, the avant-garde paradigm of secession
assumes that the historically sedimented rules and general expectations that underlie academic art have become overly rigid and so
demand some form of renovation. Secessionism treats academicism as
a stagnated, dead tradition, but it gives itself the task of reanimating
remnants of that tradition. De Duve asserts: "Academicism, far from
representing the law and order against which the avant-garde poses
itself as a transgressive force, is that which remains of previous avant-
gardes when they have run out of their scissional energy."[79] The
secessionist reinterpretation of traditional art forms is not conceived as
an effacement of memory, as a definitive rupture with the past, or an
"assassination" of tradition, but as the opening up of museum art
(Hollywood cinema for Roeg) to differential interpretations and amal-
gamations. Secession side-steps a sharply drawn opposition between
so called official and independent art and so allows for their mutual
contamination. The ghostly remains of tradition are not killed off, but

are presented anew by being reassembled in strange, historically inco-
herent ways. This is why de Duve stresses the "curious chronological
disorder" manifested by art practices that operate according to a paradigm of secession.

It seems to me that an ethos of secession is indicated by the way I
have interpreted the operations of genre in *Bad Timing* and specifically
the ironisation of Hollywood romance that the film articulates.
Although Roeg's films and the director's self-commentary tend to
endorse an aesthetic ideal of a free, individualistic, entirely self-producing artist/author, they also maintain a relation to that interpretation of the film director promoted through the now dismantled structures of studio based filmmaking, where the slow acquisition and
demonstration of technical skill are privileged. Certainly Roeg's
lengthy training as a filmmaker remains closer to this model.[80] The
contradictions of this situation—whereby a traditional emphasis on
craft, the repetition of pre-existing rules, apprenticeship and the hand-
made, is forced to operate within the structures of industrial production, including a strict division of labour, that characterise most forms
of cinema production—are irresolvable. Here the director is deeply
entangled in economic and symbolic exchanges and so subject to a
partial, uncertain interpretation of authorial agency. A wry recognition of this unsettled and unsettling situation inflects Roeg's response
to the commercial failure of *Bad Timing*. He has said he really thought
this film was "one for the streets," destined to be both a critical and
box office success—but as he admits, film audiences had other ideas.[81]

1   Director: Nicolas Roeg, Producer: Jeremy Thomas, Script: Yale Udoff,
     Photography: Anthony Richmond, Editing: Tony Lawson, Music: Richard
     Hartley; World Northal (U.S.), Rank (U.K.) 1980. Starring Theresa Russell
     (Milena Flaherty), Art Garfunkel (Dr. Alex Linden), Harvey Keitel
     (Inspector Netusil), Denholm Elliot (Stefan Vognic).
2   For examples of the latter response see Stuart Cunningham, "Good Timing:
     Bad Timing," *The Australian Journal of Screen Theory*, no. 15/16 (1982),
     101–112, Teresa de Lauretis, "Now and Nowhere: Roeg's *Bad Timing*,"
     Alice Doesn't: Feminism, Semiotics, Cinema (London: Macmillan, 1984),

84–102, Jan Dawson, "*Bad Timing*," *Cinema Papers*, no. 28 (August–September 1980). For a review that oscillates between praise and skepticism regarding the "feminism" of the film see Susan Barber, "*Bad Timing*/A Sensual Obsession," *Film Quarterly*, vol. XXXV no. 1 (Fall 1981), 46–50.

3   Cunningham, ibid., 164.

4   For a Foucauldian approach to this topic see Ian Hunter, "Aesthetics/Ascetics," ed. Wayne Hudson, *Aesthetics After Historicism* (Brisbane: Institute of Modern Art, 1993), 93–111.

5   Philippe Lacoue-Labarthe and Jean-Luc Nancy, *The Literary Absolute: The Theory of Literature in German Romanticism*, trans. Philip Barnard and Cheryl Lester (New York: State University of New York Press, 1988), 15.

6   Robert Sinnerbrook assumes the overcoming of Kant in his account of a similar exercise in the desublimation of liberal humanist aesthetics by another British art cinema auteur in Peter Greenaway's *The Cook, The Thief, His Wife and Her Lover*. Robert Sinnerbrook, "*The Cook, The Thief, His Wife and Her Lover*: A Discourse on Disgust," ed. Adrian Martin, *Film—Matters of Style, Continuum*, vol. 5 no. 2 (1992), 352–365.

7   Cunningham, "Good Timing: *Bad Timing*," 104.

8   David Silverman, "Unfixing the Subject: Viewing *Bad Timing*," *Continuum*, vol. 5 no. 1 (1991), 21. Teresa de Lauretis, "Now and Nowhere: Roeg's *Bad Timing*," More recently the Aboriginal artist Tracey Moffatt has acknowledged the impact of Roeg's work on her films. In an interview with John Conomos and Raffaele Caputo she speaks of her admiration for the "open texture" and "non-linear" temporality of *Walkabout* (1971) and *Performance* (1970), *Cinema Papers*, no. 93 (May 1993), 30.

9   David Bordwell, *Making Meaning: Inference and Rhetoric in the Interpretation of Cinema* (Cambridge: Harvard University Press, 1991), 268.

10   de Lauretis, "Now and Nowhere: Roeg's *Bad Timing*," 95.

11   Frances Ferguson, *Solitude and the Sublime: Romanticism and the Aesthetics of Individuation* (New York and London: Routledge, 1992), 31.

12   Ibid., 3.

13   Immanuel Kant, *Observations on the Beautiful and the Sublime*, trans. John T. Goldthwait (Berkeley: University of California Press, 1991), 76–77.

14   Angelika Rauch, "The *Trauerspiel* of the Prostituted Body, or Woman as Allegory of Modernity," *Cultural Critique* (Fall 1988), 80.

15   Joseph Lanza, *Fragile Geometry: The Films, Philosophy and Misadventures of Nicolas Roeg* (New York: PAJ Publications, 1989), 92. Roeg is quoted thus: "Whoever is in charge of editing a film really plays God."

16   Carrie Richey, "Tic, Tic" *The Village Voice* (Sept 24–30, 1980), 52.

17   Tom Gunning, "An Aesthetic of Astonishment: Early Film and the (In)Credulous Spectator" *Art and Text*, no. 34 (Spring 1989), 31–45. Gunning has turned over this more or less forgotten strand of early silent cinema which in his view has been buried by the later dominance of narrative forms. He argues that the cinema of attractions envisaged film as an especially powerful medium for producing visual shocks and thrills which persists in later narrative film "even if it rarely dominates the form of a fea-

ture film as a whole." Gunning proposes that the cinema of attractions developed a rhetoric based on an exhibitionist acknowledgment of the spectator, effects of direct and violent stimulus and a fascination with "unbeautiful and repulsive" sights.

18 Unpublished interview with Nicolas Roeg by Toni Ross and Lisa Trahair, 1987.

19 Thomas Weiskel, *The Romantic Sublime: Studies in the Structure and Psychology of Transcendence* (Baltimore: The Johns Hopkins University Press, 1976), 5.

20 Ibid., 3.

21 Bordwell, "The Art Cinema as a Mode of Film Practice," *Film Criticism*, no. 4 (Fall 1979), 60.

22 Noel King has pointed out that Roeg's tendency in *Bad Timing* to abruptly cut into flash-backs on the look of characters engenders some ambiguity as to whether Alex's "ravishment" of Milena actually happened or whether this scene comprises a phantasmatic projection of Netusil's desires. Noel King, "Critical Occasions: David Bordwell's *Making Meaning* and the Institution of Film Criticism", *Continuum*, vol. 6 no. 1 (1992), 174. My reading, to come, of the links between Alex and the painting *Death Comes to the Maiden*, at moments when Netusil's fantasies are not an issue, tends to view the "ravishment" scene as *authentic*.

23 Cunningham, "Good Timing: *Bad Timing*," 109.

24 Ibid., 110.

25 Silverman, "Unfixing the Subject: Viewing *Bad Timing*," 17.

26 Naomi Schor, *Reading in Detail: Aesthetics and the Feminine* (New York and London: Methuen, 1987), 19.

27 Silverman, "Unfixing the Subject: Viewing *Bad Timing*," 21–22.

28 Lacoue-Labarthe and Nancy, *The Literary Absolute*, 33.

29 Ibid., 33.

30 Samuel Weber, "Criticism Underway: Walter Benjamin's 'Romantic Concept of Criticism,' " ed. Kenneth R. Johnston et al., *Romantic Revolutions: Criticism and Theory* (Bloomington: Indiana University Press, 1990), 305.

31 Ibid., 311.

32 Weber, "Criticism Underway:....," 312–313.

33 Donald Kuspit, *The Dialectic of Decadence* (New York: Stuxpress, 1993), 57–58.

34 Tony Crawley, "The Last British Film maker," *Films Illustrated* (July 1980), 396.

35 Naomi Schor, *Reading in Detail*, 29.

36 Ibid., 35.

37 Immanuel Kant, *Critique of Judgment*, trans. and introduced by Werner S. Pluhar, foreword by Mary J. Gregor (Indianapolis: Hackett Publishing Company, 1987), 135.

38 Ibid., 123.

39 Joseph Lanza, *Fragile Geometry. The Films, Philosophy and Misadventures of*

Nicolas Roeg (New York: PAJ Publications, 1989), 91.

40 For example, the mythical cinematic status of *Casablanca* is invoked, along with the hitchhiking scene from *It Happened One Night*.

41 Patricia A. Parker, *Inescapable Romance: Studies in the Poetics of a Mode* (Princeton, Princeton University Press, 1979), 8. See also Stanley Cavell, *Pursuits of Happiness: The Hollywood Comedy of Remarriage* (Cambridge, Massachusetts: Harvard University Press, 1981), 49. Cavell names the secluded bower of romance "Connecticut" in the Hollywood romantic comedies of the 1930s and 1940s he discusses. Connecticut is described therein as "a place removed from the city of confusion and divorce."

42 Maria Laplace, "Producing and Consuming the Woman's Film: Discursive Struggle in 'Now, Voyager,' " ed. Christine Gledhill, *Home is Where the Heart Is: Studies in Melodrama and the Woman's Film* (London: BFI Publishing, 1987), 160.

43 Neil Hertz, "The Notion of Blockage in the Literature of the Sublime," *The End of the Line: Essays on Psychoanalysis and the Sublime* (New York: Columbia University Press, 1985) 44–45.

44 Ibid., 53.

45 Ibid., 60.

46 Kaja Silverman, *The Acoustic Mirror: The Female Voice in Psychoanalysis and Cinema* (Bloomington and Indianapolis: Indiana University Press: 1988), 214–215.

47 Roeg informed Joseph Lanza that during the making of *Bad Timing*: "Art Garfunkel came up to me and said he realised he was really playing me". But Roeg told Garfunkel that "he was only part of it. I challenged him to decipher when I was wearing the trousers and when I was wearing the dress." Lanza, *Fragile Geometry*, 131.

48 Lacoue-Labarthe and Nancy, *The Literary Absolute*, 33,66.

49 Ibid., 69.

50 Ibid.,68.

51 Ibid., 67.

52 Ibid., 71.

53 Ibid., 71.

54 Ibid., 73.

55 Ibid., 73.

56 Quoted in ibid., 77.

57 Ibid., 69.

58 Gilles Deleuze, *Cinema 1: The Movement Image*, trans. Hugh Tomlinson and Barbara Habberjam (Minneapolis: University of Minnesota Press, 1986), 87.

59 Ibid., 95–97.

60 Ibid., 92.

61 Roland Barthes, "The Face of Garbo," *Mythologies*, trans. Annette Lavers, (London: Granada, 1982), 56–57.

62 Deleuze, *Cinema 1*, 98.

63 Ibid., 99.

64 Samuel Weber, "Genealogy of Modernity: History, Myth and Allegory in Benjamin's *Origin of the German Mourning Play,*" *MLN* (1991), vol. 106 no. 3, 480.

65 Friedrich Nietzsche, *The Birth of Tragedy and The Case Of Wagner,* trans. by Walter Kaufmann (New York: Random House, 1967), 17–27.

66 This concluding link between Milena and the world of nature continues a tendency that I have charted within the fabrication of Milena's character that makes her a symbol of an uncompromised, authentic model of self-hood. This goes back to Frances Ferguson's discussion of Kant's aesthetics and the philosopher's siting of aesthetic pleasure and pain in nature rather than the socio-cultural activity of art. Ferguson argues that Kant's account of the sublime in nature proffers a model of individuality that remains uncompromised, proof against all efforts to re-present and therefore divide its true being from itself. She writes:

> From Burke's account of the self-preservative purposes of sublime terror to Kant's dynamical sublime, nature's might provides the model for an extraordinarily productive confusion. The theatrical world of society may make it appear than one cannot [accurately] represent oneself to oneself. The world of nature makes it appear that talking only to objects with which one shares no language guarantees individuality.

Frances Ferguson, *Solitude and the Sublime: Romanticism and the Aesthetics of Individuation,* 130–131.

67 Weber, "Genealogy of Modernity...", 481.

68 Ibid., 481.

69 Weber, "Genealogy of Modernity...", 481.

70 Lacoue-Labarthe and Nancy, *The Literary Absolute,* 115.

71 Weber, "Genealogy of Modernity...", 482.

72 Cited by Weber, ibid., 484.

73 Philippe Lacoue-Labarthe, "On the Sublime," ed. Lisa Appignanesi, *ICA Documents 5. Postmodernism* (London: ICA, 1986), 8.

74 Philippe Lacoue-Labarthe, "The Caesura of the Speculative," *Glyph,* no. 4, 65.

75 Ibid., 65.

76 Thierry de Duve, "Resonances of Duchamp's Visit to Munich," in *Marcel Duchamp: Artist of the Century,* ed. Rudolf E. Kuenzli and Francis M. Nauman (Cambridge Massachusetts; The MIT Press,1990), 56.

77 Teresa de Lauretis, "Now and Nowhere...", 101. De Lauretis has also drawn attention to the scar but with a strange slip she locates it on Milena's chest rather than her throat.

78 Thierry de Duve, "Resonances of Duchamp's Visit to Munich," 45.

79 Ibid., 45.

80 In 1947 Roeg began working in London's Marylebone Studios, dubbing French films and doing odd jobs around the studio. After W.W. II he gained

employment at MGM's Boreham Wood Studios where he worked as a clapper boy first and then as a member of the camera crew on H. C. Potter's *The Miniver Story*. From 1961 up until his directorial debut in 1968 he consolidated a reputation as a spectacularly innovative cinematographer and then made a relatively late transition into film directing.

81 Brian Baxter, "The Significance of Mr Roeg,"(Interview) *Films and Filming*, no. 30 (July 1985), 16.

"Life is a Dream"

Raul Ruiz was a Surrealist in Sydney: A Capillary Memory of a Cultural Event[1]

Laleen Jayamanne

"One doesn't decide to make a Surrealist film; one is either Surrealist or not."[2]

Robert Benayoun, 1981.

"I am not an ideologue of the baroque. I am simply Latin American. I can't help but be baroque. Allegory for me is much more than a game or an element of a style."[3]

Raul Ruiz, Sydney, 3 February 1993.

Presenting Raul Ruiz the Chilean-born filmmaker based in France as a surrealist was a canny move on the part of the Australian media.[4] I

doubt that billing him as, say, a late twentieth century baroque allegorical filmmaker would have been good publicity for the retrospective
of his work held in 1993 as part of Carnivale, a festival of multiculturalism, because "surreal" is now part of our everyday language in a
way in which "baroque" and "allegory" are not. Besides, there are
many surrealist elements in Ruiz's oeuvre.

But Ruiz says that though he puts things together in a surrealist
manner, he does so without conviction, attributing it purely to the
speed at which he has to work.[5] It is interesting that in the literature
in English on his cinema there are very few readings of his work; the
tendency is more towards enumerating the special effects.[6] When
Surrealism is used as an exhaustive term it does not enable readings,
except perhaps at a literal level.

So, in order to understand how Ruiz's cinema works it is necessary to situate Surrealism itself within the ambit of the baroque and
allegory via the work of Walter Benjamin. This is so because
Benjamin's work on baroque allegorical drama provides certain central theoretical concepts for the understanding of baroque allegory
as an aesthetic form which corresponds in some ways with
Surrealism. Susan Sontag draws out the implications of the link
between Benjamin's theorisation of baroque allegory and of
Surrealism in the following:

> Both the Baroque and Surrealism, sensibilities with which
> Benjamin profoundly identified, see reality as things.
> Benjamin describes the baroque as a world of things
> (emblems, ruins) and spatialised ideas ... The genius of
> Surrealism was to generalize with ebullient candour the
> baroque cult of ruins; to perceive that the nihilistic energies
> of the modern era make everything a ruin or fragment—and
> therefore collectable ... He drew from the obscure, disdained
> German baroque drama elements of the modern sensibility:
> the taste for allegory, surrealist shock effects, discontinuous

utterance, the sense of historical catastrophe.[7]

For both Benjamin and Ruiz, what Sontag calls the "taste" for allegory is really something like an affliction.[8] So Benjamin can say that "the only pleasure the melancholic permits himself, and it is a powerful one, is allegory."[9] Ruiz corroborates by saying that he tends to see life as a museum,[10] echoing Benjamin's Baudelaire who said "Everything for me becomes Allegory."[11]

Sontag clinches the link between baroque allegory and Surrealism in saying: "The melancholic always feels threatened by the dominion of the thing-like, but surrealist taste mocks these terrors. Surrealism's great gift to sensibility was to make melancholy cheerful."[12]

When Ruiz spoke of the two baroque diseases, namely melancholy and enthusiasm, he was probably speaking of the Spanish tradition and not the Germanic.[13] Benjamin is himself explicit about the absence of the ludic in the German Baroque plays. I will take this point up later. But for now I will return to "Raul Ruiz the Surrealist,"[14] as Adrian Martin calls him, with a sense of the affinity between the two modes of vision as highlighted by Sontag.

According to Martin, Ruiz's cinema has:

> conjured up, as in a feverish dream, the images and obsessions of historic and eternal Surrealism alike. Some caution is necessary, however, in any global roundup of the properly surreal. Since Surrealism does have an historic dimension, some of its most familiar gestures and images have inexorably become repetitive, congealed, vulgar and empty.[15]

Martin goes on to assert the necessity of separating the banal manifestation of Surrealism from the profound one. To do this he borrows the phrase, "decorative and stereotypical aspects"[16] from Ruiz and inserts it within his own sentence: "We must separate the purely *decorative*

and stereotypical aspects of Surrealism from the deeper more fertile surrealist impulse."[17] Here Martin implies that Ruiz is endorsing the jetti-
soning of the "decorative and stereotypical aspects" of Surrealism
when in fact what he says is quite different. The context is a rhetorical
question asked of Ruiz in an interview: "You also cite Buñuel as one of
your major film makers. But you aren't a surrealist ...?" Ruiz replies: "I
would have loved to have made *The Exterminating Angel.* But I am not
a surrealist. What interests me in Surrealism is the slapstick aspects,
decorative and stereotypical aspects, everything that was recovered by
Dali through advertising. I am not at all convinced by the surrealist
metaphysics."[18] In this reply Ruiz is neither endorsing nor rejecting
the pop banal aspects of Surrealism, rather he leaves open the possibility of using them for his own allegorical practice. So that if and
when they do return they would be recognisable perhaps as surrealist stereotypes, that is to say, drained of their putative marvellous life
and therefore allegorised. As Martin points out: "the medium of cinema was for the surrealists a privileged gateway to the realm of fantasy, the unconscious, dreams and desire,"[19] whereas for Ruiz, cinema
is an allegorical system—which is why its figures are ghosts, shad-
ows, zombies, the dead. This is the perverse logic that Ruiz draws out
of the ontology of the medium which he sees as allegorising.[20]
Martin concludes his piece "The Artificial Night: Surrealism and
Cinema" with the following:

> Surrealists have always loved the "walking undead" of the cin-
> ema, from Boris Karloff to the Zombies of George Romero's
> *Night of the Living Dead* films. This is doubtless because the
> merry undead live out the fine message once delivered by Ado
> Kyrou that "with everything possible, everything is fundamen-
> tally simple."[21]

Yet looking at a film like *Three Crowns of a Sailor* one can see that
Ruiz draws the opposite conclusion from a similar premise. The cin-

ema is a ghosting medium, its figures are dead, thus making every-thing possible—and fundamentally complex.

Explaining what the baroque is, Ruiz said: "Let's take the point of view of an enemy of the baroque, say any French citizen. A baroque point of view would say 'why be simple when you can be complex.' "[22] He went on to say that baroque is a multiplication of points of view, of an object of a space, a body. One can locate in this baroque possibility all of Ruiz's special effects, which he refuses to call special effects but rather natural effects. The close-up, for Ruiz, shows that the part is bigger than the whole,[23] while the cinematic instant can be longer than the day. These cinematic capabilities which have a baroque dimension form the basis of a method for Ruiz.

He pointed out that the baroque period in Spain was a time of dictatorship and political repression when religious and political simulation arose as forms of resistance and survival. He added that the baroque is fashionable now and has been so a couple of times in the last twenty years. But as distinct from this fashion, he maps out his relationship to it in the following way, which is implicit in the opening quotation.

For Ruiz, the baroque is not only a European mode of art production, it is also a contemporary living popular folk tradition in Chile, which he says is connected to the popular traditions of the baroque in Europe. In the popular tradition baroque modes of construction are related to a system of economy rather than the opulence and social privilege of the high baroque with which it is usually associated. He explains this in an everyday image of a certain small restaurant that packs in the maximum number of tables and chairs in order to maximise profit at a particular time of day. The idea is to put the maximum into the minimum.[24] So baroque excess may be understood as a practice of economy.[25]

He says that he became self-consciously aware of this tradition as a result of the Chilean nationalist revival of the 60s and adds that he was always reluctant to use the folk traditions of myth and legend as a basis for his films. It was his discovery that some of these practices were in fact part of an unbroken tradition from the Spanish popular baroque that permitted him to lift his reserve.[26] It is worth remembering here that he was outspoken in his criticism of the valorisation of the folk in the nationalist revival and spoke against the Quilapayun culture,[27] a kind of left kitsch (which is what a section of the Australian left loved to love in the late seventies). The baroque aspect that he found still operative has, according to him, more to do with games and rules for improvisation. He says that this tradition offers a complex way of developing art when one realises that art has to be a game of making things more and more complex.[28] He speaks of the initial indigestion that the canonical high Chilean allegorical mode— which was mandatory for all school children—gave him; and he also speaks of the pleasure he finds in popular baroque allegorical emblematic epigrams, such as "the scattered body," "the siesta of the saints," "the world in reverse," on the basis of which the folk tradition still improvises poetry.[29] The baroque is also important for Ruiz because of its relationship to Arabic culture.[30] All of these indicate that the baroque is a complex cultural process and method for Ruiz, and not just a set of surrealist special effects.

If polyvalence and polyphony are attributes of the baroque, is there not something contradictory in the conjunction of a baroque vision with an allegorical one? Most major theoretical texts on allegory speak of it in a somewhat contradictory way, as Ruiz does. Benjamin defined allegory in the following way: "any person, any object, any relationship can mean absolutely anything else."[31] For Ruiz the problem of allegory is that, unlike metaphor, allegory is a "one way street,"[32] requiring a clear idea of the kind, "this means that." If metaphor is polyvalent, permitting many associations and works associatively (in a realm of correspondences, both sensuous and non-sensuous), then allegory is the severing of any such associative link—a severing of name and meaning. Therefore a sense of the arbitrary is highlighted in allegorical conjunctions. Because of this logic, allegory often seems willed, reductive and heavy. Ruiz can, however, create an extraordinary experience of lightness when working in such a mode because of the alchemy produced by embedding allegory into baroque spatial rhetoric and the correspondingly dense temporality he draws out from the cinematic apparatus. This is perhaps why he can say, apparently contradicting himself, that allegorical bodies are both complex and always open in the sense that further arbitrary connections between one thing and another can be deliriously multiplied.[33] Ruiz elaborates:

> This connecting aspect of allegory is one of the things that fascinated me ... you make an allegory and this allegory touches an element of real life and makes this element become an allegory of something else, of some distant object and when this object is touched it becomes an allegory and so on ... it seems to me that in this moment, especially, most of the arts have refused this form of allegory which was such an important element in the history of culture."[34]

Cinema for Ruiz is a way of connecting many kinds of cultural elements that are usually separate. He points out that *Il ponte* (bridge) was a very important word in the baroque.[35]

The allegorical mode is generous to its obtuse reader because it often carries with it an interpretive context, it shows us how it puts itself together, more out of a kind of exhaustion[36] with the will to allegory, than for any more modernist reason; for example, "a coffin is like a bed, a boat, a tooth brush, a car, a handkerchief ... a coffin is like a coffin" says the sailor in *Three Crowns of a Sailor*. It is the same with the chocolate sauce poured over the green apples in *TV Dante* after a delirious sequence of allegorical images, of body parts being cooked like food. I am reminded of that certain small restaurant packed to capacity; one more table and the whole system will collapse.

Torment of the Flesh, the Suffering of the World

The theme of the "torment of the flesh,"[37] identified by Benjamin, is
one that persists across medieval and baroque allegory well into Ruiz's
work. According to Benjamin:

> The allegorisation of the *physis* (nature) can only be carried
> through in all its vigour in respect of the corpse and the char-
> acters of the *Trauerspiel* die because it's only thus as corpses
> (ghosts) that they can enter into the homeland of allegory.[38]

In this we can see why Ruiz perceives cinema as an allegorical system. If the cinematic bodies are not already dead and ghostly, then at
least they have to be anomalous bodies like that of the virgin prostitute, the femme fatale with only one orifice, Dr.Wepayoung (the old
man in the body of a young child), the impersonator whose identity is
mercurial, to mention a few such in *Three Crowns of a Sailor*.

Thinking about allegorical vision and changing allegorical intention I feel the need as a Sri Lankan Australian[39] to mention an image
of the corpse that is past all mourning, past all capacity for mourning,
in Ruiz's cinema.[40] This is the recurrent image of a mangled corpse
being eaten up by dogs who often stop to scratch themselves. No
thoughtful skeleton here (I am thinking of *Dark at Noon* and *TV Dante*)
who broods over this image as skeletons do over piles of skulls in
medieval and even early 20th century emblems. But in *TV Dante* the
poet does cry out once in an ostentatious act of lamentation at seeing
this image beyond grief. Grief is personal, whereas mourning is a public act which presupposes an audience, thus a certain sense of
theatre.[41] It follows then that the emblematic allegorical figures come
with the injunction, *Read me*. Allegories and ghosts are temporal
phantasms that sustain the act of mourning. Benjamin says that they
have an "affinity for mourners, for those who ponder over signs and
over the future."[42]

In the context of discussing the disparity and dissonance central to the Spanish Baroque aesthetic of Balthasar Gracian, Ruiz comments on the function of death for him:

> I try to remember that disparity exists. And this is done well in remembering death. But as such death becomes a completely other thing than a complaisance of dying, something other than melancholy. On the contrary it becomes an implement for working, a tool. In fact, if there were a general manifestation of death, let us say a kind of annihilation wherein something is wiped out, then death may have other representations such as sleep, forgetting, absence, discontinuities in cinematic montage ... Once formalised these forms of death become rhetorical tools for an audio-visual medium.[43]

Ruiz has drawn from the disintegrating power of death a cinematic life; he has been able to read the apparatus in death's shadow and has thereby been able to enrich the affective experience of allegory as well as film. The ludic element is perhaps a direct result of his ability to draw so much play/life from a putative dead, that is, immobile, apparatus.

In Ruiz it is the ludic aspect that makes real the reality of eternal passing which, according to Susan Buck-Morss, is the temporality of allegory as distinct from that of the aesthetic symbol.[44] The impersonator in *Three Crowns of a Sailor* who insists that the person who jumped overboard yesterday was not him but "The Other" is a good example of these shadowy beings without qualities created according to the logic of the cinematographic instant which is multiple—because it is articulated through multiple moments of "death," every twenty-fourth fraction of a second.[45] Here it's useful to mention Ruiz's notion of the unconscious as something that happens between people rather than in dreams—which he offers as a critique of identity. So the psychical apparatus is envisaged as an intersubjective space. The correspondence that may be drawn between the psychical and the cinematic apparatus here suggests a sort of limitless space/time of production.

Talking about the ludic in Ruiz and the thematic of the torment of the flesh is a good moment to turn to that great tormentor of flesh, that mythical avatar, the femme fatale in *Three Crowns of a Sailor*. Lisa Lyon, the American body builder/performance artist made famous by Robert Mapplethorpe in *Lady*,[46] gives body to the femme fatale, who in Ruiz's hands becomes an allegory of art. It goes without saying that one can enjoy this segment as well as the whole film at a literal level without seeing its allegorical structure. But I want to try and read it as allegory to see where it would go.

According to Cysarz, whom Benjamin quotes, allegorical emblems work in the following way: "Every idea, however abstract, is compressed into an image, and this image however concrete, is then stamped out in verbal form."[47] An allegorical construction thus must be both concrete and abstract at the same time. Lisa Lyon as an allegory of art conforms to these principles of construction.

The man without a name and qualities, the sailor, is taken to see Mathilde the femme fatale at a dance hall by a friend who sets the allegorical scene by saying: "Here you forget all the cares of the world. The only true heaven is art, beauty." The sailor's narrative voice-over comment about the femme fatale is an allegorising one, "Mathilde was nudity made art, the cursed woman made me suffer so much that I forgot all my cares."

The sailor, aroused by the femme fatale's deliriously sensual mambo dance, is audibly moved to emit a spoken commentary of a very tentative kind:

> Yes that's it, or rather you see what I mean ... yes. I thought
> that ... I was feeling good. No rather ... You see what I mean.
> Yes that's it, or rather ... you see what I mean ..."

Diegetically this commentary could be read as belonging to the framing story of the sailor's narration to the student about seeing the femme fatale; at the same time it could also be read as an expression of the ineffability of art.

When they meet, the femme fatale, true to form—unmoved by the sailor's agitation—speaks eloquently in maxims and "beautiful, interspersed, apophthegms"[48] which are a familiar baroque idiom. For example, her opening gambit, "Nudity is an art, besides art is only nudity," has the generality and finality of a maxim and functions here as a "flash of light"[49] does in baroque painting (Benjamin's insight). The maxim is according to him "a flash of light in the entangling darkness of allegory,"[50] it creates a temporal moment where a constellation can form between unrelated images. In the baroque *Trauerspiel*, these terse and pithy sayings are, according to Benjamin, its very pillars, thus central to its structure. Here too it is through these rhetorical figures that the femme fatale is metamorphosed allegorically into an emblem of art in a quite explicit and humourous way. What Benjamin says—quoting Birken in relation to a form of music drama—is certainly applicable to how the allegory works in this film: "the spoken word makes no pretence to be dialogue, and is primarily a commentary on the images, spoken by the images."[51] The conversation between the femme fatale, the sailor and his friend is structured according to such a logic, though it does also work as dialogue. The wonder of the scene is in the performance, which imbues the allegorising procedures with a delicious ambivalence and consequent lightness.

When the friend tries to break the ice by saying, "He admires you like one admires art" the allegory replies with "There is no more art, only too much civilization. Art is barbarous." Then she stops to ask the sailor: "I don't know what your opinion is." To which he replies, "Same as yours." And she rejoins, "That's what they all say but nudity scares them sooner or later." We will see very soon this prophecy fulfilled. The friend mediates again and says: "My friend would like to stay alone with you," a statement which Mathilde the femme fatale immediately allegorises with "He is right, art is loneliness." There is a nice break in the sequence at this point when she says: "I will see you tomorrow, when and where I choose." The break functions like a sign for suspense without the corresponding affect. When they meet again the purple prose of the allegorical emblem enunciates a 19th century romantic view of art as transcendence of which allegory is the very ruin:

> This disgusts me. We should have met outdoors in the eye of the storm, far from the prejudices of the world, at the supreme moment lightning would have annihilated us. Nothingness is perfect nudity. I'll render your desires transcendent.

This emblem is highly aware of its immanence, even as it articulates the desire for transcendence in the idiom of high romantic agony proper to a *Tristan and Isolde*, encoded in the temporality of the symbol which is that of "fleeting eternity."[52] This is the famous doubleness of allegory in operation. The sailor then responds obtusely: "I want to see you naked"; the allegorical emblem, trying to educate the sailor as to how to read her, responds: "Tangible nudity is the skin which clothes the being." Unable to follow a line of abstract enquiry to do with, say, intangible nudity and where that might lead etc., he can only come up with the simple and in this allegorical context entirely simple-minded, "I want to make love to you"—so he has to listen to the devastating maxim, "Love can't be made, love is." Not quite devastated, because obsessed with complete revelation, he says, "I have never seen someone completely naked." Then the allegory, naked woman as art, says, "But I am not naked" and proceeds to disrobe by rehearsing a gesture performed by Magritte in his painting *The Rape*. In Magritte the gesture is a metaphoric operation, condensing one orifice into another. In *Three Crowns of a Sailor*, when Lisa Lyon as the Mathilde, the femme fatale, detaches her nipples and vulva from where they naturally belong and places them on a table with stars, they do not form a new constellation as they do in the ambiguously gendered head of Magritte. The body denuded of its sexual anatomy—thus subject to "the disjunctive atomising principle of allegory"[53]—becomes more eloquent than ever: "You see, I have only one orifice. I do everything with my mouth." This is baroque economy (putting the maximum in the minimum) at its ludic best. Because allegory does not work like metaphor, the two things (Lisa Lyon as femme fatale as art) do not perfectly transfer (the meaning of *metapherein* from which metaphor derives). Because of the methodological impossibility of a complete fusion it is impossible to forget the tangible cinematic image of Lisa Lyon's built body,[54] her particular form of willed corporeality, even as she enunciates in verbal form an abstract romantic ontology of art.

Benjamin says that nakedness as an emblem appeared in the Middle Ages as a radical attempt at the subjugation of flesh in Catholic allegory. This was so because flesh was suspect in the fall from grace and was also associated with the daemonic.[55] According to Bezhold (quoted by Benjamin), "whenever medieval scholarship came across unclothed figures, it sought to explain this impropriety with reference to a symbolism which was frequently far-fetched, and generally hostile."[56] But in Ruiz's allegorical practice of presenting Lisa Lyon's body as an emblem of art, the equation is anything but far-fetched. In fact there is something quite familiar in presenting the naked female form as art—which points to a whole genre of western painting. I want therefore to call this aspect an inconspicuous practice of allegory, drawing on the distinction Benjamin makes between conspicuous and inconspicuous allegorical constructs.[57] The proscenium theatre space within which the elaborate baroque configuration of Lisa Lyon's mambo dance is displayed renders it in a certain way an amalgam of both conspicuous and inconspicuous allegory. While this sequence has the ostentation and hyperbole proper to allegory and the emblem, it simultaneously operates in another register related to the theatricality of the setting itself, which in effect naturalises the grandiloquent. This stereotype is given the proper illusionist space to play in, to display her virtuosity, so that she returns in a register of the ludic. I want now to return to Benjamin's comment that German allegory of the *Trauerspiel* knew nothing of inconspicuous allegory, only the ostentatious—unlike the Spanish allegory of Calderon which is inconspicuous and light. Benjamin says that "Because of its obsession with earnestness the German Trauerspiel never mastered the art of using allegory inconspicuously. Only comedy could lighten the gravity of the allegorical will."[58]

Ruiz is a master of the inconspicuous use of allegory. One of his contributions to the history of the stereotype in cinema is that he has given us the fatal woman in a ludic register without diminishing her power to fascinate. It is this toxic mixture that gives her allegorical embodiment such a miraculous lightness.

At the very moment when the femme fatale begins to disrobe we are made aware of an everyday image of a man (uncommonly like Ruiz in shape) reading a newspaper and watching TV in that same baroque room with no windows, who finally intervenes in the scene to eject the besotted, hence, too ernest sailor from this world of allegorical play governed by the arbitrary rule of dead objects.

The breasts and vulva of the femme fatale, simulacra all, have been ceremoniously discarded as exhausted allegorical emblems, while the orifice where nature and history meet, whose emissions are an "eternal passing," is allegorised with all the wonder of a miracle.

That Surrealism should still find so much life in these exhausted emblems of female mythic nature suggests that it has lost an awareness of the tension between repetition and change in the problem of returning to the stereotype. Ruiz's cunning allegorical practice, in contrast, offers a form of realism (believability) for the moment and Lisa Lyon, as femme fatale as art, is for me its most memorable emblem.

Perhaps the figure of the femme fatale survives as trickster here because she returns as allegorical emblem rather than in the more familiar form of mythic symbol. As mythic symbol she would of course have to die. But as emblem she activates a form of daemonic agency (neither human nor divine but in-between) which is said to be proper to all allegorical heroes.[59] This means among other things that agency and image become closely linked, even to the extent of being fixed; femme fatale equals trickster, but this very fixity also permits the move of ascribing a certain kind of action to allegorical images.

What then is the emblematic action or trick that this allegory of art performs? She is an allegory simulating an aesthetic symbol in order to lure the sailor, to ruin his impossible desire. This simulation is achieved partly via her commentary which espouses a romantic notion of art consonant with the valorisation of the aesthetic symbol. This then is also the famed stereotypic duplicity of the femme fatale mirroring the doubleness of allegory.

In staging the antique battle (and here I assume that the nineteenth century is our antiquity) of the claims of the symbol versus those of allegory through the late twentieth century body of Lisa Lyon, is Ruiz giving us in a ludic register (play, enthusiasm, frenzy[60]), what was first staged as melodrama in the nineteenth century romantic debates where the symbol killed the taste for allegory? Perhaps he is. But I don't think this is simply an instance of reversal and play with genre. For in staging this reversal, both in a nineteenth century dance hall with a proscenium stage and in a baroque boudoir that recedes into infinity, Ruiz and Lyon are able to allegorically metamorphose the mythic symbol "Woman" and the spaces and temporality that have traditionally defined that symbol.

The placement of this scene is an index of its centrality to the film as a commentary on Ruiz's own allegorical practice. As such it may be read as an allegory about allegorical efficacity.[61] It is I think important that this whole scene is placed between two scenes of the loss of the maternal, a space/time charged with phantasy. The sailor, learning of the death of his real mother in numerous fictional accounts, stumbles into the dance hall seeking forgetfulness. It is soon after this scene with the femme fatale that the sailor finds the rented mother on board the ghost ship, a substitute for the loss of the real one, but really an allegory of memory.[62]

The Maternal as Emblematic Memory

With historical Surrealism there is a willed and enabling break with tradition and in this it complies with the general meaning of the avant-garde, the desire of which is forever to create the new. In the cases of Ruiz and Baudelaire, the break with tradition was anything but willed. Baudelaire's allegorical work was a response to the shock of modernity, while for Ruiz the loss of tradition is marked by the Chilean diaspora. It is from a position of loss of country, language and identity that Ruiz begins to recover the loss by allegorising the moment of rupture in a film such as *Three Crowns of a Sailor*. But for the allegorist there is really no return to a moment of plenitude, as Ruiz expresses in the following anecdote. Asked how he felt on returning to Chile after 10 years of exile, he said:

> The first time was a shock. I felt like one of the living dead. It wasn't a feeling of nostalgia, it was more like *saudade* —you could call that nostalgia for something that was never there. It's a mixed feeling—you're also glad it was never there.[63]

This paradoxical mixture of remembering and forgetting, this peculiar non-retentive multiple temporality seems to create an affective register for turning towards tradition, towards a cultural memory as a precondition for invention. As there seems to be a correspondence between *saudade* and Proust's involuntary memory I will read it via Benjamin's commentary on the latter. "An experienced event is finite, at any rate confined to one sphere of experience; a remembered event is infinite, because it is only a key to everything that happened before it and after it."[64] But if what evokes *saudade* was never there, either in experience or memory, then does this not transform the past into a pure virtuality and thereby make it inexhaustible? Memory's work would thus not be retention or recovery but invention across a temporal abyss.

The rented mother as allegory of memory is reminiscent of Benjamin's angel of history, who according to Irving Wohlfarth is also an allegory of memory (that is, remembrance, *"Eingedenken"*).[65] Therefore I will frame my reading of this sequence on a hunch—namely, that the rented mother as allegory of memory may be to Ruiz's film what the corpse was to baroque allegory, and what the whore was to Baudelaire's notion of allegory. She is something like an allegory of allegory, its very matrix.[66]

There are two letters read out in *Three Crowns of a Sailor*, one written by the sailor to his mother as he departs on the ghost ship, with haunting lines like: "I forgive you for not giving me a name, I forgive you the nights without electricity, I forgive you Valparaiso." The other is from the rented mother to her sons on the ghost ship, after she has been made to disembark for having inadvertently caused a fatal fight over the question of access to her. The spaces in which these two letters are heard echo each other in subliminal ways, partly a function of *mise-en-scène*, the tonality of the images and of the music. Both letters are read out over images of the ocean and sky that at all times are intersected by human constructs such as steel bridges and parts of the ship itself. So we see nature through a grid of delicate steel decorative motifs, as it were. The film plays with the similarity of the French word for sea and mother (mer, mère) and yet does not succumb to an oceanic surrender to the maternal as mythic symbol.

The doubling of the absolutely singular is, according to Benjamin, a sign of the tenacity and fanaticism of the allegorical will.[67] The doubles—the real mother and the rented mother—are a testimony to such a will. This doubling is different from a splitting operation. The split-

ting of the symbol "Mother" usually produces the good and the bad
mother of both myth (Pattini and Kali) and some versions of psychoanalysis. The doubling here instead produces a delicious sense of non-
sense, which is perhaps an affective precondition for allegory to begin
its work of signification, while its humour certainly enhances our
receptivity to these anomalous figures.

What function does the rented mother perform in this film
described as an allegory of contemporary exile? Why does she pop up
in a ship of the dead, a place where memory would have no function
at all? But the essential question to ask here under Benjamin's tutelage
is: "what kind of memory does she emblematise?" For Benjamin has
shown us how memory itself has mutated under certain historico-
technological pressures and that therefore it is not whole. He maps out
this process of the fragmentation of memory in his essay "The
Storyteller"[68] which may be summarised thus: Since the disintegration of the epic, *Mnemosyne* (the rememberer, muse of the epic art of
the Greeks) has been separated into *Gedächtnis* and *Eingedenken*, the
memory of the many and the remembrance of the one.[69] Benjamin
maps this out in detail in the following:

> memory is the epic faculty par excellence ... Memory creates
> the chain of tradition which passes a happening on from gen-
> eration to generation. It is the Muse-derived element of the epic
> art in a broader sense and encompasses its varieties. In the first
> place among these is the one practiced by the story teller. It
> starts the web which all stories together form in the end. One
> ties on to the next, as the great storytellers, particularly the
> Oriental ones, have always readily shown. In each of them
> there is a Scheherazade who thinks of a fresh story whenever
> her tale comes to a stop. Such is epic memory (*Gedächtnis*) and
> the storyteller's muse.[70]

Gilbert Adair has aptly called the Ruiz of *Three Crowns of a Sailor,*

Scheher*uí*zade,[71] for he has drawn both Chilean and European seafaring tales into a *mise-en-abîme* structure that seems truly inexhaustible. Ruiz thereby happily contradicts Benjamin's melancholy reflection on the demise of storytelling as oral practice in an era dominated by the technological manufacture of information and the consequent loss of a capacity for experience. Yet in a sense Ruiz does confirm a certain Benjaminian conviction about cinema's double-edged capacity for destruction and creation of experience.[72]

Benjamin describes further the mutation and fragmentation of memory in the following passage:

> Against it (the storyteller) is to be set another principle, the Muse of the novel, which initially—that is to say in the epic—lies concealed, not yet differentiated from that of the story. In epics it can at most be occasionally divined, particularly at such solemn Homeric moments as the initial invocations of the Muse. What these passages prefigure is the perpetuating memory of the novelist as opposed to the short-lived reminiscences of the storyteller. The former is dedicated to the one hero, the one odyssey or the one struggle; the latter to the many scattered occurrences. It is, in other words, remembrance (*Eingedenken*) that, as the novelist's Muse, joins memory (*Gedächtnis*), the storyteller's, their original unity having come apart with the disintegration of the epic.[73]

With this theory of memory and its vicissitudes in mind I want to analyse the sequence of the rented mother. The first captain who rents the mother introduces her in this way: "There are two types of contamination, contamination of solids like furniture and this ship and the contamination of the gaseous, air, the wind," and adds that "only one thing is pure, our lady, the sea and alcohol," thus drawing our lady, the sea and oblivion into some sort of equivalence. Gestures of cutting a picture from a magazine and choosing an

uncontaminated cigarette from a contaminated pack are the images
that introduce this sequence. The fiction is now well and truly in the
realm of the inflation/contamination of solids and the gaseous that
circulates from the exterior to the interior, and it is to assuage such a
state of things that the rented mother is hired.[74] Following this preliminary introduction the sailor muses, "I thought I had met a person able to explain the meaning of life." Here it is worth noting
Wohlfarth's observation that Benjamin echoes Georg Lukács in saying that "the notion of *the meaning of life* is the center around which
the novel revolves."[75]

In their actual encounter in private, the sailor and the rented
mother address each other in a shot-reverse-shot sequence where the
image rocks from side to side in a gentle movement. The rented mother asks a series of questions: "Who are you?"; "Where are you from?";
"What do your parents do?"; "What did you do in Valparaiso?" The
sailor does not respond to "Who are you?" "Nowhere" is his initial
answer to the question "Where are you from?" and silence his reply to
"From Valparaiso?" So when reminded, "You must come from somewhere, from the north? from the south?" he finally responds "Yes
south" and adds that he was doing nothing, just drinking in
Valparaiso in answer to the question "What did you do there?" This
elicits a smile of recognition and the rented mother christens the
nameless sailor "lumpen proletariat." This is the rented mother as
remembrance (*Eingedenken*) offering the amnesiac sailor a rudimenta-
ry sense of personal memory, a sense of spatio-temporal coordination.
So it is also the moment of the birth of desire: "I wanted to see her
every day" he says.

But there is a problem of access to the maternal as memory. As
a result of this problem the sailor fights and kills the first captain
and narrates the fatality of the act in the following way: "Maybe I
already told you, but to get on the boat you had to kill on land and
sea. It was the secret rule and I obeyed it unknowingly. I spent two
weeks in chains. When I was set free my mother had been made to

leave the boat. She had written us a letter." Access to the maternal as memory is costly. In fact, it is at the price of death that she can now be accessed, albeit indirectly, via the letter she leaves for the sailors, read by the man without qualities *par excellence*, the impersonator.

In her letter she no longer speaks in the form of memory as remembrance of the one (*Eingedenken*), but as epic memory or a variant thereof (*Gedächtnis*). "You will follow her precepts," says the impersonator, before he reads her letter. "Develop the *memory* which belongs to everyone. If someone remembers something forgotten by the others let him forget it too. You will honour her with *understanding*: let everyone understand the same thing. If someone seems to understand something the others do not, let him admit his ignorance. You will honour her with *feelings*: you will love and hate at the same time. You will honour her with *imagination:* invent new ways of being and acting together. Never forget that memory, feeling, imagination and understanding must be used for an honest and productive life."

This enunciation of memory as a series of techniques or practices by the impersonator is important because the precepts—which have the ring of something sacred and perhaps even pious at the very end—cannot be taken at their face value as truths. The rented mother speaks with a forked tongue. She is both epic memory (*Gedächtnis*), memory of the many, of the storyteller as well as memory of the one (*Eingedenken*), remembrance, novelistic memory. Memory itself has now been allegorically marked by a destructive, fragmenting power.

If there is a desire here it is the wish to remember dismembered and forgotten memory itself. In emblematising memory as a contradictory, ambiguous and difficult practice via the allegory of the rented mother, Ruiz is not only redeeming the wish for memory in all its fragmented, irreconcilable complexity, he also offers something to a maternal imaginary as well—which is why I've pursued this analysis.

Though at first she did remind me of Benjamin's angel of history it is now clear to me that she is no angel. If anything she is rather more like the medieval devil, saying one thing and meaning something else, which is of course one way of defining allegory.

What of my hunch that this maternal allegory of memory is central to Ruiz's own allegorical practice? Let me offer as confirmation what Benjamin says about the structure of creativity he sees active in Baudelaire's allegorical practice, which I think is applicable to Ruiz as well. "If it is fantasy which presents the correspondences to memory, it is thinking which dedicates allegories to it. Memory brings the two together."[76] The two might be either fantasy and thinking or allegories and correspondences—this is not very clear; but what is clear is the centrality given to the function of memory itself, memory as technique/method and also as governed by chance, that is, memory in both its voluntary and involuntary aspects. From the point of view of voluntary memory (*Erinnerung*), involuntary memory (a variant of *Eingedenken*) may for Benjamin be more like a forgetting.[77] This makes intelligible the power attributed to forgetting in Ruiz's allegorical practice.

Her forked tongue, her discourse on memory performed by the impersonator—the improviser *in extremis*, wielding a hammer like an arhythmic baton—suggests that the solace this avatar of the maternal offers is not that of braiding the two types of estranged memory into an organic totality. This maternal allegory of memory, therefore of time and of experience (*Erfahrung*), exhorts her sons via her letter to invent a provisional collectivity across the figure of death itself, this death who is now an ally of both forgetting and of the will to remember.

The victory of allegory over symbol, whether staged via the emblem of the naked woman as art or that of the rented mother as memory, thus clarifies a facet of allegorical will and intuition, which is its methodological capacity to create memory and forgetting. Would Surrealism ever be able to even dream of emblematising the mythic symbol "Mother" as allegory of memory, in close proximity to the other myth, the femme fatale, as Ruiz does? I think not, because eternal surrealism is still enthralled by what Patricia Mellencamp calls the " 'MacGuffin' [red herring] of female sexuality."[78]

The maternal as emblematic memory is an image of time, a time-image in the Deleuzian sense.[79] Ruiz has extracted a sonic time-image from the mythic symbol Mother via allegorical doubling and the device of the letter performed by the impersonator. Hence she is no longer the dark continent, the silent body nor the guardian of tradition. This mater/matter as memory effects "incorporeal transformations"[80] on those who listen to her speech, the ghosts on the ghost ship. She does not lull, she speaks of the conditions that might make a possible future.

The fiction of the maternal body as "semiotic chora"[81] has sustained a formidable modernist history of male creativity. For women that fiction may not be that generative.[82] But Ruiz's allegory of the maternal as speech act (hence a pure cinematographic utterance in Deleuzean terms[83]) is certainly more enabling. This speech act which has detached itself not only from its sender but also from its receiver passes into a seascape. This floating utterance touches the image formed of sea, sky and steel. I too am touched by the corrosive allegorical impulse. So all I can see in the final image (of this sequence), the rusty ghost ship cutting a passage through the sea, is an image of memory as a writing on water.

I wish to thank Suhanya Raffel for introducing me to the work of Lisa Lyon with Robert Mapplethorpe. This paper was written for the "Breath of Balsam; Reorienting Surrealism" conference convened by the Museum of Contemporary Art and the Humanities Research Centre, in 1993.

1   *Life is a Dream* is a play by Calderon which Ruiz adapted in his film *Memory of Appearances*. Ruiz has said that "there is a way of using dreams and one of using memory. They are not the same, even though they are often confused ... Memory is a method/technique, machinery/mechanism. The mnemotechniques are linked completely by chance,"(Buci-Glucksman, 103, see note 16). Ruiz structured his film *Memory of Appearances* on the basis of this technique, which was derived from Frances Yates' book *The Art of Memory*. Given the surrealist celebration of dreams I want here to foreground Ruiz's concern with making a distinction between working with dream and memory.
    An explanation of my title is I think required. I use the notion of a "capillary memory" as a minute memory trace, which works like capillary veins bringing blood to larger blood vessels. In this particular instance it is a memory trace that hurt for a while. Capillary bleeding however is not fatal but if the ceaseless irritation is not heeded there may be some substantial loss. This paper comes out of a need to deal with some unfinished business (call it non-fatal bleeding) related to the forum with Raul Ruiz organised by the Australian Film Institute (chaired by me) on 3 February 1993, in Sydney. This essay is also a reading of two sequences, those of the femme fatale and the rented mother, from Ruiz's film *Three Crowns of a Sailor*, France (INA), 1983, 117 mins, 35mm.

2   Robert Benayoun, quoted by Adrian Martin in "The Artificial Night: Surrealism and Cinema," *Surrealism, Revolution by Night*, catalogue for exhibition curated by Michel Lloyd et al. (Canberra: National Gallery of Australia, 1993), 190.

3   Raul Ruiz forum, Australian Film Institute, Sydney, 1993.

4   "Who is Raul Ruiz?" *Sydney Morning Herald*, 29 January 1993, 1. The Australian Broadcasting Corporation, Radio National's program *Screen* on "Surrealism and Cinema" included an interview with Ruiz, 14 January 1993. The Australian Film Institute flyer for the Ruiz retrospective has the line "The films of Raul Ruiz, A Surreal Journey."

5   *Screen*, ibid.

6   The only exceptions I know of are the following: Suzana M Pick's "The Dialectical Wanderings of Exile," *Screen*, vol. 30 no. 4 (Autumn 1989), 48–64 and Libby Ostinga's "Exile and Metamorphosis, the magical cinematic practice of Raul Ruiz," unpublished honours thesis, Department of Fine Arts, University of Sydney, 1992.

7   Susan Sontag, Introduction to Walter Benjamin's *One Way Street*, trans. Edmund Jephcott and Kingsley Shorter (London: NLB, 1979), 16–17.

8   It is curious that when modern allegory is theorised it is most often accompanied by an affect, namely, melancholy. A student asked me why, which set me wondering as well. The conjoining of melancholy and allegory introduces a pathological dimension to this mode of signification. The pathology of melancholy is analysed by Freud in his essay, "Mourning and Melancholia" (*Sigmund Freud*, The Standard Edition, trans. James Strachey, vol. XIV, 1914–1916, London: Hogarth Press, 1986), 243–260. As point-

ed out by Strachey in his editor's note to the essay (249), Freud suggests that "there was a connection between melancholia and the oral stage of libidinal development" (249–50). Also see note 36 for Freud's distinction between mourning and melancholia.

9 Walter Benjamin, *The Origin of German Tragic Drama*, trans. John Osborne (London: NLB, 1977), 185.

10 Raul Ruiz forum, Australian Film Institute, Sydney.

11 Baudelaire as quoted by Susan Sontag,"Introduction," 20.

12 Ibid., 20.

13 Raul Ruiz forum. Ruiz said that "Enthusiasm" and the "ludic" are synonymous, much to my surprise. Interestingly Freud in his essay on "Mourning and Melancholia" makes a connection between melancholy and mania, (joy, exultation, triumph) 253–54. Freud says, "the most remarkable characteristic of melancholia and the one in most need of explanation is its tendency to change round into mania—a state which is the opposite of it in its symptoms ... the content of mania is no different from that of melancholia, both disorders are wrestling with the same "complex," but ... in melancholia the ego has succumbed to the complex whereas in mania it has mastered it or pushed it aside." (254) One could take enthusiasm and mania to be more or less the same affect vis-à-vis melancholy. What all of this suggests is that melancholy and enthusiasm are complex affects. Perhaps something Italo Calvino has said in his essay on "Lightness," in *Six Memos for the Next Millennium*, (1988, 18) may clarify the link that seemed so obvious to Ruiz. Calvino refers to "the special connection between melancholy and humour studied by Raymond Klibansky, Erwin Panofsky, and Fritz Saxl in *Saturn and Melancholy*" (1964). He clarifies this: "As melancholy is sadness that has taken on lightness, so humour is comedy that has lost its bodily weight." The ludic as a species of the comic then is inextricably intermingled with melancholy. "Enthusiasm" which the ancients called "poetic inspiration" is here reinvented to be a compound, "a veil of minute particles of humours and sensations, a fine dust of atoms ..." (Calvino, 20). The idea of melancholy humour feels right in relation to the kind of ludic register in which *Three Crowns of a Sailor* operates. This notion may also be quite a useful one with which to think the work of some of the great silent comedians like, for example, Buster Keaton.

14 Adrian Martin, "The Artificial Night," 191

15 Ibid., 191.

16 *Raoul Ruiz*, "Interview with Raoul Ruiz," Christine Buci-Glucksman and Fabrice Revault D'Allonnes (Paris: Editions Dis Voir, Sarl, 1987), 103, unpublished trans. Marie Ramsland.

17 Adrian Martin, "The Artificial Night," 191.

18 Buci-Glucksman,"Interview with Raoul Ruiz," 103.

19 Martin, "The Artificial Night," 193.

20 Raul Ruiz forum.

21 Martin, "The Artificial Night," 195.

22 Raul Ruiz forum, see published version in *Agenda*, vol. 30 no. 31 (May

1993), 50–53.

23   If allegorical bodies are fragmentary in structure then an allegorical figure
     is a part which is greater than the whole. Thanks to Jodi Brooks for point-
     ing out this analogy between the fragmenting power of allegory and the
     close-up and for reminding me of how this connects with Balazs' and
     Eisenstein's notions of the close-up.

24   "Interview with Raoul Ruiz," by Pascal Bonitzer and Serge Toubiana,
     Cahiers du Cinéma, no. 345, (March 1983).

25   Most of this section is a summary of what Ruiz said at the Sydney
     Australian Film Institute forum.

26   Libby Ostinga, unpublished interview with Raul Ruiz, Sydney 1993.

27   Michael Chanan, *Chilean Cinema* (London: BFI, 1976), 32.

28   Ostinga, unpublished interview.

29   Buci-Glucksman, "Interview with Raoul Ruiz," 96–98.

30   Ostinga, unpublished interview.

31   Benjamin, *The Origin of German Tragic Drama*, 175.

32   Raul Ruiz forum.

33   Ibid.

34   "The Cinema of Raul Ruiz," interview by Adrian Martin, *Cinema Papers*, no.
     91 (January 1993), 61. I am greatly indebted to this interview by Martin
     for having raised the issues of the baroque and allegorical aspects of Ruiz's
     cinema, perhaps for the first time in English.

35   Ibid., 35.

36   This notion of exhaustion of the will to allegory and the affliction of allego-
     ry or the compulsion to allegorise are related. They may be understood via
     the comparison Freud makes between mourning and melancholy. (Freud,
     "Mourning and Melancholia" see note 8.) In the case of mourning one con-
     sciously knows what is lost but the melancholic subject grieves at the loss
     of an object and does not know what it is that s/he has lost. According to
     Freud, "it is an object loss withdrawn from consciousness." (245) This loss
     of the object is like a double loss because of the attendant amnesia. Freud
     suggests that this loss causes a narcissistic disorder because the loss of the
     object also means a loss in regard to the ego. The internal work of the
     melancholic which Freud says is akin to that of the work of mourning con-
     sumes the ego. (243) This may be a reason for the "exhaustion" that marks
     the tenacious will to allegorise. There is here a correspondence (somewhat
     difficult to grasp), between the absent, forgotten object of the melancholic's
     grief and the positive power attributed to forgetting in the construction of
     allegory in Ruiz's film. Could this be called sublimation?

37   Benjamin, *The Origin of German Tragic Drama*, 220.

38   Ibid., 217.

39   It is as a result of the Raul Ruiz forum that I have been impelled to refer to
     myself thus, after having lived in Australia for some eighteen years.

40   Recent Sri Lankan history is littered with such corpses burnt on tyres as
     emblems for the living to see and smell. In such a context there was an odd
     coincidence which I relish. On 1 May 1993 as I was going out to see *Three*

Crown of a Sailor, in order to write about it, we heard on ABC news that the Sri Lankan president had been blasted into oblivion by a bomb. Rumour has it that all that was identifiable was a hand which had the president's ring on it. The president, during whose regime bodies were used as allegorical emblems, lessons for the living, was himself left with hardly a body trace. Macabre Sri Lankan humour has it that some of the body pieces put into his coffin may in fact have been those of his assassin, there was no way of telling.

41 Freud, "Mourning and Melancholia," note 1, 243. The editor says "the German 'Trauer,' like the English 'mourning,' can mean both the affect of grief and its outward manifestation." In this section I am more interested in the theatrical dimension of public mourning which no doubt has its own necessity and efficacity. As a child I remember going to a funeral of a fisherman in my mother's village. As we approached the house we saw the dead man's wife looking out the window and registering our arrival. As we entered the house, which was until then quiet, the bereaved wife started her loud lamentation (which had set phrases and non-verbal sounds). I think my mother understood both codes of mourning (the affect and its outward manifestation) but I judged that woman as being insincere for having displayed her grief for our benefit. In the last seventeen years, having been to many Australian funerals, I have returned with a sense of a loss of something like a ritual act to mark this momentous rite of passage into oblivion and memory.

42 Benjamin, *The Origin of German Tragic Drama*, 193.

43 Buci-Glucksman and Fabrice Revault D'Allonnes, "Interview with Raoul Ruiz," 95.

44 Susan Buck-Morss, *The Dialectics of Seeing; Walter Benjamin and the Arcades Project* (Cambridge and Massachusetts: MIT Press, 1991), 167.

45 Paul Garcia, David Bolliger, Nick O'Sullivan, "Cinema, Prosthetics and a Short History of Latin America: An Interview with Raul Ruiz," Sydney (unpublished). Ruiz has said in passing that the cinematic apparatus necessitates a critique of Bergson's idea of duration, because in every 24th fraction of a second there is a black space, a death, an instant of forgetting. This suggests that there is the possibility of multiple beginnings. Benjamin's critique of Bergsonian duration could function here as an elaboration for Ruiz. In his essay "On some Motifs in Baudelaire" (*Illuminations*, 187), Benjamin says:

> If Baudelaire in *Spleen and Vie anterieure* holds in his hand the scattered fragments of genuine historical experience, Bergson in his conception of the durée has become far more estranged from history. "Bergson the metaphysician suppresses death." The fact that death is eliminated from Bergson's durée isolates it effectively from a historical (as well as prehistorical) order ... The durée from which death has been eliminated has the miserable endlessness of a scroll. Tradition is excluded from it. It is the quintessence of a passing moment that struts about in the

borrowed garb of experience. The spleen, on the other hand, exposes
the passing moment in all its nakedness.

46 Robert Mapplethorpe, *Lady, Lisa Lyon,* (New York: The Viking Press,
    1983),
47 Benjamin, *The Origin of German Tragic Drama,* 199.
48 Ibid., 196.
49 The maxim as a rhetorical device is marked by an economy that can link
    up with Ruiz' understanding of baroque visual economy. The idea of a
    "flash of light," as Jodi Brooks has pointed out to me, is a complex one in
    Benjamin's writing. Irving Wohlfarth relates this mode of involuntary per-
    ception to what Benjamin calls "presence of mind," in the following: "But
    presence of mind as Benjamin conceives it both collects itself and recollects
    the past in a flash too instantaneous to be called self-reflexive." So, "the
    flash of light" seems to be a modality of involuntary memory. Irving
    Wohlfarth, "On the Messianic Structure of Walter Benjamin's Last
    Reflections," *GLYPH,* Johns Hopkins Textual Studies, no. *3* (Baltimore:
    Johns Hopkins University Press, 1978), 164.
50 Ibid., 197.
51 Ibid., 195.
52 Susan Buck-Morss, *The Dialectics of Seeing,* 166.
53 Benjamin, *The Origin of German Tragic Drama,* 208.
54 Body building may be thought of as a form of nudity that makes the dis-
    tinction between the inside and the outside irrelevant and in this sense
    may be likened to the allegorical body because the latter does not have an
    interiority. The naked body may be said to be a vulnerable body while the
    built body as a form of armature may make the body a non-vulnerable sur-
    face so it becomes in some sense perfect material for allegorical metamor-
    phosis. Here one may see a shift in the very genre of the nude, because
    nudity in this instance has become a dress that may not be taken off but
    reveals nevertheless a magical capacity to metamorphose via a process of
    fragmentation.
55 Ibid., 222.
56 Ibid.
57 Ibid., 191.
58 Ibid.
59 Angus Fletcher, *Allegory: The Theory of a Symbolic Mode* (Ithaca: Cornell
    University Press,1982), 50.
60 Raul Ruiz Forum, Australian Film Institute, Sydney. Ruiz's description
    matches Erwin Panofsky's account of melancholy both as pathology and
    as description of a form of creativity in his book *Saturn and Melancholy,* co-
    edited with Raymond Klibansky and Fritz Saxl. (London: Thomas Nelson,
    1964), 17, 40, 41.
61 It is necessary to sketch out what I understand by allegorical efficacity. It
    seems that the melancholic temperament perceives in a heightened way
    transience, the flux of time and things. It seems that allegorical constructs

are temporal forms imagined and willed in order to perceive, make tangible the operations of time as incessant flow and decay, hence the privileged emblems of modern allegory, the corpse, the ruin and the ghost. Perhaps an allegory is efficacious if it can provide an emblem that can make one play with time, wrest an "instant" to reflect on its inexorable movement. Also it is efficacious if it can create a process whereby involuntary memory can be generated. In such a dynamic, remembrance and forgetting would have to be necessarily related.

62 It amazes me to realise that the allegory of the femme fatale has been placed between two figures of the maternal and that it is by pursuing my fascination with this figure that I inadvertently stumbled on the figure of the rented mother. There is a logic of phantasy here that is generative, seemingly inexhaustible. If the propensity to melancholy is connected with a disturbance with the oral function (according to Freud) then the maternal and the loss of the maternal must surely figure prominently in this pathology. Ruiz has been able to sublimate (not repress) this loss via the melancholy humour of his film. Perhaps this is why there is no logic of a secret to be revealed in this film, despite the mystery and enchantment of the film.

63 Ostinga, Interview with Raul Ruiz.

64 Benjamin,"The Image of Proust," in *Illuminations*, 204.

65 Irving Wohlfarth, "On the Messianic Structure of Walter Benjamin's Last Reflections," *GLYPH*, Johns Hopkins Textual Studies, no. 3 (Baltimore: Johns Hopkins University Press, 1978), 154.

66 The matrix of allegory unlike that of the human embryo would have to be a temporal form that can sustain incommensurable temporalities. Memory as imagined by both Benjamin and Ruiz is such an entity. Unlike Benjamin however, Ruiz is able to imagine the maternal in a manner that is untouched by the Oedipal.

67 Benjamin, *The Origin of German Tragic Drama*, 193.

68 Benjamin, "The Storyteller," *Illuminations*, 83–109.

69 Irving Wohlfarth, "On the Messianic Structure," 150.

70 Benjamin, "The Storyteller," 97. Just the final sentence is as translated by Wohlfarth.

71 Gilbert Adair, *Sight and Sound*, vol. 53 no. 3 (Summer 1984), 162.

72 Benjamin, "The Work of Art in the Age of mechanical Reproduction," *Illuminations*, 240.

73 Benjamin, "The Storyteller," 98. Here again I have used Wohlfarth's translation of this passage as it is clearer than the one in *Illuminations*.

74 Gilles Deleuze, *Cinema 1: The Movement Image* (Minneapolis: University of Minnesota Press, 1986), Ch.12, 206. I read Ruiz's notion of "contamination of the gaseous" as being equivalent to what Deleuze calls the "inflation of images both in the external world and in people's minds."

75 Wohlfarth, "On the Messianic Structure," 169. This is because the "isolated bourgeoise subject is haunted by the loss of objective meaning."

76 Benjamin, "Central Park", *New German Critique*, (no.34, 1985), 40.

77 Wohlfarth, "On the Messianic Structure," footnote no.12, 199. Wohlfarth
    also draws the analogy between voluntary and involuntary memory and
    the Freudian distinction between the conscious and the unconscious
    where the latter is more like a forgetting from the perspective of the former.
78 Patricia Mellencamp, "Five Ages of Film Feminism," p.25 in this volume.
79 Gilles Deleuze, *Cinema 2: The Time Image* (Minneapolis: University of
    Minnesota Press, 1989). Though Deleuze does not theorise allegorical or
    baroque temporality in his books on the cinema one could use his ideas
    about the time image and combine it with what Ruiz says about allegory to
    come up with a particular time image deriving from allegorical forms
    (which are temporal constructs), as I have done in this paper. Ruiz also
    spoke about the importance of the distinction between allegory and mon-
    tage at the Sydney forum and said that the movement of the former was
    centrifugal, while that of the latter was centripetal but added that he had to
    think about it further. I have hardly touched on the *mise-en-scène* of the
    femme fatale sequence but if I did, it would be necessary to work out how
    allegory relates to the structure of montage, which would also be a ques-
    tion about time. If according to Deleuze the time-image is a sensory event
    before action takes hold of it then allegories are endlessly open sensory
    events that seem to go on forever. This is, however, not the logic of inter-
    minable analysis familiar from psychoanalysis. I have this feeling that I
    can spend the rest of my professional life analysing this film and yet not
    exhaust it. It is a bit like the way the black father from Dacca feels about
    the act of narrating his life in *Three Crowns of a Sailor*, i.e. that there is not
    enough time.
80 Deleuze's idea of "incorporeal transformations" is explained by Ronald
    Bogue (in *Deleuze and Guattari*, Routledge, 1989, 137), as deriving from
    both the Stoic idea of incorporeals and from Austin's speech act theory.
    According to the latter saying something is a way of doing something. As
    for the Stoics, according to Bogue, they "recognise two simultaneous and
    coextensive readings of the universe, one in terms of bodies, causes and a
    perpetual present, the other in terms of incorporeals, surface effects, and a
    perpetually contracting and expanding past and future."(68) While words
    are bodies they have an incorporeal dimension, that of sense/meaning that
    can haunt bodies, this is partly because of the peculiar temporal dimension
    within which they operate. It is the temporality encoded within the utter-
    ance that effects the incorporeal transformation in the sailor.
81 Julia Kristeva, *Desire in Language: A Semiotic Approach to Literature and Art*
    (New York: Columbia University Press, 1980), 133, 174, 284, 286–287.
82 This may be so because there is no possibility of experiencing difference
    through such a fiction, without which it would be impossible to begin the
    work of signification.
83 For Deleuze a "pure" sonic image is one that is separate from the visual
    image but reaches it at some moment in a manner to be deciphered. A
    question has plagued me: Why doesn't Deleuze deal with his fellow
    migrant compatriot's cinema when analysing the time-image? When this

impossible question was put to Ruiz at a Melbourne forum he laughed and mentioned that they had had a fight (a physical one) many years ago! But beyond this it is possible that the chaos, and the irreducible multiplicity in Ruiz's baroque allegorical work is still difficult to deal with within philosophy, even one of multiplicity. Could this also be due to the French difficulty with the baroque that Ruiz spoke of?

Meditation on Violence

Lesley Stern

> We had to delay if not avoid what we thought of as the moment of cas-
> tration in the editing suite. That was 1968, editing became a byword for
> a reformist moment which attempted to contain the revolutionary one
> we lived in the streets where we shot. Editing tended to block and freeze
> material that was vital and came to us "red hot" from the laboratories.
> For me, the editing room was a cross between a slaughter house and an
> autopsy room; it was the closest moment I could think of (in the process
> of film-making) to death and embalming.
>
> Bernardo Bertolucci[1]

The blood is leached from *Raging Bull* and yet it comes to us 'red hot,' too
hot to handle, still too red for a body slashed excessively and bled to black
and white.

A woman twirls, flies through space, compelled by the red shoes she
wears to dance forever. A newspaper flutters into the air, into her arms,
transforming there into a human shape. The couple dance together
and in the circulation of desire there is a transference: her dress is slowly imprinted, assumes the texture of windblown newspaper.

Like the woman dancing, *Raging Bull* bears an imprint, can be read
in terms of *The Red Shoes*; it is as though *The Red Shoes* has bled sublim-
inally into *Raging Bull*.

Too Hot to Handle

There is a film I often show. I load this film onto the projector and tell the students to watch carefully, they are about to see a film about the cinema. There's a moment of blackness when the lights in the room are switched off, then—for a moment—the beam from the projector illuminates the screen and I hold my breath. Then there is redness, flesh, butchered corpses. Or so it seems. I try, every time, to watch. Part of me indeed is fascinated and attracted by these images, but also—they repel. I have to look away, close my eyes, sometimes I have to leave the room. Later they say: how can you talk about this film, how can you claim to have seen it, presume to teach it, when your eyes are closed? "But I am watching," I say. And it's true. The images are insistent, even when my eyes are closed the images seem somehow imprinted on my retina. And although I tell myself "these are only images of bloody bodies, only images embalmed that you are seeing, you aren't seeing—with your own eyes, for yourself—real bodies truly bleeding" it makes no difference. But, of course, this Brakhage knows. There is a documentary quality to *The Act of Seeing with One's Own Eyes*[2]—set in a mortuary and documenting autopsy procedures it is uncannily reminiscent of Bertolucci's "cross between a slaughter house and an autopsy room," but the documentary dimension is almost a pretext for fictionality. It is a film about the way the cinema engages the imagination, about a dynamic of repulsion and attraction, about the imbrication of images and imagination.[3]

Bertolucci, in the quotation that prefaces this paper, is talking primarily about how editing, in the heady days of 1968, was experienced as an act of violation, interfering with the primacy of the real and deadening all vital impulses. When I read this the film that came first to mind was *The Act of Seeing with One's Own Eyes* which is odd because although it thematises and depicts a version of death and embalmment it is hardly an instance of cinematic "still life"; on the contrary it never fails to disturb, to bring images and fantasies alive.

To then superimpose *Raging Bull* and *The Red Shoes* over *The Act of Seeing with One's Own Eyes* might seem at first to simply exacerbate the oddness, insofar as these are films characterised by virtuoso editing which is hardly "reformist," certainly does not "block and freeze." But Bertolucci speaks not only of editing, he is actually articulating something more general about the cinema, using editing to focus a particular fear and thrill involved in filmmaking. He conveys an excitement about cinema's ability to transmit something that is "red hot," and also a fear of cinema's capacity to deaden and embalm. Now despite arguments about the tendency of any representational mode, and of continuity editing in particular, to contain disturbance and literally "reform" the castration threat, editing is not intrinsically deadening.[4] But it might be—and here's the danger. It might be deadening not exactly in the sense suggested by Bertolucci (i.e., numbing) but in another, though related, sense—in the sense of articulating a death threat, of enacting a death drive. If the cinema does not simply reconstitute a presence of bodies, but if it participates in a genesis of the bodily then it also can dismember bodies, disperse bodily fragments like Actaeon torn limb from limb by his own hounds and scattered in pieces through time and space. Moreover the film itself can materialise as a body of sorts, a body that bleeds—metaphorically, but with sensible affects, producing for instance sensations of illness, fear, ecstasy. Making a film, then (and making it up as a viewer—in the act of seeing with your own eyes), involves the risk that in generating the thrilling and ecstatic you will go beyond the pleasure principle and encounter a death threat. Bertolucci himself articulates this—to a large degree through editing—in *Before the Revolution* (1964), most particularly in the famous jump cut sequences and in the opera sequence where the force of desire between the young protagonist, Fabrizio and his beautiful aunt is conveyed through a dizzyingly ecstatic orchestration of camera movements and cuts. But it's double edged, this desire, razor sharp; the other side of ecstasy is danger, the threat of annihilation and death, a fate intimated by the operatic setting.

Raging Bull and *The Red Shoes* were provoked into being for me, I suspect, by these words of Bertolucci's not because they deaden, but rather because they also pose a death threat, and in that very posture they invoke the ecstatic. The association with *The Act of Seeing with One's Own Eyes* pivots around the notion of slaughter, cutting as dismemberment and bleeding; but also (and this is part of it, crucially so) they are all films obliquely—through enactment one might say, rather than through direct discursive means—about cinematic experience. Just as the pivotal sequence of *Before the Revolution* takes place at the opera thus enticing us into a heightened dramatic mode as it simultaneously foregrounds our place as audience, so *Raging Bull* and *The Red Shoes* are also about performance and viewing. The former is about a spectator sport—boxing, and the latter is about ballet, and in both the viewing position is doubly articulated as we occupy the position of audience both inter- and extra-diegetically. But such thematic concerns are merely indicative—it is in their enactments that both films explore the act of seeing in the cinema.

This paper is partially concerned with cutting, or editing. But also it revolves around the question of what makes a film "red hot." Let me briefly indicate the range of these two concerns. First, cutting. As already indicated, cutting carries threatening connotations. However, this is not all that cutting implies, and in this paper I will also be concerned with the relationship between editing and motion. In both films editing itself is used almost magically to create sensations of velocity; but more particularly I am interested in the way editing is frequently combined with the speed of filming (employing both resolute slowness and rapidity) to enact a compulsive drive. Second, the question of what makes a film "red hot." Insofar as the phrase "red hot" implies "too hot to handle" there is an evocation of touch. Bertolucci is speaking literally, about handling celluloid in the editing room; but I intend to deploy the phrase as a figure of speech—to explore the relation between what it is that makes it difficult to get a handle on these films, and the way in which the films themselves obsessively enact a drama around the taboo on touch. In *Totem and Taboo* Freud argues that the principal prohibition is against touching.[5] The totemic object, which is simultaneously sacred and unclean, inspiring veneration and horror, must not be touched for fear of its capacity for contagion and transference. The offender who touches runs the danger of being possessed. Many critics (and the cinephiles that lurk in most of us who here are reading, and writing), actually yearn to be possessed and in much writing on Scorsese, and in Scorsese's writing on Michael Powell, there is a kind of mimicking of the films in a critical discourse that obsessively repeats terms such as "immediacy," "intensity," "danger," "excess" as though repetition in itself constitutes evidence and validation. It is as though contact with the films produces a kind of adjectival delirium tantamount to possession. It is a phenomenon that intrigues and irritates me, no doubt because I find myself implicated, compelled to repeat. So it is that the notion—or rather, the question—of immediacy, the immediacy of touch (what we might call the "critical touchy feely" phenomenon), constitutes the starting point for this work around Scorsese.

I argue that *Raging Bull* and *The Red Shoes* themselves enact, in an obsessive mode, a death drive and thus implicate the viewer or would be critic in a dangerously mimetic relation. What I shall concentrate on, however, is the way in which both films dramatise the relation between obsession and the totemic object. Freud stressed the relation between obsessive behaviour and forms of behaviour instituted by the totem-and-taboo dynamic by locating both the prohibitions of neurotics and taboos in touching, and extended the sense of this to include the notion of coming "in contact with."[6] This paper will focus, then, on a series of totemic objects—boxing gloves, red shoes, *Raging Bull* and *The Red Shoes*.

That's Entertainment

The totemic object—insofar as it implies an ordinary object invested with extraordinary qualities—summons a context of ritual, of ceremony, of theatre; a context realised in sharp opposition to the everyday. The gloves and the shoes both indicate an arena of performance, an arena in which the ordinary body is transformed. On the stage, in the ring—boxing, dancing—for an audience, the body is ceremonialised. Both films revolve around the relationship between art and life as has frequently been discussed; but what interests me is the way in which their enactment (rather than simply their thematic) renders familiar distinctions—between artifice and naturalism for instance, between public and private—perilously uncertain. In both cases it is the body, the "decided body," to borrow a term from the language of performance, that paradoxically becomes the site of radical uncertainty. But before going further into this notion of the decided body, a reminder of what these films are "about."

The Red Shoes, made by Michael Powell and Emeric Pressburger in 1948, opens with a crowd waiting outside a stage door. As the doors are opened the crowd turns into a mob, literally storming the theatre. Tension builds as we anticipate the performance. In the audience, i.e., as spectators, are the three main protagonists of the film, who do not yet know one another, but who are destined to become entwined in a drama of desire, ambition, creativity and possession. There is Boris Lermontov (played by Anton Walbrook in a steely mode of restrained stylisation), the impresario who presides over a prestigious ballet company and who incites the young composer Julian Craster (Marius Goring) to write a ballet called "The Red Shoes" for an equally young and unknown dancer, Victoria Page, whom he intends to make into a great star. Vicky was played by a ballet dancer not an actress (Norma Shearer), which creates a fascinating performative tension in *The Red Shoes* itself,[7] and across the energy field mapped by both films (there is a kind of inversion in *Raging Bull* where the main protagonist is played by an actor not a boxer, but a method-oriented actor, Robert De Niro, who learnt how to box and literally reshaped his body to an extraordinary degree in order to play the part—a rite of passage that has now entered the annals of Hollywood legend). The ballet of "The Red Shoes" within the film *The Red Shoes* dramatises a girl's desire—she yearns for a pair of red shoes but when she gets them they take her over, body and soul, so that she can neither take them off, nor stop dancing. This tale is mirrored in Vicky's "everyday" life, in the framing story. In their first meeting Lermontov asks her, "What do you want from life? To live?" "To dance," she replies. Dancing is her life, but it is also a compulsion that poses a threat to "ordinary" happiness and in the end it drives her literally over the edge—to her death.

Raging Bull, made by Martin Scorsese in 1980, is encapsulated in its opening. It begins[8] in a dressing room in New York City, 1964, where Jake La Motta, ex-middleweight boxing champion now grossly overweight, is reciting his lines in preparation for a performance (in a night club).[9] The words are faded in before we see him—"I remember those cheers/They still ring in my ears." The poem, with its stumbling repetitions, lasts the length of a single take, in medium long shot, with La Motta puffing on a fat cigar. It ends thus: "So give me a stage/Where this bull here can rage/And though I can fight/I'd much rather recite/That's entertainment." Cut to a medium close up with a title over—JAKE LA MOTTA 1964. Cut to a shot of a much younger, sinewy La Motta, in the ring (also in medium close-up, but from the obverse diagonal). Over the image of him at the ready, gloved hands poised, is the title: JAKE LA MOTTA 1941. On the soundtrack we hear, softly, the line repeated: "That's entertainment." Then there is an explosion of sound and movement—blows, flash lights, the crowd roaring. At the end of the fight the ring is mobbed (as the theatre is stormed in *The Red Shoes*), people trampled underfoot, chairs sent flying through the air. *Raging Bull* is a film based on the life of boxer Jake La Motta, but more accurately, I think, it is a fiction about a man who lives in order to fight, just as Vicky lives in order to dance. In fact only about fifteen minutes of the film are devoted to boxing. Violence, however, is dispersed into the everyday, into the way that Jake lives out his closest relationships, enacts his paranoid delusions and jealous obsessions.

***

There exists in many European languages an expression which might be chosen to epitomise what is essential for the actor's life. It is a grammatically paradoxical expression, in which a passive form comes to assume an active meaning, and in which the indication of an availability for action is couched in a form of passivity. It is not an ambiguous expression, but an hermaphroditic one, combining within it action and passivity, and in spite of its strangeness it is an expression found in common speech. One says in fact, "*essere deciso*," "*être décidé*," "to be decided." And it does not mean that someone or something decides us or that we undergo decision, nor that we are the object of decision. It doesn't even mean that we are deciding, nor that we are carrying out the action of deciding.

Between these opposing conditions flows a current of life which language does not seem to represent and around which it dances with images.[10]

***

Eugenio Barba in here discussing the "decided body" points to a paradox: this body performs by virtue of training, discipline, yet in the act of performing it appears as possessed, almost as an involuntary presence. There is something hard to grasp, something other than technique even though it includes technique (thought of as a repertoire of acquired skills), that differentiates this body from the everyday body. It is to do with the particular way of deploying energy, and includes context—the presence of an audience, the marking out of a quasi-ceremonial or ritualistic space. "The actor gives himself [sic] form and gives form to his message through fiction, by modeling his energy."[11] The performing or extra-daily body is distinguished from the daily body by the kind and range of techniques, and the ways in which they are used. The distinction is *not* made on the basis of presence or absence of technique, i.e., the extra-daily "having" technique, the daily "without" or "natural." On the contrary, quotidian techniques are profoundly cultural, but usually learned and acted out on an unconscious and habitual level. What is interesting to performance theorists[12] is that within the Occident the distance which separates daily body techniques from extra-daily ones is often neither evident nor consciously considered (unlike in India, Bali or Japan for instance).

Boxing and ballet provide us with two instances of clear theatrical differentiation within a Western context—sites for a particular modeling of energy. Hence it seems useful to draw on an understanding of acting (using the term broadly to include a range of performance modes) that focuses on the way energy is deployed by and through the body, rather than privileging psychological or mimetic principles. But there is another reason for this detour, this allusion to a tendency within performance studies that is peculiarly attentive to cultural constraints and conventions. *Raging Bull* and *The Red Shoes* are about performance, about the way in which bodies are transformed and "possessed" by performing—in the ring, on the stage. The red shoes and the gloves, as totemic objects, derive their force from this performative, quasi-ritualistic context. But the films also, it seems to me, enact a dilemma that is peculiarly cultural, that has precisely to do with the fact that in the Occident the distance which separates daily body techniques from extra-daily ones is often neither evident nor consciously considered. If we think of performance as a way of converting and transforming energy, then it seems that in these films there is a demonstrable excess—energy that is not contained by the performance arena is transformed differently in the quotidian, ecstasy is repeated, but with ruinous reverberations.

Faced with *Raging Bull* and *The Red Shoes*, let us contemplate the fiction of a decided body. What is interesting in Barba's discussion is the peculiar combination of passive and active, voluntary and involuntary. The decisiveness of the performing body, carried over into the daily by Vicky and Jake, is transformed into a catastrophic indecision or inability to contain a compulsive and deadly drive. Although they are extremely active, they are also gripped by passivity, in the thrall of obsession—by its nature involuntary. But we are not just speaking of the protagonists; the films themselves are textual bodies, at once decided and potentially out of control.

***

There exists a primary level of the actor's dramaticity which has nothing to do with intellectual categories but which relates uniquely to the way in which the actor manipulates his energy. The way he exploits and composes the weight/balance relationship and the opposition between different movements, their duration, their rhythms, permits him to give to the audience not only a different perception of the body but also a different perception of time and space: not a "time in space," but a "space-time."[13]

***

Raging Bull and *The Red Shoes* both articulate this "space-time," not just thematically, as films about performers, but through their modes of staging different movements, their duration, their rhythms. They permit the viewer a different perception of the body—cinematically spaced out. There are other films whose techniques are similarly extra-ordinary—think of Cassavetes' *Opening Night* and Rivette's

L'amour fou. Deleuze, in discussing "the cinema of the body" cites both these directors and says that sometimes this cinema "mounts a ceremony, takes on an initiatory and liturgical aspect, and attempts to summon all the metallic and liquid powers of a sacred body, to the point of honour or revulsion ..."[14] Remember that vivid and painfully sensational scene in *Opening Night* in which Gina Rowlands, caught between the arena of the stage and the everyday, bangs her head repeatedly against a door frame—a focusing of energy at once voluntary and involuntary, not dissimilar to the scene in which La Motta enacts a similar gestus in the prison cell. Of *L'amour fou* Deleuze writes, "Rivette invents a theatricality of cinema totally distinct from the theatricality of the theatre (even when cinema uses it as a reference)."[15] We might say the same of Scorsese, and Powell and Pressburger.

But The Gloves Are Red

It all begins with the telling of a story, with several stories and various beginnings. And in every beginning there is an ending (or two).

One of the stories goes like this: whilst preparing for *Raging Bull* Marty shot some 8 mm while Bobby was training in a gym, and he showed this footage to Michael Powell. "As the film ended, Powell turned to Scorsese and said, 'But the gloves are red.' "[16]

***

When, in *The Red Shoes*, Boris Lermontov, the impresario played by Anton Walbrook, tells the story of Hans Christian Anderson's "The Red Shoes" (to Julian Craster the young composer), he fondles a statuette of a pointed foot in a ballet slipper. It is a severed foot—set on a pedestal. Julian asks, "What happens in the end?" Lermontov shrugs the question off, tosses his answer into the wind—"Oh, in the end she dies."

***

Scorsese's version of watching the 8 mm footage goes like this:

> I remember we were looking at this, projected on the back of a
> door in my apartment on 57th Street, and Michael Powell was
> sitting on the floor watching it with us. Suddenly Michael said,
> "There's something wrong: the gloves shouldn't be red." Back
> in 1975, he'd written to me after first seeing *Mean Streets* to
> say that he liked it, but I used too much red—this from the
> man who had red all over his own films, which was where I'd
> got it from in the first place! But he was right about the boxing
> footage, and our cinematographer Michael Chapman also
> pointed out how colour was detracting from the images.[17]

There is a generic underpinning to these explanations of how
Raging Bull came to be shot in black and white. Today's fighters usually wear red gloves and pastel-coloured trunks but our memories of
boxing in the forties and fifties are in black and white, partly because
of grainy documentary footage and newspaper photographs and films
like *Body and Soul* and *Champion*. But in these anecdotes there is something in excess of genre explanation. "But the gloves are red" coming
from Michael Powell immediately evokes the red shoes. There is an
intimation of the relation between the shoes and the gloves, realised
through redness. The identity between these two objects cannot be
reduced simply to a question of colour, but the decision to repress
colour in *Raging Bull* produces a ripple of reverberations and disper-
sals. The black and white film seems to vibrate with colour, most especially with red, though it is not the gloves that we see as coloured, but
rather the redness of blood that we see spurting through the cuts and
slashes, dripping off the rope, seeping through the black and white
images (literally so in the title). The boxing gloves echo the red shoes
as agents of compulsion, compelling and even seducing us to look

even whilst forcing us to look away, to avert our gaze from intolerable
mutilation. Both films are at once exhilaratingly magical and cruelly
violent, they enact cinematically both balletic and pugilistic impulses.

***

To begin then: a pair of shoes, a pair of boxing gloves.

***

At the heart of *The Red Shoes* there is a ballet, also entitled "The Red
Shoes." In this ballet a woman in white dances, in a spotlight, past a
shoemaker's shop where her attention is caught by a pair of crimson
ballet slippers. She is transported by a reverie imagining herself in
them, she dances beseechingly for the shoes as though at a shrine,
until at last she pulls away and tries to forget by dancing with a lover.
But the shoes remain, attracting her back into their orbit. In an extraordinarily audacious and breathtaking shot the woman runs headlong towards the camera, leaps in mid-flight into the shoes and continues dancing without interruption, although the mood and quality of
her dancing suddenly becomes more vivacious and joyful as though
she is absorbing into her being the nature of the red shoes. A sense of
the red shoes as magical is strongly conveyed in this scene, but as the
ballet progresses the magical dimension takes on a more sinister cast
for it becomes apparent that she cannot take off these shoes which
have a will of their own, which keep dancing and dancing and dancing. She is driven inexorably—through episodes of frenzy, exhaustion,
hysteria, despair—to death. The Hans Christian Anderson fairy tale on
which the ballet is based, puts it thus:

She was very much frightened, and tried to throw off her red shoes, but could not unclasp them. She hastily tore off her stockings; but the shoes she could not get rid of—they had, it seemed, grown on to her feet. Dance she did, and dance she must, over field and meadow, in rain and in sunshine, by night and by day.

At the end of the ballet she tries to cut off the shoes, cut off her feet with a large and lethal looking knife, but the knife turns into leaves on a vine wrapped around her ankle; when it turns back into a knife in her hand she throws it, like a dagger—point-first, into the wooden floor. There is nothing left for her then but to dance until she dies, and so the ballet ends.

***

The key in her hand turns into a knife; a flashed image, almost subliminal, haunting—a knife in the bed; her face reflected in the blade; her throat slit: *Meshes of the Afternoon*, Maya Deren and Alexander Hammid, 1943.

***

At the end of the film, the heroine, Vicky, who has played the lead role in the ballet, also dies. In a headlong rush towards the camera she plunges to her death, flying over a balcony and onto the train tracks below. This event takes place a few moments before the curtains are about to open on a production of "The Red Shoes" in which she was to have repeated the performance that made her famous. The ballet goes ahead without her, an empty spotlight dancing over the stage, illuminating her absence. She lies on the railway track, her legs gashed and bloody, bound by the scarlet ribbons of the ballet shoes, wrapped up in ribbons of blood. "Take off the red shoes," she says and as they are lifted from her feet she dies. Meanwhile on stage the ballet is ending, the spotlight is still, centre stage, and in the centre of the spot: a pair of red shoes. Thus the ending of the ballet is the end of the film.

The shoes appear initially as ordinary, recognisable objects. But before long their supernatural dimension becomes apparent. They are intensely desirable but once taken up, put on, there's no stopping and no going back; they have a life of their own—compulsive and all consuming—so that ultimately they destroy, through a kind of contagion, that which they touch. "Cinematic techniques are employed to give a malevolent vitality to inanimate objects."[18] Attainment of the object of desire simply provokes further desire and sets in motion a pattern of compulsive repetition.

Once Jake La Motta dons boxing gloves he is doomed to a cycle of obsessive repetition, playing out round after round, in the boxing ring. In the end he does not die, but still has to compulsively repeat his performance, although in the end it is lines he repeats and not blows. In the nightclub that masquerades as a theatre he plays out atonement and expiation. De Niro repeats the words of the young Brando[19] and in doing so he repeats the fate of Brando—to become old and bloated. "The obsessional act is ostensibly a protection against the prohibited act; but actually in our view, it is a repetition of it," says Freud.[20]

In both films the shoes and the gloves clearly figure as supercharged objects, almost magical in their effects. However, the very fact that they are so apparently significant might alert us to the fact that they *mean too much* and thus, paradoxically, rather than containing meaning they indicate a process of signification whereby excess (of various sorts—excessive desire, ambition, pleasure, colour, speed ...) is made manifest. Another way of saying this is that they do not, in and of themselves, mean anything; rather, they function as cinematic tropes. In rhetoric a trope is a figure of speech, and by "cinematic trope" I mean to imply a specifically cinematic articulation (thus, a process in excess of representation—the shoes don't simply stand *for* or *in place of* something else but are a form of process, of cinematic energy). Although they are both objects of attachment—attaching to the body, to hands and feet, we need to guard against the temptation to attach them too closely to the characters who possess and wear them. For one thing it is quite clear that this is a double-edged process, to possess these objects is to be possessed and ultimately it will be more rewarding to pay attention to this dynamic, and its operation through the filmic texts, than to try to read the objects in terms of individual characters. This is not to exclude the fact that in some instances and on certain levels they might well serve to articulate something about both Jake La Motta and Vicky, but the point is that this is not their only function. Driving desires and rampant ambitions are dispersed through the body of the texts, and this means that on the narrative level a variety of characters are implicated (this is particularly the case in *The Red Shoes*). But it is not simply in terms of characters (one or many) and narrative *raison d'être* that these objects function; they are objects of investment par excellence, that is they provide an anchor or point of crystallisation for various unattached and often excessive energies, and by doing so they provide a psychic safeguard against madness.[21] An objection could be raised here, it could be pointed out that neither Vicky nor Jake are saved from madness or at least tragedy. But this is just it—although the characters are not saved in some senses the films are, they don't disintegrate into the madness and death of eternal repetition; although the films engage us in a death drive they actually release us from the logic of their own perversity and restore us to an economy of pleasure. I would argue that this is partly because the energies (both ecstatic and destructive) unleashed by the films are invested through these tropes. This means that we too, watching the film, are exposed to the death threat but also offered the possibility of investment via these objects or tropes. We can objectify what we experience as the emotional, but might also think of as psychic drives. Put like this the object status of the shoes and the gloves is

clearly cast in terms of the figurative. That is to say, it is not simply as
functional and denotative objects that they exist, but as totemic.

The charm and mystery of *The Red Shoes* is surely derived from its
basis as a fairy tale. The ballet itself, lasting a full fifteen minutes or so,
is an extraordinarily fantastical *tour de force*. The heroine, propelled by
her red shoes, seems to fly through space passing from night to day
encountering characters who dissolve into one another in landscapes
that merge and transform before our very eyes. The cinematic
momentum produces a sense of exhilaration that is way in excess of
the narrative drive, it is as though we are being swept along, literally
propelled by the movie. This of course is a familiar "move" in the musi-
cal genre, a move that we might refer to as a flight of fancy; but what
makes the difference here is that the fantasy mobilised by this flight
goes on too long, incorporating paranoiac projections, repeating the
movements to an excruciating degree, such that extreme perturbation
is registered. This reverberates beyond the ballet and into the framing
story, but already the reverse is also operating, the ballet is permeated
by "the everyday life" that surrounds it diegetically, by the desires of
the three protagonists (for each other and for their "art," as dancer,
composer and impresario). If, for a moment, we superimpose *The Red
Shoes* over *Raging Bull* the perturbation that we have registered comes
into focus as perversity. *Raging Bull* is much more clearly driven by
perversity, the imbrication of pleasure and pain is foregrounded more
directly, but the circulation of energies is not so different—compulsive
repetition is still the dominant motif in both films. If, then, the reflection of *Raging Bull* inflects the fairy tale fantasy of *The Red Shoes* with
an element of perversion, so the reverse process superimposes over the
perversion of boxing a fairy story fantasy. Both the extremely lyrical
slow motion balletic sequences of *Raging Bull*, and the terrifying speed
and violence of some of the sequences in *The Red Shoes* can be conceived as flights of (furious) fancy. The "masculine" world of boxing is
a fairy story, the "feminine" world of ballet is refracted in a boxing
ring.

A Young Girl's Hands

The boxing gloves both protect and conceal the boxer's hands, and they substitute for bare hands, in the process becoming weapons, actually enabling the man who wears them to fight. Fairly early in the movie Jake confides to Joey as the two men sit at the kitchen table, "What's the matter with me? My hands. I got these small hands ... a young girl's hands." This involves him in a paradox—it means he can't ever be the best because he'll remain always a lightweight— "I'm never gonna get a chance to fight the best there is"—but it also means he has to box, is driven to somehow negate and conceal, by wearing gloves, these "young girl's hands." He has to use the component of femininity as a weapon, a missile. Immediately after he has confessed (his "problem," his weakness, his secret) he asks Joey to hit him in the face. Joey is reluctant and has to be cajoled and bullied into complying. Eventually, with a tea towel wrapped around his hand in lieu of a glove he hits him—repeatedly—in the face in a series of tight shot-reverse-shots. It is as though Jake is expiating his sins, inviting and enduring punishment for having "girl's hands." But also it is as though there is a substitution of face for hands. Later (after an early defeat by Sugar Ray Robinson) we see him flex his hand in a bucket of iced water (echoing the scene where he pours cold water down the front of his pants to dowse desire and preserve energy for fighting). Ostensibly an act of protection and preservation the slow clenching of his fist in the water (depicted in close-up, the camera very slowly and slightly zooming in) suggests a massive effort of repression, an effort to negate these "young girl's hands." The repression and the expiation go together—"I done a lot of bad things Joey. Maybe it's coming back to me," he says, his hand in the water ("The obsessional act is ostensibly a protection against the prohibited act; but actually in our view, it is a repetition of it"). If there is a fear of castration in *Raging Bull* there is also (and these drives are not incompatible) a will to self-destruction, or at least a will to negate and destroy that part of the self that suggests femininity.

***

The room is lit by lamps—an elegant room of wine red tones and deep blues. In the middle of this room a figure reclines on a *chaise longue*. A man's hands are clasped tightly together, fingers intertwined, forming a rigid steeple. But the thumbs escape, dancing in agitation. It is Lermontov and he has just received news of Vicky's marriage. He crumples the telegram in his right fist, thumping it several times into his other hand. The sound of the blow reverberates, as do the groans of pain, issuing in a staccato manner from this body held so stiffly, so restrained. He walks towards the camera into medium close-up, pulls his arm back and then lunges violently forward, his fist coming straight at us. A quick cut registers the fist smashing violently into glass. Now, with the camera behind his head, we can situate the previous shot as a mirror image. He holds his fist still for a few moments, clenched in the posture of impact. The glass is shattered. As he drops his arm the fragmented image of a man's face looks back at us.

***

Gloves figure elsewhere, in another movie. Remember that famous scene from *On the Waterfront* where Brando is walking with Eva Marie Saint to whom he is very attracted but he's nervous, shy, doesn't know what to do or say. She drops one of her gloves—tight-fitting and of the thinnest white leather—and he picks it up and fondles it, fiddling absentmindedly, slipping his own hand into it. It is as though through this gesture he conveys an intimacy not apparent in his halting speech. Or this is how it is usually read, celebrated as a great moment of method improvisation in Hollywood cinema.[22] But something else besides naturalism is conveyed here. Within the context of this scene the glove is a very felicitous object. Its circulation transforms the relations between inside and outside, renders boundaries uncertain. The glove functions within the diegetic space as a magical object, enabling Brando—as Terry Malloy, as character—to invest undirected energy. But it also functions for Brando the actor as a kind of super-natural device; in the very process of investment (enabling the audience too to focus energy and disperse tension) the ordinariness of the object and the gesture is transformed, to some degree ceremonialised.

***

A ballet shoe is put on, over the foot, just as a boxing glove is put on, over the hand. But once the red shoes are put on they can never be taken off—they conceal and cover but also become one with the body, indeed they come to "possess" the moving body. There is no way of saying where the body ends and the shoe begins, no way of distinguishing between inside and out. Derrida, after Heidegger, spends a long time pondering Van Gogh's shoes, noticing the tongue of the shoe, the traces of a body, of labour, of cultural inscription, teasing out this relation of inside and outside.[23] Here too there is a problematic of inside and outside, but also of daemonic possession and the shoes and gloves of which we speak fall within a different lineage—that of cartoons and fairy tales. And, as with those objects invested with magical properties in cartoons and fairy tales, they draw attention to the mystery and instability of sexual identity.

***

The gloves which Camille wished to try on were of the thinnest white leather and tight-fitting. The woman ... brought one of the gloves to her mouth and breathed into it before handing it across the counter to Camille ... Filled with her breath, the

glove took on the form of a hand which suddenly and deeply
frightened Camille. It was a languid boneless hand, a hand
without a will, a hand floating in the air like a dead fish with its
white stomach uppermost. It was a hand she did not want. It
was a hand that could not clench itself. It was a hand which in
caressing would in no way be a hand and would not caress; it
would lead away. At that moment she knew what he was
offering her. He was offering her the possibility of being what
she pretended to be ...

The gloves fitted her perfectly. The leather across her
tiny bony knuckles was so tight that it shone as if it were
wet.[24]

***

If we understand this confession scene (confessing to "girl's hands") as
an attempt to articulate a sense of subjectivity or experience of the self,
then clearly it is also about a sense of self as inadequate, requiring confession (of a culpability for something that is lacking—i.e., masculinity
and power as embodied in powerful hands) and punishment.
Subjectivisation, for Jake, coincides with the experience of his own
powerlessness, of his own position as that of a victim of destiny:

> No matter how big I get no matter who I fight no matter what I
> do I ain't never gonna fight Jo Louis. I'm never gonna get a
> chance to fight the best there is. And you know something? I'm
> better than them.

In the face of this natural deformity he is powerless, there is nothing he can do. We could say that Jake blames the feminine in himself
(as embodied by his hands) for preventing him from realising his ambitions of greatness. But it's not quite as simple. For one thing Jake as

character is not so self-conscious, but more to the point the film text never posits masculinity as simply dependent on repressed femininity. This film, along with other Scorsese films, exhibits an obsessive fascination—as well as repulsion—for the problem and experience of masculinity, and whilst it mobilises a variety of masculine fantasies it is most fascinating in exploring masculinity as fantasy. Puzzling over how this happens (i.e., why the fascination?—or rather, intersecting fascinations, mine, Scorsese's, intradiegetic characters ...) my mind wandered to another instance of ambivalent fascination conventionalised in the cinema—the femme fatale figure most familiar in the film noir genre. This might seem like an odd place to start (insinuating a connection between Jake la Motta and the femme fatale) but I think now that the reverberation was not accidental. Though the connections might seem abstruse they will lead us back with utter simplicity to Jake's request to Joey, after his confession: "Do me a favour. I want you to hit me in the face."

***

Slavoj Zizek discusses the coincidence of subjectivisation with the experience of one's own powerlessness in terms of the femme fatale in the hardboiled detective novel (but he interestingly illustrates his point by an example from elsewhere—Adorno's discussion of *Carmen*, specifically of that moment where Carmen as "bad-fatal object" is subjectivised, felt as victim of her own game.)[25] He writes:

> in the best novels of this genre, a certain reversal happens when the femme fatale as "a bad object" is subjectivised ... What gives her power of fascination to the femme fatale is exclusively her place in masculine fantasy. She is only "mastering the game" as an object of masculine fantasy. The theoretical lesson that one should get from this is that subjectivisa-

tion coincides with the experience of one's own powerlessness, of one's own position as that of a victim of destiny.[26]

Now what exactly is this theoretical lesson, and how is it arrived at? It is fairly clear how a conception of subjectivity as powerlessness is derived from the instance of the femme fatale—we can illustrate repeatedly the fact that when she thinks she masters the game she is in fact as much a victim as her victims. However, Zizek makes the point that this form of subjectivity (the woman's realisation of her own powerlessness) is part and parcel of male fantasy. In other words the threat posed by the femme fatale (she devours men, uses her sexuality to gain power over them) which also elicits fascination, is neutralised for the masculine subject when he casts her in the position of experiencing herself as powerless, when a particular form of subjectivity is ascribed to her. Now this implies a certain form of contorted identification. He (the male subject), in the process of protecting himself, places himself in the perspective which is hers; or, to put it another way, he realises her position. This identification must involve him, paradoxically, in experiencing himself as powerless. From this can be derived the theoretical lesson of, as Adorno puts it, "the original passivity of the subject." That is to say, we can extrapolate from the particular to note that in general the experience of subjectivity coincides with the experience of powerlessness.

What interests me here is what Zizek implies, but doesn't explore, about masculinity. Many critics have noted that if, within the film noir genre, there is a compulsion to punish the femme fatale (through killing her off, or through neutralising her), there is also a partial exposure of that compulsion. This is why feminists have been so interested, or indeed fascinated, by the genre, arguing that it is interesting for the way it disturbs the filmic ordering and containment of sexual difference. The personification process (bad-object personified in *femme fatale* exerts fascination and simultaneously threatens *hero*) means that the focus has been primarily on the figure of the woman as site for examining the construction of sexual difference. The men in film noir tend to be pale in comparison (classically, the detective who becomes caught up in the investigation and thus undone). This focus means that some of the questions implied in Zizek's argument haven't really been examined. What, for instance, happens when the male subject experiences himself as powerless? The film noir genre generally resolves this question narratively, and in terms of characters. The woman is punished or saved, i.e., the bad-object is negated or reformed. But what are the general theoretical implications of the aporia which is opened up when a system posited on mastery—i.e., masculinity—is exposed as, in fact experienced as, illusory; when "mastering the game" is posited on a fundamental condition of powerlessness? How, under these conditions, does masculinity continue? What fantastic structures are necessary to sustain it?

I suspect that it is the process of personification itself that has deflected these questions. They surface, however, precisely in those filmic texts where the bad-object figures as a strong presence, but unattached so to speak, not personified in the person of the femme fatale, not invested. They surface particularly in a film like *Raging Bull* and other Scorsese films revolving around protagonists frequently unreconciled; on the edge of psychosis they play out, obsessively, a game of mastering the threat, of mastering masculinity. The femme fatale might not be much in evidence in Scorsese films, but an understanding of the way she figures in masculine fantasy can very usefully illuminate the Scorsese dynamic. And conversely, these films provide a useful way of developing issues around masculinity that might have been raised initially by an analysis of the femme fatale. There might not, in Scorsese, be a femme fatale to serve as bad-object before whom the masculine subject feels fascination and fear, but it might be that the bad-object is internalised in the Scorsese hero (think particularly of J.R. in *Who's That Knocking at my Door?* Charlie in *Mean Streets*, Travis Bickle in *Taxi Driver*, Jimmy Doyle in *New York, New York*, as well as Jake La Motta). This is not quite as simple as saying that the Scorsese hero is fascinated by and simultaneously fears his own repressed femininity (though this might not be inaccurate). Rather, it is to argue that he is involved, still, in a fantastical construction of the bad-object, but one that exacerbates and foregrounds the problem of masculinity precisely because there is no external "other" to be "objectified," to be the bad-object.

In the case of the femme fatale, identification with the bad-object allows structural resolution. Identification as a process here involves transformation and rehabilitation—either she is turned into a good object or she is punished, but either way the masculine subject is confirmed as subject. However, it's a precarious project and just how precarious can be seen when the bad-object is integral to the self. Rather than rehabilitation (under the guise of acting upon the other) there is the threat of being undermined from within. If she is me, then masculinity must be experienced as a double inscription of powerlessness or passivity. But this experience totally contradicts the knowledge of masculinity—posited on self-possession and the exercise of power. The contradiction opened up here cannot be easily resolved through projection, through a rehabilitation of the self in terms of (through differentiation from) an other. Nevertheless, there is of course a drive to reclaim subjectivity, and what this means paradoxically is a desperate, obsessive and frequently violent "acting out" of masculinity in a repetitive attempt to negate the horror opened up by this internalised bad-object. The desperation, obsession and violence are born of engagement in a game that can never be mastered. This is the real force of masculinity as fantasy. It is not simply that the association of masculinity with power is illusory; it is rather that masculinity itself corresponds to the structure of a game that can never be mastered but must be played out, a game in which each manoeuvre is provoked by the force of a bad-object, the annihilation of which would amount to an annihilation of self. The force of the bad object is registered through fear and fascination, and through a punitive dynamic that frequently mimics what we too often assume to be the masochism of femininity.

***

And so we are returned to the scene of "domestic intimacy" between the brothers, the confessional "hit me" scene. Before passing on to *The Red Shoes* I want to pause for a moment to note the way in which the scene is diegetically framed. Joey arrives in the midst of a violent marital quarrel, the wife is ejected from the room and before the men sit down at the table Jake yells at her through the closed door, "I'm gonna kill ya!" She is then out of the scene (obscene?) but returns at the end. The sequence ends with a fleeting shot of her watching and listening secretly. Her absence is secured through a violent threat and yet she returns, like the repressed, present as a silent witness. Later, in his second marriage, Jake—jealously obsessed about his wife Vickie's absence—interrogates her about her movements. She tells him she's been to see (has witnessed) *Father of the Bride*, another film, as we know, about troubled and suspicious masculinity.

***

Like A Girl Committing Suicide Or Like A Ballerina?

That masochistic inflection of femininity is manifested in *The Red Shoes* in the logic of Vicky's suicide flight. I say logic because the dynamic of the film has set up a pattern of repetition that seems thematically to revolve around choice (will she choose dancing or living an ordinary "everyday" life? Which man will she choose? and so on), but in fact the psychic logic (which is what propels and drives the film) actually enacts the impossibility of choice. Compulsion cannot be helped, obsession precludes choice and culminates in death and ecstasy.

The Red Shoes and *Raging Bull* both spin intricate tensile fictions in which obsession and ecstasy are enmeshed. In *Raging Bull* the connection is enacted most particularly in the fight sequences, but the overall narrative is structured like a classical tragedy in which the rhythm of rise and fall (of the hero) opens up, in the end, an elegiac space for mourning (the loss of male beauty? of ecstasy itself?[27]). The man himself, however, doesn't die. *The Red Shoes* is much more explicit about the imbrication of ecstasy and obsession and death.

Just before the curtains are about to open for the first time on the ballet of "The Red Shoes" Lermontov holds Vicky's hands to his chest, as though in supplication, confession or declaration. He wants from her ecstasy—"ecstasy I've seen in you only once before." He admits to having seen her at the Mercury Theatre on a wet afternoon, dancing Odette in *Swan Lake*. She might not have been aware of him in the audience on that occasion, but we as the film audience are hardly likely to have forgotten a sequence so charged with the energy and dangerous desire of dance. It is the first time in the film that we see a body transformed from the daily, a spectacularly "decided body"; and it is the first time that we witness balleto-cinematic effects. The scene in the Mercury Theatre lasts for a few minutes, but the crucial sequence—for the way it introduces and prefigures the action of the film—lasts only 28 seconds and is composed of a dozen shots.[28] After setting the scene—a poster outside the theatre, the gramophone playing, the small audience—we are shown the stage. In long shot Vicky, as Odette, in her white swan's costume, enters screen left (stage right), dances across the stage and begins to pirouette back. This is almost a "proscenium" shot, i.e., respectful of the stage, it is full frontal and almost static. Cut to a medium close up moving shot as she twirls twice; and then there is a whirl of abstract colours and shapes interspersed with flashes of the audience. This is clearly a subjective series, but what matters is not what she sees, or even primarily the perspective (it is not set up as a point of view shot), but the sensation—a vertiginous experience of "space-time." We are drawn into this sensationalism, but also drawn, albeit imperceptibly, into an exchange of energy—between actants on the stage and in the auditorium. The flash-shots of the audience move progressively round, and in, closer. From the audience we cut to a medium close up of Vicky twirling, and then a close-up—her head slightly back, spinning, a smile of bliss appearing in the movement. There is another subjective shot—flashing lights and colours—which eventually settles and comes into focus on Lermontov in the audience. In long shot, static, she holds her pose—back where she began. Cut from this to a close-up of Lermontov watching intensely, and then an abrupt cut into Vicky in extreme close-up. This shot always evokes for me the shocking experience of the close-up in so called "primitive cinema"—it is as though all the intensity, the flagrant momentum that has been generated, is here distilled—precariously. Her lips are vividly scarlet (prefiguring the red shoes), her mouth like a wound, and her elaborately painted eyes are wide and wild (a look that will reappear in the suicide flight). She appears possessed, transported, ecstatic. Possessed by the obsession that is dancing or the desire that is Lermontov's? There is no answer, or rather—it is impossible to give an answer that chooses one or the other. And this is the impossibility that kills. There is something curiously frightening in this shot (although not purely "in" it; the effect is also derived from its placement in the sequence, the way it is cut in), an intimation of the deadly aspect of ecstasy.[29]

***

Shots are held together not by the constant identity of an individual performer, but by the emotional integrity of the movement itself, independent of its performer.[30]

The cutting in this sequence, the spacing of shots, the rhythm and timing is reminiscent of many sequences of *Raging Bull* where the viewer is drawn into the ring, as it were, implicated in the subjectivity of the shots, in the sensation of deadly ecstasy. In fact nothing could be more repetitious and circular (and therefore potentially tedious) than boxing—round after round after round; nothing that is, except ballet—pirouette after pirouette after ... Indeed, it is partly the aspect of obsession that renders this material interesting (that gives a charge to the endless repetition); but it is the cinematic rendering of obsession that engenders ecstasy.

***

The scene in the Mercury Theatre anticipates Vicky's suicide flight. She is in her dressing room where she has been practising in her new red shoes. Her dresser hands her the normal peach-coloured slippers that she is to wear for the opening of "The Red Shoes." ·

> So much for realism. I now brought the Red Shoes into play as a magical image with a power over their wearer, exactly as in the fairy tale. I went close on the Red Shoes with the camera and worked out with Jack Cardiff a high intensity of colour and light, which seemed to give the shoes life. So I invented the action where Moira takes a step towards the camera and the shoes stop her dead and then turn her round exactly as if they were the masters. The flashing light and the flaring colour get more and more intense, and she starts to run in the opposite direction to the stage.[31]

She rushes along the corridor, around a corner, down stairs, into the sunshine, down more steps and over a balustrade. In order to capture the sense of continuous movement as Vicky runs down the stairs, of compulsive dancing, (and to ensure that her feet stayed in view), Powell mounted a twenty-five-foot high spiral staircase on a turntable which was turned slowly as she ran down. Two takes were shot and edited together almost invisibly. This rush to death is extraordinarily fluid, exhilarating and balletic, but it is also—or at least I find it to be—nauseating. Perhaps this is because of the anticipation, because the ending is so strongly inscribed in the flight itself as, precisely, a repetition (many contemporary reviewers chastised the film makers for the "bad taste" of this bloody ending, but I wonder if their troubled response doesn't register this very tension—between artifice and naturalism, public and private). In this flight, just as in the ballet of "The Red Shoes," we witness the traversing of an imaginary space, the charting of "a geography that never was,"[32] and it is this cinematic rendering of "space-time" that is at once so magical and catastrophic.

***

"Mr Powell! Shall I jump like a girl committing suicide, or like a ballerina?"

I thought. "Like a ballerina."

She is only in the air for about eight frames, but it is one of the most beautiful cuts in the film.[33]

***

It *is* thrilling, this flight through the air, but there's a risk: that in going beyond the pleasure principle you will fly in the face of death.

***

Throughout this writing a voice has whispered, ghostly images have hovered—flitting between the lines, shadowing the text. The ghost of Maya Deren, for whom "the condition of the ecstatic was 'the incandescence of obsession.' "[34] The title of this paper has been taken from a twelve-minute film she made in 1948—*Meditation on Violence*. Like most of her projects it explores and stretches the relation between dance and film, but what makes it particularly pertinent is that it is derived from boxing (Chinese boxing). In reflecting upon the film she pointed out that insofar as the film is a meditation its location is an inner space, and its concerns are more with the idea of violence, rather than with the act. "However," she writes, "meditations investigate extremes, and life, while ongoing and non-climactic in the infinite sense, contains within it varieties and waves of intensity."[35]

***

The gloves and the shoes, then, serve to focus and crystallise unattached energy. They also indicate, as in totemic rituals, an aspect crucial to spectatorship and performance—that is, the ceremonial. Both gloves and shoes mark out the body and an arena of performance—the stage and the ring. They imply a trained and disciplined body, an extra-daily body. But when techniques of the body appropriate to the stage and the ring disperse into the quotidian there are no boundaries to contain these single-minded desiring bodies. Hence, the perverse logic of ecstasy. It is dangerous, and the danger for us is that we might be infected by coming into contact with the ecstasy, by touching what is "red hot." Going to the movies is an event, a way of ceremonialising. But as part of life we take movies away with us, project after-images elsewhere, and onto the movies we project scenes and memories and forgotten sensations. Or should I say we use the movies as objects of investment, like the red shoes and the boxing gloves. And that might save us from madness, but it might also open up glimpses of horror, moments when the cutting is palpable and we must avert our gaze. I am reminded, whilst not looking, that looking—at the screen—constitutes an activity, a performance, a potentially dangerous encounter.

In the movie theatre the act of seeing with one's own eyes is always more than it seems.

This is a version of a chapter in my forthcoming book, *The Scorsese Connection*, published by the British Film Institute, 1995.

1   Enzo Ungari, *Bertolucci by Bertolucci*, trans. Donald Ranvaud (London: Plexus, 1987), 71.
2   Stan Brakhage, USA, 1971.
3   It seems to me one of the most interesting manifestations of his theory of "closed-eye vision."
4   And we've known this from early days, both from the movies and from such theorists as the Soviets—Eisenstein, Pudovkin etc., and more contemporary writers such as Tom Gunning and Andre Gaudreault who have theorised the dynamic and demonstrative (rather than strictly narrative) function of editing in early cinema. See for instance their article, "The Cinema of Attractions: Early Film, Its Spectator and the Avant-Garde," *Wide Angle*, vol. 8 no. 3&4 (1986), 63–70; and Gunning, " 'Primitive' Cinema—A Frame-up? or The Trick's on Us," *Cinema Journal*, vol. 28 no. 2 (Winter 1989), 3–13.
5   Sigmund Freud, *Totem and Taboo*, trans. and ed. James Strachey (New York: W.W. Norton, 1950), 27 ff.
6   Ibid., 27.
7   For a very entertaining (and somewhat caustic) account of the on-set/off-screen clash between the high art of ballet and the low art of celluloid occasioned by this casting, see Michael Powell, *A Life in the Movies. An Autobiography* (London: Heinemann, 1986), 656.
8   I refer here to the opening scene, as was the case with *The Red Shoes*. However, both films have significant credit sequences, prior to these scenes. *The Red Shoes* depicts a series of painted flats culminating in flames—emerging out of a pair of red satin ballet slippers. The credits of *Raging Bull* are laid over a scene of a lone boxer (in long shot) in cloak and hood rehearsing his moves in extreme slow motion, accompanied by a hauntingly elegiac soundtrack. The film title itself—RAGING BULL—appears in scarlet, the only moment of colour in the entire film.
9   It is from her dressing room that Vicky flees at the end of *The Red Shoes*—to avoid performance.
10 Eugenio Barba, *Beyond the Floating Islands*, trans. Judy Barba, et al. (New York: Paj Publications, 1986), 149–50.
11 Ibid., 94.
12 A particular tendency that includes Meyerhold, Brecht, Barba—all influenced by non-European traditions.
13 Eugenio Barba, *Beyond the Floating Islands*, 95.

14 Gilles Deleuze, *Cinema 2. The Time-Image*, trans. Hugh Tomlinson and
    Robert Galeta (London: The Athlone Press, 1989), 191.
15 Ibid., 194.
16 Thomas Wiener, "Martin Scorsese Fights Back," *American Film*, vol. 1 no. 2
    (1975), 31–34, 75.
17 David Thompson and Ian Christie, ed., *Scorsese on Scorsese* (London, Faber
    and Faber, 1989), 80.
18 Maya Deren discussing *Meshes of the Afternoon* (the emphasis is mine). See
    Maya Deren, "Notes, Essays, Letters," *Film Culture*, no. 39 (Winter 1965), 1.
19 From *On the Waterfront*—"I coulda been a contender."
20 Sigmund Freud, *Totem and Taboo*, 50.
21 This notion of "investment" is used in the Freudian sense where it serves as
    a translation of the German *"besetzung."* A more common English transla-
    tion is "cathexis," but I find this term overly technical and wish to retain
    the sense of everyday usage that pertains to the German.
22 James Naremore's discussion which dissents from this view is interesting.
    See James Naremore, *Acting in the Cinema* (Berkeley, Los Angeles and
    London: University of California Press, 1988), 193–195.
23 Jacques Derrida, *The Truth in Painting*, trans. Geoff Bennington and Ian
    McLeod (Chicago: University of Chicago Press, 1987). Martin Heidegger,
    "The Origin of the Work of Art," *Poetry, Language, Thought*, trans. Albert
    Hofstadter (New York: Harper and Row, 1971). The extensively glossed
    Van Gogh shoes in themselves cohere precariously as a fascinating
    instance of critical *mise-en-abîme*. See also Fredric Jameson's essay,
    "Postmodernism, or the Cultural Logic of Late Capitalism," *New Left
    Review*, no. 146 (July-August, 1984). Jameson compares the Van Gogh
    shoes and Heidegger's approach to them to Andy Warhol's *Diamond Dust
    Shoes* which he posits as all surface, refusing a depth reading. Nevertheless,
    shoes of various kinds, and their indeterminate relations with bodies, pro-
    liferate in this essay.
24 John Berger, *G* (London: Penguin, 1972), 190–191. I am grateful to John
    Frow for reminding me of this passage.
25 Slavoj Zizek, "The Limits of the Semiotic Approach to Psychoanalysis," ed.
    Feldstein and Sussman, *Psychoanalysis And...* (New York and London:
    Routledge, 1990), 89–110.
26 Ibid., 108.
27 For an essay that explores these questions, and is certainly the most inter-
    esting piece of critical writing that I know on *Raging Bull* see Pam Cook,
    "Masculinity in Crisis?" *Screen*, vol. 23 no. 3–4 (September, October,
    1982), 39–53.
28 As accurately as I can determine. Because of the combination of camera
    movement, focus and cutting it is hard to tell precisely.
29 There are two very similar shots of Kathleen Byron in *Black Narcissus*
    (Powell and Pressburger, 1947)—her febrile hysteria transfigured as dead-
    ly desire.
30 Maya Deren, "Ritual in Transfigured Time," *Dance Magazine* (December

1946).
31 Michael Powell, *A Life in the Movies*, 652.
32 Maya Deren, describing the movement of the dancer in her film *A Study in Choreography for Camera* (1945), in "Notes, Essays, Letters," 30.
33 Ibid., 653.
34 Annette Michelson, "On Reading Deren's Notebook," *October* 14 (Fall, 1980), 54.
35 Maya Deren, "Notes, Essays, Letters," 18.

NOTES ON THE CONTRIBUTORS

Patricia Mellencamp is a Professor of Art History & Film at the University of Wisconsin at Milwaukee. She is the author of *High Anxiety: Catastrophe, Scandal, Age & Comedy*, and *Indiscretions: Avant-garde Film, Video, and Feminism* and *A Fine Romance: Five (St)Ages of Film Feminism or what Snow White, Cinderella and Rapunzel Forgot to Tell Thelma and Louise*. She has edited four collections of essays, including the recent *Logics of Television*, and is coeditor with Meaghan Morris and Andrew Ross of the series "Art and Politics of the Everyday" published by Indiana University Press.

Jodi Brooks is a lecturer in Cultural Studies at the University of Melbourne.

Needeya Islam is a post-graduate student in the Power Department of Fine Arts at The University of Sydney. She is writing a PhD thesis on gender, youth and representation in American cinema.

Melissa McMahon is a post-graduate student in the Department of General Philosophy at The University of Sydney. She is writing a PhD thesis on the concept of the outside in recent French philosophy.

Lesley Stern lectures in Theatre and Film Studies at the University of New South Wales and is the author of *The Scorsese Connection*, published by the British Film Institute, 1995.

Michelle Langford is a post-graduate student in the Power Department of Fine Arts at The University of Sydney. She is writing a PhD thesis on the allegorical cinema of Werner Schroeter.

Toni Ross lectures in Art History and Theory at the Queensland University of Technology.

Laleen Jayamanne lectures in Film Studies at the Power Department of Fine Arts, The University of Sydney. She has made several short films including *A Song of Ceylon* (1985).